THE
HAY DAY
COOKBOOK

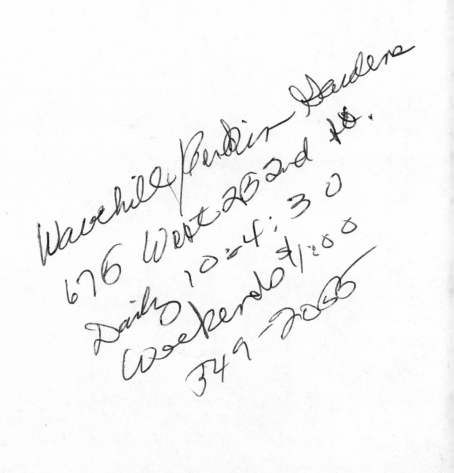

THE
HAY DAY®
COOKBOOK

Maggie Stearns
&
Sallie Y. Williams

Foreword by Lydie Marshall

ATHENEUM   NEW YORK

1 9 8 9

Atheneum
Macmillan Publishing Company
866 Third Avenue, New York, N.Y. 10022
Collier Macmillan Canada, Inc.

Library of Congress Cataloging-in-Publication Data
Stearns, Maggie.
    The Hay Day cookbook / Maggie Stearns & Sallie Y. Williams ;
foreword by Lydie Marshall.
        p.   cm.
    Includes index.
    ISBN 0–689–70815–7
    1. Cookery. 2. Farm produce. I. Williams, Sallie Y. II. Hay
Day (Firm) III. Title.
TX714.S74 1989
641.5—dc19   88-39190   CIP

Macmillan books are available at special discounts for bulk purchases for sales
promotions, premiums, fund-raising, or educational use. For details, contact:

Special Sales Director
Macmillan Publishing Company
866 Third Avenue
New York, N.Y. 10022

10 9 8 7 6 5 4 3 2 1

Printed in the United States of America

ACKNOWLEDGMENTS

Many people helped with the preparation of this book. Helen Brody read the manuscript, tested recipes, and selected, from many superb products she has created for Hay Day, the recipes that are included here. Christina Baxter, our merchandising genius, tested recipes and created the display on the back cover on one hour's notice; Rick Gutlon's thoughtfulness and expertise were indispensable throughout the whole process.

Helpful and responsive Hay Day customers offered suggestions as we tested products in the store. Talented Hay Dayers like Mimi Boyd, Bill Connell, Mary DeSantie, Ashley Drouet, Paul Heintz, Bruce Kinnaman, Mary Kay LaFlèche, Sue Nyakas, Diane Pearson, Peter Schott, Judy Stearns, and Graham Whitney not only helped establish high standards for all our stores but worked hard to perfect Hay Day products and recipes for this book.

Gloria Drouet, Gary Fertig, Erica Griffin, Genny Pearce, Patricia Pelton, Sallie Schacht, and Pam Van Rensselaer tested recipes and administered them to their patient families with tireless enthusiasm.

And without Larry Sheehan, of course, there would be no *Hay Day Cookbook* to begin with.

Maggie Stearns
Sallie Williams
Alex and Sallie Van Rensselaer

FOREWORD

When I began teaching cooking in the United States fifteen years ago, most of the produce I bought in the supermarket came wrapped in cellophane. How I missed Hay Day in those days!

The store, a wonderful cornucopia of vegetables, fruits, herbs, and flowers, is the answer to every cooking teacher's prayer. On my first visit it reminded me of the first time I went shopping in the market in Cannes in my native France, where I went wild over the abundance, the aromas, and the colors and overbought everything; when I got to Hay Day I wandered around like a child in a toy store, wanting one of everything. No wonder I love to teach cooking classes there!

Now we have this charming book, which allows all cooks to enjoy the spirit of Hay Day as Alex and Sallie Van Rensselaer have nurtured it over the past decade. Many of us read cookbooks as if they were detective stories, searching for the clues which make the recipes successful. In the case of the *Hay Day Cookbook*, the first-class ingredients are themselves the main clue, and that's why reading the book gave me a feeling of well-being—I could smell and taste each dish. But be warned: it's the fresh ingredients, not the cook, that are the real stars in these recipes. In trying such appetizing concoctions as Barbecued Oysters, Fettuccine with Prosciutto and Mascarpone, Charcoal Grilled Rosemary Chicken, or the wonderful Tomato Baked Eggs, remember that even the greatest cooking skills cannot compensate for second-rate ingredients.

The book is organized by seasons, and coming from a market that prides itself on the best and the freshest in each season, that is as it should be. Each group of seasonal recipes is accompanied by a kind of mini-encyclopedia of shopping and storing information that is useful for home cooks and even for gardeners.

Not all of us can live near a Hay Day market, but with the *Hay Day Cookbook* in our kitchens, we can come close. Bon Appetit!

LYDIE MARSHALL
author of *Cooking with Lydie Marshall*,
and director, À La Bonne Cocotte cooking school,
New York City

Published Seasonally at HAY DAY, Westport and Greenwich, Connecticut   Vol. VIII No. 7   July 1985

BEACH AND BATHING NUMBER

The Bathers. *Harper's Weekly.* August 2, 1873.

ABOUT THIS BOOK

When the first Hay Day opened in Westport in 1978, it was just a produce stand. I had spent most of my professional life as a marketing executive, but recently Sallie and I had had some success in Ohio and Georgia as pioneer growers of hydroponic lettuce and tomatoes, superb products that needed—and weren't finding—mass distribution. We thought an attractive country produce market might grow into an outlet for bringing the beautiful results of the new hydroponic technology into traditional American households.

Hay Day grew, all right, but not the way we expected. People were settling here in southwestern Connecticut precisely because it *was* still the country—there were farms here, and fresh air and vegetable gardens, and fishing in Long Island Sound, but none of the flavor of the place was reaching the mass merchandisers on the Post Road. Everybody in this neighborhood knew all about fresh produce, but they weren't finding it in their supermarkets.

So we were welcomed, and we flourished, and realized we were dealing with something a lot bigger than hydroponics—Hay Day was part of a general sea-change in the industry. The produce market burgeoned in Westport; we added a bakery, then a cheese department and a charcuterie. We opened the store in Greenwich in 1981 and started cooking classes in its tremendous kitchen; kindred spirits Lydie Marshall, Paula Wolfert, Bert Greene, Jacques Pepin, Giuliano Bugialli, and Richard Sax came out to raise everybody's consciousness about cooking with beautiful food.

The Hay Day team grew, too, and their collaboration has produced this book. Southerner Sallie Williams, author of several cookbooks, who had lived in France for a number of years, was the director of the well-known La Varenne cooking school in Paris when Sallie Van Rensselaer went there in

1979. When we all returned to the United States it seemed natural to ask her to contribute recipes and seasonal menus to the *Hay Day Rural Times*, the newspaper we give our customers at the checkout counter. Maggie Stearns, a Connecticut freelance writer and national press director for Opera Theatre of St. Louis, joined the team in the fall of 1982 to edit the paper and report on what's new in the stores.

The recipes, which have all been thoroughly tested, come from France, Italy, Germany, and all corners of the United States; there's a lot of the savor of classic New England seasonal cooking, with a dash of Sallie Williams's strong Virginia heritage. They are easy to prepare (many can be made ahead), simply and logically set forth, and based on an appreciation of the finest-quality ingredients. None of them takes a lot of time—the premise is that good food doesn't necessarily mean hard work—but they're sophisticated enough to be interesting.

Recipes for some of Hay Day's own best-selling entrées and desserts are printed here for the first time. Mimi Boyd, the founder and presiding genius of our original bakery in Westport, contributed ideas and bread recipes. Helen Brody, the architect of everything that comes out of the Greenwich kitchen, adapted Chicken Chèvre, Shrimp and Pasta with Champagne Vinaigrette, Lemon Mousse, and other Hay Day products into proportions for home cooking. (She even put in our special recipe for Spicy Chicken Salad because the kindergarten teacher up the hill asked her to!)

Drawing on the expertise of our produce managers, we have highlighted the fruits and vegetables that are the inspiration for this book with detailed charts on individual varieties and descriptions of the items we like best each season. Not that these things are unobtainable the rest of the year—most seasonal produce can now be had virtually year-round if you pay enough and know where to look—but there are still peak periods for most fruits and vegetables, and that's what the book is based on.

Whether you're an experienced cook or a beginner (and there are plenty of both among our customers), we hope you will find pleasure here. It's not just a matter of flavor and nourishment, although that's certainly paramount; we all know by now that there's a lot more to salad than iceberg lettuce and cardboard tomatoes. This book also celebrates the fact that cooking with natural, unprocessed ingredients is fun. After a long day at the office there is something tremendously appealing, and even therapeutic, about a gorgeous heap of eggplants and tomatoes piled in a basket. Savoring their textures while you make them into ratatouille is a tranquil way to end a complicated day.

A few of the recipes will seem astoundingly simple—Cranberry Sauce, for example, or Pesto, or Old-Fashioned Parsley-Buttered New Potatoes—and as you read along you may find yourself saying a little grandly, "*I* know how to do *that*." That's the point. There are lots of new ideas here, but there are some others—old friends, perhaps—that are worth remembering because they're really special when they're made with gorgeous vegetables. You may have done one of them just the other day, but the person next to you hasn't, and this book is for both of you.

Some of us are part of the generation that remembers margarine in squeeze bags with dreadful little buttons of orange dye; we were wide-eyed children when cake mix was a new idea and teenagers when somebody first made California Dip with powdered onion soup. But America's long love affair with processing is over at last, and it is the age of real food that we celebrate with this book.

We hope you like it.

ALEX VAN RENSSELAER

Contents

FALL

WINTER

THE
HAY DAY
COOKBOOK

The Story of Hay Day

WE opened for business on Memorial Day weekend 1978, in a former carwash on the Post Road in Westport. We had made one trip to the produce market at Hunts Point in the Bronx for "hardware" (things that will keep, like onions and potatoes) and another the next night for perishables. Then, cautiously optimistic and bleary with sleeplessness, we opened the store on Friday morning—and sold almost everything. We couldn't believe it. There was no way to restock until Hunts Point reopened on Sunday night, so we spent all day Saturday apologizing, hoping our first customers would come back again.

All that summer we went to market two or three times a week, experimenting and gradually adding to the fruits and vegetables we sold. We bought a huge wheel of cheddar in the fall, mainly for display; the whole thing disappeared the same day, and we started the cheese department. A couple of loaves of Mimi Boyd's homemade bread led to a bakery; one pepperoni sausage and some local smoked bluefish were the beginning of the charcuterie.

We've learned a lot since that first year, and much of it would make experienced commercial operators roar with laughter. We set out to be homespun and accommodating, and that hasn't changed, but we found out the hard way that a two-person bakery can't take orders for ten figgy puddings in one afternoon without paralyzing the kitchen and that if you scrawl more and more special orders for chestnut stuffing on the wall without writing down anyone's phone number, there's no way to avoid staying up till three in the morning peeling twenty pounds of chestnuts.

We gradually learned to keep proper records and walk the thin line between homestyle and professional, but we still peel our own chestnuts, and keep our fresh bread, unwrapped and unweighed and unlabeled, out in the open on bakers' racks. We went to a bakers' convention once, but one look at all the sacks of white bread mix and the massive dough-grabbers that can turn out hundreds of loaves an hour made us realize we were walking on the moon. One salesman choked when he heard we used nothing but sticks of unsalted butter and made cookies by hand on cookie sheets. "How do you scale [weigh] them?" he asked. "We don't," we said. "But how do you know if you're making any money?" he asked. "Well," we said, summoning what dignity we had left, "we just look in the register and count it up at the end of the day."

We've come a long way in eight years. We run five stores, and we now sell hundreds and hundreds of loaves of bread every day, but we're still determined to maintain our particular style—making things by hand, accommodating customers, selling the best quality we can find in the market—and sometimes it gets complicated.

Take the matter of food samples, for instance. We've always thought they were a good idea, especially in the cheese department where even the most sophisticated customers enjoy tasting new cheeses. If labeled samples are available, people can compare varieties without having to bother the staff, and if they like, they can engage the whole department in discussions of the relative merits of Cambazola Blue and Saga, Brillat-Savarin and Saint-André.

So we take whatever we think is exceptional that day and put out little pieces, garnished with appropriate fruits or crackers—but sometimes you have to watch your fingers. If it's close to lunchtime and the samples run out, customers have been known to seize the knife and whack off chunks of cheese for themselves, which can be downright dangerous.

And some people do, frankly, come to graze. They move slowly down the counter, savoring each variety, and sometimes circle back and do it again.

One small child went through half a jar of imported Italian sun-dried tomatoes before his mother finally found him. We were even featured in a magazine article on Good Cheap Food, in which the author pointed out that free
samples of smoked turkey, Dan's Mustard, and several cheeses, topped off
with a glass of mulled cider or a cup of Hay Day coffee, could make a nice
light lunch. Certainly, he said, the price was right.

But most people get the idea, and there's no question that samples are as
much a part of the scene here as Bach and Vivaldi and fresh flowers. Somewhere out there are the puzzled customers who once took some homemade
cheesecake we were sampling and spread it on crackers, thinking it was Brie,
or the people who picked up and ate handfuls of coffee beans (what could
they have thought they were getting?) while Alex was putting new labels on
the jars. We thought whoever it was might have complained, but we never
heard a word.

Like most other merchants, we've had our share of flimflam artists and
quiet little ladies with bags sewn under their coats where their pockets ought
to be, or crazies who eat half a loaf of cranberry bread or Doux de Montagne
and stash the rest under the broccoli. It took us some time to discover that
someone in the neighborhood was selling Christmas trees off our lot after the
store closed, telling people we'd asked him to look after the place and oh, yes,
of course he would give us the money in the morning. One year gypsies dis-
tracted the store manager so confederates could take a crowbar to the safe,
but our primitive offices are so overpopulated that the scheme didn't work;
their car was spotted as they fled, and they were caught and brought back
almost immediately. The police conducted the lineup right in the parking lot;
most of the customers were enjoying the spectacle, heightened by the flashing
lights of four police cars parked outside, but in the middle of the drama one
plaintive little voice was heard from way in the back of the store: "Can somebody please slice me half a pound of salmon?"

The pies at Hay Day have quite a reputation, and competition for them
gets pretty fierce, especially around national holidays. One day just before
Thanksgiving the bakery in Westport had all the special-order pies ready to
go in boxes labeled with customers' names; other last-minute customers were
obediently lined up outside the window, reading the *New York Times*, waiting for the next batch to come out of the oven. One of them decided to beat
the system. Reading a name at random off a box, she pushed to the head of the
line and said, "I'm Mrs. Cartwright—I'm here for my pie." It turned out the
real Mrs. Cartwright had ordered several hundred dollars' worth of other
casseroles and desserts, and as the bakery staff piled it all in the cart, there was

nothing for the impostor to do but mutter something about being "the other Mrs. Cartwright," abandon everything, and flee.

Although we've grown a lot, Hay Day's style hasn't changed much; we still do most things the way we did when we started, and run the office with a lineup of mushroom baskets for in-boxes. Our intelligent young staff make the place more cheery just by being there, and seem to enjoy the work, even at times like the day before Thanksgiving when gridlock hits the parking lot and some of them are buffeted by the surge in the aisles like swimmers in the breakers off Nantucket. It's fun to be in the store when somebody like Paul Newman or Gilda Radner or Harry Reasoner is shopping, and the customers and staff are all so busy Pretending Not To Notice that they keep crashing into the counters. We enjoy helping provide for Thanksgiving, and Christmas, and the Fourth of July, and being, in a way, a part of people's households.

Above all, the name Hay Day has come to stand for a lot more than just groceries. Like the event we're named for, the summer feast that marked the first hay crop safe in the barn, we like to think we are a celebration of good things, of a bountiful year-round harvest, of a quality of life that somehow manages to be both simple and sophisticated at the same time. Hay Day bears the same relationship to supermarkets that cross-country skiing does to the snowmobile; we're all out in the same weather, but we think we get a lot more out of it.

Preliminaries

SET forth here are definitions of some of the cooking terms referred to throughout this book, with brief discussions of the tools, techniques, and materials we find most useful in our own cooking.

ACIDULATED WATER

Usually used to keep peeled fruits and vegetables from discoloring, "acidulated" water is water to which a little vinegar or lemon juice has been added. Use about 2 tablespoons of either to a quart of water.

BLENDERS AND FOOD PROCESSORS

Each has its uses, and throughout the book we indicate a preference if there is one. Blenders are great for handling small quantities, making hollandaise (see page 18), and puréeing light soups and sauces; we even use ours for whipping cream, which can't be done in a standard-size food processor and is

[7]

tricky in a large one. Food processors, of course, are great for chopping, slicing, kneading, and puréeing heavier foods.

BRAISING, PARBOILING, AND BLANCHING

Braising produces a finished product by cooking meats or vegetables for a long time slowly in a small amount of liquid. *Parboiling* is usually an inter-mediate step; it means partially cooking something in water for a short time, usually to tenderize it or to shorten cooking time in a later process. *Blanching* vegetables for a very short time in a large quantity of boiling water sets their color and cooks them very slightly; they are then refreshed in cold water and frozen or set aside to be reheated in butter, cream, or a little liquid.

BROTH AND STOCK

Broth and stock are both rich liquids in which meats, poultry, or fish and bones have been simmered with vegetables; *stock* is the raw material, and *broth* is stock that has been concentrated and seasoned with herbs, salt, and pepper to be served at the table or used as a cooking liquid. *Bouillon* is a con-centrated, unclarified broth usually made from beef or veal bones, and *con-sommé* is a clarified broth.

CHICKEN BROTH

The character of a soup depends in large part on the broth that goes into it. Most canned broth tastes like nothing more than salt water, as far as we're concerned, and you'll get a much richer result if you make your own.

1 three-pound chicken, cut up, or five pounds chicken necks, backs, and wings
8 cups water
1 cup dry white wine
4 cloves
2 teaspoons salt
2 carrots, cut up
2 stalks celery with leaves, cut up
2 leeks, cleaned and halved
1 clove garlic (optional)
6 sprigs fresh parsley
8 peppercorns

Simmer the chicken in water and wine for 30 minutes. Add remaining ingredients and simmer 2 hours. Cool, strain, and remove fat. Break chicken meat up into broth for a hearty soup. Add salt to taste.

Chicken broth can be frozen or stored in the icebox for later use in soups and sauces. If it is to stay in the icebox more than a day or two it should be boiled again for about ten minutes, or frozen.

BUTTER

We have not specified salted or unsalted butter in many of our recipes because we know that it's often difficult to find good unsalted butter. We use unsalted butter at Hay Day because we find it sweeter and less watery than salted and we have a good supplier, but—perhaps because we have been spoiled by the European variety—we have yet to find a satisfactory brand in a supermarket. Unsalted butter doesn't keep as well because salt acts as a preservative. So use the best quality you can find in your market, and remember to adjust the amount of salt in each recipe to your own taste.

Flavored butters are made with herbs or strongly flavored fruits, and we sell a lot of them. Our herb butters are made with unsalted butter and finely minced herbs such as tarragon, dill, rosemary, or parsley. Fruit butters are made by puréeing and draining fresh fruits and stirring them into softened butter.

COOKING WITH CHEESES

There are two watchwords for cooking with cheeses—low and slow. You are only trying to heat and melt the cheese, not cook it, so gentle treatment is in order; cooking too long or too fast leaves it oily on top or rubbery and stringy inside.

Very soft cheeses like ricotta and cottage cheese can be beaten or processed directly into other ingredients. Soft cheeses like Muenster, Brie, and mozzarella should first be sliced or cubed—the smaller the pieces, the smoother the final result. Semihard cheeses like cheddar and Gruyère should be shredded before stirring into sauces and soups or layered in other dishes. They will become stringy if they are overcooked.

A really fine aged cheddar has as much character as robust old brandy, and many people have never tasted one. A good cheddar is made from unpasteurized milk and aged anywhere from nine months (mild) to three years (sharp) and is never bitter. Bitterness comes from using pasteurized milk, or aging cheese in the package instead of the rind, or a number of other sins against quality.

Hard cheeses like Parmesan or Romano should be grated very fine and are usually added to the other ingredients at the last minute. People who keep a can of commercially grated Parmesan in the icebox door don't know what they're missing; instead, keep a chunk of good aged Italian Parmesan tightly wrapped in the cheese drawer and grate it as needed with a hand grater or food processor. For a tiny bit more effort you will get a lot more flavor. Some good "Parmesan-type" cheese comes from Wisconsin, but the great stuff is Italian—Parmigiano Reggiano in particular. True aged cheese will be grainy and light yellow; younger cheese, or stale cheese, will be almost white.

COOKING OUTDOORS

We do all our outdoor cooking on an open grill and start it with an electric starter. There is an easy way to tell how hot a fire is: place your hand about four inches above the coals, and if you can hold it there two seconds it is very hot, three seconds medium hot, four seconds medium, and five to six seconds slow.

Shorten cooking time by bringing meat, fish, or poultry to room temperature before grilling, and control the cooking temperature by raising or lowering the firebox or the grill. Use water in a small plastic sprayer to control flareups, but don't soak the coals or the temperature will drop dramatically. When cooking large pieces of meat, add coals around the edges periodically, moving them to the center when they begin to glow.

Large roasts must rest after cooking; plan enough time so the meat can stand for fifteen to twenty minutes before being carved. Allow enough cooking time, too—it's better to serve meat lukewarm but perfectly cooked than to torture the guests while the host copes with meat that is still blue in the middle.

There are hundreds of combinations for barbecue sauces and marinades that add spice and flavor to grilled meats. Remember that *marinades* are designed to impregnate the meat with the flavor of the sauce, while glazing meat with a *barbecue sauce* while it cooks will add a tasty outer coating but will not have much effect on the flavor of the meat inside.

What charcoal should you use? We recommend mesquite or hardwood charcoal. Use briquettes only as a last resort; they give a chemical taste to grilled meats and fish.

Although it has long been used as a cooking fuel in Mexico and the American Southwest, mesquite only recently reached the East. Mesquite is a natural hardwood that grows like a weed in the Southwest, and mesquite charcoal burns very hot to sear meats and seal in flavor. It suffuses even the simplest foods with a wonderful smoky fragrance. A mesquite fire will get hotter faster than briquettes will, and puts out more heat over a longer period. Use a wire screen to keep small bits from falling through. We love it for swordfish.

If you want a more intense smoky flavor than you can get from charcoal alone, add water-soaked hardwood chips (hickory, apple, cherry, grapevine, or mesquite) to the fire, but experiment with a little at first—too much can be overpowering.

Finally, don't let the cook be stuck in the kitchen while everyone else is outdoors. Almost anything can be finished on the grill or kept warm on it while the meat is cooking.

MAKING A COURT BOUILLON

The classic mixture for poaching fish is 2 cups of white wine, 2 cups of water, 1 stalk of celery chopped with its leaves, 1 chopped onion, 1 chopped carrot, 1 bay leaf, 10 peppercorns, and a little salt, simmered together for ten minutes before proceeding with the recipe.

HEAVY CREAM *vs.* "WHIPPING CREAM"

It's getting harder to find heavy cream in supermarkets because ultra-pasteurized "whipping" cream has a much longer shelf life. Although heavy cream doesn't last as long, it contains more butterfat and we like it much better. We've specified heavy cream in our recipes, but "whipping" cream can be substituted if it's all you can find.

CRÈME FRAÎCHE

A cultured, slightly acid cream, crème fraîche is gradually becoming more widely available all over the United States. It's very rich, but it has less fat than butter! Crème fraîche is interchangeable with heavy cream or sour cream in any recipe and wonderful on vegetables, berries, and fruit. It makes superb sauces—you just stir it into the pan juices as you would butter.

The only trouble is that it's usually expensive. You can make crème fraîche yourself by adding 1 tablespoon of sour cream or buttermilk to 1 cup of heavy cream; shake it well and leave it out at room temperature for eight hours or overnight till it has thickened. (The time will depend on how warm "room temperature" is in your house.) After that it will keep in the icebox for at least a week. Don't worry if a little water accumulates on its surface after a while—just stir it in.

If crème fraîche is made with buttermilk it is less likely to curdle when cooked. If it is made with sour cream it will be gorgeous on fruit, but there is a possibility that it may curdle in a sauce. Make crème fraîche with heavy cream instead of "whipping" cream if you can—it will be a lot richer and a lot better.

DOUBLING RECIPES

It works, but not always. Watch out for the salt and spices, for example, and don't multiply them without tasting the mixture first. You can always add more, but you can't take it away. Eggs are tricky, too; if doubling a recipe means using four eggs instead of two, it's wise to beat the second two separately in a small bowl and add them gradually in small quantities to avoid making the mixture too eggy.

DEGLAZING AND REDUCING

Deglazing means pouring a liquid—usually stock or wine—into a pan in which meats have cooked to incorporate all the juices into a sauce. *Reducing* is the next step—boiling away the excess liquid to concentrate its flavor.

COOKING WITH EGGS

Large size eggs are assumed in all our recipes—extra large will make the results too eggy. Egg whites at room temperature will mount higher when they are beaten. If eggs are put into hot liquid too quickly they will scramble, so always add a little of the hot liquid to the eggs first to warm them up a bit before stirring them into the rest.

As soon as an egg leaves the hen, it starts to "breathe" and lose carbon dioxide. The white begins to thin out, and the membrane around the yolk weakens, allowing it to flatten. For the cook, this means that older eggs are thinner and runnier; freshness can usually be judged by the thickness and cloudiness of the white and the firm, high roundness of the yolk.

Although they will keep well for several weeks in the icebox, eggs deteriorate rapidly at room temperature. As time goes on the egg loses more carbon dioxide and moisture, and the tiny air pocket at the round end (designed by nature to give the hatching chick a gulp of air to start life with) enlarges. Thus the ancient test for freshness is to submerge whole uncooked eggs in water. The freshest ones will sink the lowest (because they contain the smallest amount of oxygen), rotten ones will float to the top, and Old Usables will bob up slightly off the bottom.

To make hard-cooked eggs, put them in a saucepan with a generous amount of cold water. Bring them to a boil, then remove at once from the heat; cover and let stand for twenty minutes, then drain and peel or refrigerate.

There's a solitary egg in the icebox door. Is it hard-boiled, or is it fresh? Spin it—a hard-cooked egg is uniform inside and spins readily, while the various liquids in an uncooked one keep it from spinning easily, if at all.

Does it matter if you get some yolk in beaten whites? Yes, it does. Any fat in the white will reduce its capacity to store air and reduce its beaten volume by as much as half. Yolks are the greatest inhibitors, but any fats and oils will have the same effect, even the minute amounts that are found on the surfaces of plastic mixing bowls. Cream of tartar won't make whites mount higher, but it will certainly make them less prone to collapsing. Salt weakens the froth and destabilizes it.

Does copper matter? Yes, again. The copper in an unlined beating bowl does the same job as cream of tartar, making the egg whites more stable and less likely to collapse.

The color of the egg shell makes no difference at all. It's a matter of genetics, not nutrition: Rhode Island Reds have brown "earlobes" and lay brown eggs; Leghorns have white "earlobes" and lay white eggs. A neighbor of ours has chickens of various varieties that produce eggs that are greenish-blue and bluish-green and yellowish-brown, and they're all the same inside.

WASHING FRUIT

As a general rule, don't wash any fruit—berries, grapes, cherries, apples—until you're ready to eat it. Almost all fruits have a natural bloom, or protective coating, on their skins, and as soon as it is removed the fruit will begin to spoil.

GARLIC

Chef Louis Diat said, "Garlic is the fifth element, as important to our existence as earth, air, fire and water. Without garlic I simply would not care to exist." Garlic fans are having a field day with the popularity of the Chinese and European cuisines that rely on it heavily, but nutritionists are rediscovering its healthful properties, too, in studies that give it credit for protecting against heart disease (it reduces cholesterol and inhibits clotting), diabetes (it reduces blood sugar), and the common cold. We haven't seen the evidence ourselves, but it's nice to know that people are taking our favorite herb more seriously.

Raw garlic is pungent, of course, and best served to groups of people who will remain closely associated for several hours afterward. When it is cooked, though, garlic becomes tame and gentle, and the legendary Chicken with 40 Cloves of Garlic (see page 366) turns it into a buttery vegetable that can be squeezed out of the skin and spread on a piece of toast. (No kidding.)

The form in which garlic is used in cooking makes an enormous difference in its flavor. For just a little, use a whole clove and remove it from the hot oil or sauce once it has released some of its pungency. For more character, cut the clove in halves or quarters. Finely minced or pressed garlic gives a very intense flavor to sauces, but we think it's nearly impossible to sauté effectively—it turns brown and bitter so fast that it doesn't have time to exude its flavor into the oil. We never use garlic presses in our own cooking.

Garlic bulbs should be firm and heavy; never buy them if they are yellowed or have green shoots. The fresher they are, the milder their flavor will be. (It is widely believed in France that purple garlic harvested early in the season is milder and easier to digest. The flavor of all garlic, whether white or purple, intensifies as the weather grows cooler.) Keep garlic bulbs in a cool, dry, well-ventilated place, and use them as quickly as you can. We peel the cloves by pressing firmly down on them with the blade of a knife to loosen the skin. Chopping is easy—just sprinkle a little salt on the peeled clove to keep it together and chop it quickly with a few strokes of the knife.

Elephant garlic is a relative newcomer, grown in California and available in specialty stores from late summer through the end of March. As the name implies, the cloves are huge, but we find it has a milder, more delicate flavor than its conventional ancestor.

GINGER

Ten years ago you could only find ginger in Oriental markets; now it's all over the place. Ginger, cardamom, and turmeric are all members of the same south Asian *Zingiberaceae* family, but ginger these days is king of the kitchen.

Ginger grows underground; it's a rhizome, like a potato, a swollen underground stem that can grow new roots and plant shoots. In Chinese cooking it gives a fresh taste to fish and raw meat; it sparks any chicken or seafood dish, and gives a lovely tang to fruits, soups, and sauces.

Choose the biggest "roots" you can find; they should be fat, glossy, and very hard—never shriveled or brown. Ginger keeps well in the icebox wrapped in a paper towel and stored in a plastic bag. Slice off the littlest knobs and peel the main sections with a sharp knife or vegetable peeler, then cut into thin slices or strips, or mince or purée as specified in the recipe.

GRAINS AND FLOURS

Like Mimi Boyd, the wizard who started our Hay Day bakery, we are all great believers in whole-grain flours; we go to considerable lengths to get them from Walnut Acres, an old-fashioned organic farm in Penns Creek, Pennsylvania. Even people who are not hooked on nutrition recognize that breads made with whole grains have a more interesting taste and texture than those made from commercially milled flour or bleached cake flour.

Unbleached flour should be the basis for almost all baking—certainly for all white bread. Never use cake flour or commercially processed flour for baking bread, and make sure that any flour you use is at room temperature.

Cracked wheat is wheat kernels cut into coarse, angular fragments. In small quantities it gives whole-grain bread a nutty flavor and crunchy texture.

Rye flour is low in gluten and produces breads that are moist and compact but sticky and inelastic; it should always be combined with whole wheat or unbleached white flour or both.

Cornmeal adds flavor and moisture to all breads; it should be water-ground to retain the germ. Yellow cornmeal has a lot more vitamin A than white.

Gluten flour is a wheat flour whose starch has been removed. For a lighter loaf, combine it with nonglutenous flours such as rye or soy.

Soy flour has a high fat content, which tends to make breads brown more quickly. Very high in B vitamins and protein, it must be used in combination with other flours.

Twelve-grain flour is a high-protein mixture of whole wheat, rye, corn, barley, oat, buckwheat, rice, and soy flours with millet, sunflower, sesame, and flax seeds. It should be used in combination with whole wheat flour.

Wheat germ is high in vitamin E, B vitamins, and iron. We use toasted wheat germ from health food suppliers because it still has the vitamin E that has usually been removed from supermarket wheat germ to give it longer shelf life. Toasting also destroys the enzyme that, if left alone, will digest the starch and gluten in slow-rising breads, making them gummy.

Brewers' yeast is an excellent source of B vitamins but should never be confused with active, granular bakers' yeast.

Bakers' yeast bought from a health food store will almost always be fresher and more active than the kind that comes in packages, and bread made with it will rise faster and higher. At Hay Day we get our yeast from Walnut Acres, too, but at home we buy it very fresh from the health food store down the street.

HERBS: FRESH AND DRIED

The chart on page 129 sets forth all the important herbs in detail; use fresh ones if you can. No matter how pretty the jars they come in, even the best dried herbs do not keep their flavor very long. If you must treasure the jars, replace the contents frequently. If you're substituting fresh herbs for dried, use three measures of fresh for every measure of dried—but like almost all rules, this one is not exact. (Dried tarragon, for example, is an exception—it's stronger when it's fresh.) Just keep tasting.

Be careful when recipes call for whole fresh herbs like bay leaves or sprigs of thyme—they should be carefully removed before serving. Many cooks have now stopped breaking up bay leaves; the edges are smooth when they're whole but razor-sharp when broken, and they have been known to cause internal injuries.

HOLLANDAISE AND MAYONNAISE

BLENDER HOLLANDAISE

MAKES APPROXIMATELY ¾ CUP

A quick version of Hollandaise Sauce can easily be made in a blender. Blend 3 egg yolks with 2 tablespoons lemon juice and a pinch of cayenne or Tabasco, then slowly blend in ½ pound melted (but not boiling) butter. Serve lukewarm.

HOMEMADE MAYONNAISE

MAKES APPROXIMATELY I CUP

1 whole egg
1 tablespoon red wine vinegar
¼ teaspoon salt
¼ teaspoon freshly ground white pepper
1 cup safflower oil

Blend the egg, vinegar, salt, and pepper in the food processor until well mixed. Add the safflower oil in a slow but steady stream until emulsified.

HYDROPONICS

Hydroponics, the cultivation of plants using a waterborne nutrient solution instead of soil, has been known for centuries but has been a commercial success only in the last ten years or so. *Hydroponic lettuce,* now available virtually year-round, is tender and delicately flavored; we usually offer Ostinata, a head lettuce that is a cross between Bibb and Buttercrunch, and Waldman, a frilly, pretty leaf lettuce. Hydroponic lettuces are fragile and don't last long when they're cut from their roots, but they will keep beautifully in a plastic bag in the icebox if the roots are kept moist and intact. *Hydroponic spinach* is free of grit, has large, very tender leaves, and is full of flavor.

Growers are now producing *hydroponic tomatoes* of extraordinary quality that are the next best thing to their field-grown summer-ripened cousins. Hydroponic tomatoes are vine-ripened, and since their growing conditions are always ideal, they can sometimes even surpass farm tomatoes nutritionally. They are delicate and perishable, though, and therefore expensive.

But compare them to the rubbery nubbin that comes in a box in the supermarket, and they're worth every penny. To survive packing and shipping, mass market tomatoes are picked when they're hard and green and reddened artificially with the ethylene gas that nature would normally provide them with at a later stage. They will thus redden on the way to market, but they will not ripen—they're no riper when you buy them than they were the day they were picked.

Hydroponic tomatoes, on the other hand, are tied up in a greenhouse just as they are in a garden and are picked when they're ready. They're available almost year-round, but May and June are the peak of the growing season, which usually coincides with the first field lettuce from New Jersey.

MARINADES

Alice B. Toklas put it well: "A marinade is a bath of wine, herbs, oil, vegetables, vinegars and so on, in which fish or meat destined for particular dishes repose for specified periods and acquire virtue."

OILS

There's no escaping the fact that the rich, delicious imported oils are expensive. We use walnut oil or cold-pressed extra-virgin olive oil for salads or pasta only when their particular flavor is important; we use a variety of less expensive oils, including supermarket olive oil, as well. *Sesame oil* is often specified for salads and stir-fries. *Safflower oil* has no flavor and will not interfere with other seasonings (we often mix it with expensive olive oil to cut the cost and the intense flavor). *Peanut oil* has no cholesterol and is excellent for cooking, although some people find it distasteful in vinaigrettes and mayonnaise. *Hazelnut oil* and *walnut oil* have pronounced flavors and are generally mixed with other oils; since they burn very quickly, they should be used only in dressings or uncooked sauces.

Olive oil keeps well for about a month at room temperature, although a large quantity should be decanted into airtight bottles and refrigerated. The oil will turn cloudy and solidify in the icebox, but will liquefy again at room temperature.

PASTA

Fresh pasta takes less time than dried pasta to cook, but both must be watched and tasted carefully. To keep pasta water from boiling over, add a tablespoon of oil or butter to increase the surface tension. (This works for jams, too.) To keep the pasta from sticking together after it is cooked, add a little oil, or butter, or even a little of the cooking liquid to the drained pasta. Sauces for pasta can be made from practically anything—leftover meat, chicken, shellfish, vegetables, and so on.

COOKING WITH PEPPERS

If you should happen to rub your eyes after working with the very hottest peppers, the pain can be agonizing; always wash your hands after peeling or chopping them.

ON COOKING RICE

Method I

You lose some vitamins this way, but it's awfully easy. Just put the rice in a huge pot of boiling water, allowing one cup for every four servings, and boil for fifteen minutes. Drain in a sieve and rinse under the tap, then set aside and steam in the sieve to reheat at serving time.

Method II

Cook the rice tightly covered for exactly seventeen minutes, using one and a half cups of liquid for every cup of rice. This is the method Craig Claiborne likes (you will notice that it differs substantially from Uncle Ben), and it produces dry rice that is still a little crunchy.

Method III

Cook rice uncovered, very rapidly, using two cups of water to every cup of rice. Cook it till the water has been absorbed but the rice is still wet and sticky, remove it from the heat, put a paper or linen towel over it, and put the top on. The rice will be dry and fluffy in about fifteen minutes and will even have loosened from the bottom of the pot. This is a good method for people who worry about rice being sticky.

SMOKED SALMON

Smoked Scottish and Norwegian salmon are both magnificent, but given the choice, we prefer Norwegian. It's the same fish, but the Norwegian process uses a cooler smoke with a milder blend of woods for a shorter time than the Scottish, giving it a more delicate flavor and texture. (Scotch is the liquor, by the way. *Scottish* is the salmon.)

Smoked salmon should be firm and pink and lustrous, not dry or cracking on the edges, and the scales of the skin should be vividly colored. Be sure the salmon is wrapped in waxed paper because ordinary butcher paper will draw out the oils and dry the flesh more quickly.

SALT

Is there anyone left who doesn't know that excess salt is injurious to health? Although our recipes use relatively little in comparison with older ones, we do recommend salt in moderation to marry and intensify flavors. Never add it without tasting to a recipe that already contains salty ingredients like anchovies or Parmesan cheese, and if you are making a sauce that must be boiled down or reduced to concentrate flavor, the salt should be added as the final step.

VANILLA

Split a vanilla bean in half and bury it for a week or more in superfine sugar, and use the sugar to intensify the vanilla flavor for any recipe that uses vanilla and sugar together. We do this at Hay Day, but when we need vanilla extract we use the best quality we can buy—it really makes a difference. You can make a nice Christmas present by putting a split bean in one to one and a half cups of good brandy and infusing it for six months in a dark place; it is a welcome substitute for ordinary commercial extracts, most of which are just 50 to 60 percent alcohol.

WASHING AND COOKING GREEN VEGETABLES

Leafy green vegetables like spinach and lettuces should be washed fresh from the market, using a sinkful of water so that dirt can fall to the bottom. They should then be removed from the water, leaving the grit behind (this process may need to be repeated), then drained, spin-dried, and refrigerated in plastic bags. Like cut flowers, green beans, asparagus, and broccoli keep well in water, especially if their ends are trimmed, or rinsed and returned to their plastic bags. Zucchini, cabbages, Brussels sprouts, and peppers should be rinsed briefly and trimmed just before using.

Steaming on a rack over boiling water keeps fragile vegetables intact and retains more of their nutrients, but we often find it difficult not to overcook them. It is easier to keep them green and crunchy by plunging them uncovered into large quantities of rapidly boiling water, but they lose more vitamins and minerals that way. Leafy green vegetables like spinach, chard, and beet greens are best just covered and cooked in the water that clings to their leaves after washing, then reheated tossed in a pan with a little butter just before serving— a procedure that usually takes less than five minutes altogether.

VINAIGRETTES AND DRESSINGS

What's the difference? A *vinaigrette* is a mixture of vinegar, oil, and various flavorings—usually one part vinegar to four parts oil, with salt, pepper, and a little garlic—but if you add any other liquid, crème fraîche or yoghurt, for example, we would call it a *dressing*. A tablespoon of warm water added to a vinaigrette will help keep it from separating.

VINEGARS

Choosing vinegars is a matter of taste, and it's interesting to experiment. For vinaigrettes we use the best quality wine vinegar we can find—some of the new Italian ones are outstanding—which does not necessarily mean the most expensive. If it comes from a good wine region, it's probably a good vinegar. *Balsamic vinegar* comes from Modena, where it is aged in barrels like sherry, and the bottled vinegar is often a blend of vintages up to fifty years old. We like its strong, robust flavor in a variety of dishes, but it should be used sparingly in salads. All-purpose *cider vinegar* is very strong, too. *Rice wine vinegar* has a mild and delicate flavor; *sherry vinegars* are excellent. *Raspberry vinegar* is superb in cooking; if it is made with real raspberries it has just enough sweetness to be mixed with club soda for a refreshing, astringent summer drink. *White vinegar* is usually just a mixture of acetic acid and water, but it is sometimes useful in mustards and creamy cheese dressings.

SPRING

*The first sign of spring here is when the ice breaks up
on the inkwell in the post office. A month later, the ice
leaves the lakes. And a month after that the first of the
summer visitors shows up and the tax collector's wife
removes the town records from the Frigidaire and plugs
it in for the summer.*

E. B. WHITE, One Man's Meat

FOR some people spring starts about the end of January, when they
see the first flowers on the narcissus they got for Christmas. For others
it is a little later, when the peepers start and someone fairly small brings in
some dandelions mashed in a paper cup. We're suckers for rhubarb, ourselves. At Hay Day the first reddish-pink stalks of rhubarb mean spring no
matter what; even though we know perfectly well they come from hothouses
in Cleveland and Michigan they do the job just fine, and the whole mood of
the place changes. Right after that the crew in the bakery starts talking about
strawberry-rhubarb pie, and we know it's really here.

Spring in the produce business starts in southern and central California,
where lettuce, broccoli, celery, and strawberries get the season going till it's
time for the East Coast crops. We visit Oxnard (lemons, limes, lettuce), Wat-
sonville (asparagus, strawberries), Salinas (lettuce, broccoli, celery), and
Castroville (artichokes) every year and arrange to have the very perishable
items flown to us so our trucks can meet them in New York. In March the
spring crops start coming in from Florida, and the season moves north along
the coast through the Carolinas to New Jersey and Connecticut.

Spring has meant traveling a good deal in Europe, too, as Hay Day has evolved. One of the great treats in the business is a June visit to the Salon International de l'Alimentation (SIAL), the international fancy food show in Paris, where on seven floors in three buildings a dazzling display of the riches of France—oils, vinegars, jams, spices, cheeses—is set forth by the people who make them. We visit Rungis, formerly Les Halles, the French version of the Hunts Point Terminal Market in the Bronx now relocated south of Paris, where in a vast and astoundingly clean and efficient system (there's a whole warehouse for flowers and four or five for cheeses, and all produce is brought in fresh every morning) we buy products for Hay Day and pool them in containers for jet air shipment to New York.

We've visited cheesemakers and cheese factories, and we've learned a lot, most of it the hard way. We have always been fanatic admirers of Brie de Meaux, and on one of our first trips to France we set out for what we assumed would be the mother house at Meaux, only to find that although there is a spectacular cathedral in the town, there is no Brie whatever made in Meaux—it all moved away years ago. We've been welcomed at the almost surgically clean Edam and Gouda (they pronounce it *howda*) factories in Holland, where shiny trucks visit tidy farmhouses and take the milk back for storage in gleaming tanks at the spotless factory, and at slightly more freeform places like Martin Collet in France, where the legendary velvety Brie is produced in organized chaos by workers in hip boots cheerily hosing down the whey that sloshes over the forms.

On a cheese tour of England we tasted Stilton at the spectacular three-hundred-year-old Tuxford and Tebbutts factory in Melton Mowbray and Blue Cheshire at Hinton Bank Farm in Shropshire. We sampled Wensleydale, Double Gloucester, and Leicester at Mollington Grange in Chester, where we found the aristocratic proprietor, Sir Oulton Wade, just as affable and patient with newcomers as his confreres on the Continent. (What is it about the cheese business that makes everybody so civilized?)

We went to Italy for cheeses and olive oil and brought home porcini mushrooms and sun-dried tomatoes as well. We saw a blaze of red out the window on the way to Venice and realized we were in virtually the only place in the world where you can see fields of radicchio. Knowing that the olive oil made in Tuscany is the best in the world, we set out to visit Badia a Coltibuono, the ancient estate that sends us wine and vinegar and magnificent cold-pressed extra-virgin oil in handblown dark green bottles—but for all we know it could be Oz. Lost in the first snowstorm they'd had in those mountains in decades, we never found it.

Above all, though, there's a wonderful sense of discovery in these trips. Melons from Cavaillon in France, figs from Italy and Morocco, olives from Provence—the world really is our garden these days, and we always come home with treasures.

It's a pretty nice business.

The Spring Market

ASPARAGUS is available almost year-round from worldwide sources, but for us it will always be a springtime event; it is in season in California from March through May and then in New Jersey in May and New England in June. Tenderness in asparagus is a matter of age; fat stalks are just as juicy as thin ones (they're classified Pencil, Standard, and Jumbo in the market) if they're picked young enough. The spears should be tightly budded and green at least two-thirds of the way down.

Keep asparagus in the icebox just as you would cut flowers; cut off the bottoms of the stems and store them upright in water. If they are really young they need not be peeled—just snap off the stems at the point where they break naturally. If the asparagus is larger, or if it's a special occasion and you're really gilding the lily, peel the stems with a sharp knife or a vegetable peeler, starting with a narrow cut near the tip end that gets deeper as the skin gets tougher. White asparagus is traditionally peeled because the outside layer of the stalks is often woody.

Cook asparagus uncovered in a roaster or a deep skillet—anything that is long enough and holds a lot of boiling water—until a fork will just pierce the spears, or until they droop gently when you lift them with a fork. (Special steamers are available that cook the stems in boiling water and steam the tips, but an old coffee percolator works just as well.) Plunge them in cold water to stop cooking, and serve warm with melted butter.

Artichokes are coming in from Castroville, California, where fields of them stretch to the horizon in every direction. One of the great springtime delicacies, they are also the dieter's friend—most calorie charts list the average artichoke at only about 44 calories. Choose artichokes with firm, solid green heads and compact leaves; if the leaves are brownish or cracked, they've been in storage too long. Pull off the rough outer leaves, cut off the stem at the base, and cut off about three-quarters of an inch of the springy top. Trim the thistle spikes off the leaves if you like, but it isn't necessary. Rub all the cut surfaces with half a lemon to prevent discoloration, and keep the cut artichokes in cold water with the juice of a lemon until you're ready to cook them. Cook in a stainless steel or enamel pot—aluminum will discolor them.

Artichokes can be steamed in about two inches of water, or simmered in boiling salted water, but in either case add bay leaf, lemon juice, and perhaps a little pepper and garlic or olive oil to the cooking water. Cook anywhere from twenty-five to forty minutes until the bottoms are tender and the leaves have loosened, and cool upside down on a rack. If the artichokes are young

and very small, the bristly "choke" under the leaves is edible, but in most cases it should be cut out to reveal the silky heart underneath.

If the artichoke hearts are to be used alone as a base for seafood salads, they will not take as long to cook as whole artichokes. Remove all but the tenderest leaves surrounding the heart, trim them, scrape away the choke, and boil or steam the hearts till they are tender, about twenty minutes.

This is peak *avocado* time, too. We like the lumpy-skinned, blackish Haas avocados the best, although fans of the bright green Calavos are legion; both are rich in B vitamins and minerals, but dieters beware—they're 20 percent fat, twenty times the average for other fruits. Avocados are rarely ripe when you buy them, but they will ripen to a nice all-over softness after two or three days on the kitchen windowsill in a brown paper bag. Don't try to ripen them in the icebox—it doesn't work.

Belgian endive is available almost year-round these days, but it is cheapest and most plentiful in the spring. The beautiful cluster of pale creamy leaves is the second shoot of a plant whose first-year growth is inedible; its roots are stored after the first year, then repotted and grown in cool darkness to keep the leaves packed closely together and as white as possible. Why is endive so expensive? Not only does it take two years to bring to market, but almost all of it is flown here from Belgium, often packaged in dark paper to reduce light. Endive heads should be solid and crisply white, with no brown outer leaves. It requires almost no washing; just cut off the hard bottom stem and rinse. Endive is usually served raw in salads or with dips, but it is also delicious braised and eaten hot; it has a slightly bitter taste that goes particularly well with rich meats like roast pork.

Chocho, or *chayote* (or Christophene, Mirliton, or vegetable pear), is a lovely, long-neglected tropical squash that grows in the Caribbean and the southern United States. Chocho is never eaten raw; it looks like a large green pear and has a gentle flavor somewhere between that of a cucumber and a zucchini. Substitute it in any recipe for summer squash—it can be stuffed, steamed, or parboiled and sautéed briefly in butter, or made into soup.

Fiddlehead ferns, one of the more exotic spring items, are the first green, tightly curled springtime growth of young ostrich ferns and actually an old American favorite. People who've never eaten them have trouble believing it, but they're delicious; they have a delicate taste, not unlike that of asparagus.

Fiddleheads should be steamed or cooked very briefly in boiling water till they're just tender, then drizzled with melted butter or served cold with a garlic vinaigrette. And don't worry—ostrich ferns are wild and plentiful all over the United States, and the tops grow back easily after cutting.

It must be highly amusing to the Mexicans that people in this country are only now discovering *jicama*; for them this useful and refreshing root has been as universal as the potato for centuries. Eaten raw it is not unlike a water chestnut, and it goes well in salads. As a cooked vegetable, it can be treated like a sweet potato, although its flavor is slightly less sweet. Don't be put off by its homely appearance. Buy small, firm tubers, and store them in a plastic bag in the icebox.

Morels, the great spring mushrooms, will be in the market in April and May. Egg-shaped and spongy-looking, they are fabulous sautéed in a little butter. (See mushroom chart on page 233). Dried morels can be very gritty; they should be thoroughly rinsed under the tap after soaking.

"I recall Sydney Smith," writes M.F.K. Fisher, "who once said that his idea of heaven . . . was pâté de foie gras to the sound of trumpets. Mine . . . is fresh green peas, picked and shelled by my friends." *Peas* are at their peak from mid-March until the hot weather settles in and finishes their season. Three kinds turn up in the market: snow peas and sugarsnap, both with edible pods, and green garden peas, which must be shelled.

Thin, delicate snow peas are usually specified for stir-frying because they lie down obediently in a wok; we also like to steam them till they're just tender but still green, then refresh them in cold water and set them aside. At serving time we warm them briefly in a skillet with a little butter. Sugarsnaps are wonderful eaten raw with a dip.

Peas are like sweet corn in that their sugars start turning to starch within minutes of picking, so they should be cooked as soon as possible. As a rule of thumb, one pound of garden peas will yield a little over a cup of shelled peas, which will serve two people; a pound of snow peas will serve three, and a pound of sugarsnaps perhaps four or five.

This is the time when everybody is most grateful for greenery, and young baby *salad greens*—Bibb and Ruby lettuces, arugula, curly endive, escarole, and watercress—are both plentiful and economical. Baby spinach leaves and young spring Belgian endive are succulent in spring salads, too. Use the lightest possible dressing to avoid drowning their different tastes and textures in a complicated sauce, tossing the salad thoroughly to wet the leaves completely.

If salad greens are crisp when they're bought, most will keep well for several days if they are washed and then dried in a salad spinner. Keep them in the spinner or in a plastic bag layered with paper towels to absorb excess moisture. We often use a pillowcase for storing large amounts, and it works fine. *Arugula* and hydroponic lettuces will also keep well with their roots on, dampened with water and stored in a plastic bag.

Sorrel is the same tangy, lemony leaf we used to call sourgrass, but cultivated sorrel grows much larger than its wild relative. Used for sauces and soups in France for centuries, sorrel has caught on only recently in American markets; it used to be impossible to find unless you grew it yourself. Its tart, pungent flavor is welcome in warm weather. It makes a classic soup, or try wilting it in a pan with a little onion and then adding it to an omelet or spreading it over a gratin of potatoes. Puréed sorrel turns a sort of gloomy grayish-brown, but added to crème fraîche or a bechamel, it makes an elegant sauce for fish or meat.

When you bring home a bunch of cultivated sorrel, wash it well and cut the bunch crosswise into thick ribbons. Put it in a pot with a little butter and it will melt down almost instantly into a purée that rarely needs straining. The young leaves have the clearest, freshest taste, but the larger ones are fine in moderation.

Fresh *spinach* is at its peak now; look for the smallest dark green leaves, and try to get them fresh and springy—spinach in a package just isn't the same. We think the best way to wash spinach is to put it in an enormous bowl full of water so that the grit all falls to the bottom, then to lift it out and repeat the process as often as necessary; if you wash it in a colander, all the sand stays right there. Use a lettuce dryer to dry it for a salad, but if you have a huge amount you might consider what one friend of ours does—she puts it in a pillowcase and spins it dry in the washing machine.

To cook spinach, remove tough stalks, wash leaves well, and place in a pot with a little salt but no additional water. Cover and cook over medium heat, stir after a few minutes, and the spinach will wilt down in less time than it takes to defrost a package from the frozen food department. Drain, then press it in a sieve or squeeze it dry with your hands, and reheat it very gently with a little butter when you're ready to serve. Spinach can be steamed in just a few minutes, too, or blanched in a large quantity of rapidly boiling water, although many of the vitamins and other nutrients go down the drain with the cooking water.

May and June are peak times for tender, fragile *hydroponic tomatoes*, which come along just in time to go into salads with all those lettuces (see page 37). Hydro tomatoes sometimes have the edge on their field-grown cousins because their greenhouse conditions are always ideal; rooted in a soil-less medium such as gravel, sand, or peat moss, they are fed nutrients in a waterborne solution several times a day and picked from the vine only when they are fully ripe.

Most of the onions in the chart on page 39 are available year-round, but delicate, perishable *Vidalia onions* come only from Vidalia, Georgia, in May and June, and unlike other onions, they cannot be stored. They are so sweet they can almost be eaten like apples and with no adverse social consequences. Be sure they're real Vidalias (the sacks are always marked) before you experiment, but do try them. They are glorious sliced with hydroponic tomatoes.

Papayas are not easy to ripen at home. We buy them almost ripe in the wholesale markets and put them out only when they're soft and yellow and just about ready to eat. A solid green papaya will never ripen well, but one with a touch of yellow will ripen in a paper bag if there's a cup of water in with it to enhance the humidity. Although they're often cooked and puréed for sauces and desserts, ripe, sweet papayas may also be eaten raw with a sprinkling of lime juice. We sometimes scrape out the seeds and put a scoop of vanilla ice cream in the hollow or serve them instead of melon for breakfast. Papayas sometimes redden human skin; this is an allergic reaction to an enzyme present in the juice.

Rhubarb, our favorite early spring dessert, isn't really a fruit at all—its beautiful pinkish-red stalks are close kin to celery. There are actually two kinds—the pink one and an older, yellowish-green variety—but although the pink is prettier, they taste exactly the same when they're cooked. Rhubarb is incredibly easy to prepare. Just trim off the leaves and dice the stalks, let them stand with a little sugar to extract the juice, then simmer till tender (the detailed recipe is on page 105). Don't ever eat the leaves, though; they can cause serious gastric distress.

Strawberries pour in from California in April and May until the crop from New Jersey takes over for late May and early June. Driscoll is the picturebook variety (it's bigger than most, with a pretty green cap), but Douglas and Pajaro are two other very successful recent varieties that may have the edge on flavor. Don't be seduced by appearance when buying strawberries; some that look spectacular can taste like plywood when you get them home. They should be sweetly fragrant and very slightly tender but not squashy. Like any fruit, strawberries with high sugar content break down more rapidly, so the ripest, sweetest ones must be flown here from California and therefore cost more in the market, but the difference in flavor makes it easy to rationalize the price. Keep strawberries in the icebox, and never wash or stem them until just before they are served; they spoil very quickly.

SALAD GREENS

VARIETY	DESCRIPTION	SUGGESTED USES IN SALADS
BIBB LETTUCE	Soft-leaf variety of Butterhead lettuce. Mild flavor. Leaves susceptible to bruising easily. Light green color. Limestone lettuce is Bibb grown in limestone soil, especially in Kentucky.	Leaves lay flat to make a nice bed for composed salads. Toss with a sharper and deeper color green for contrast.
BOSTON LETTUCE	Soft-leaf variety, but a slightly compact head.	Use a light dressing of walnut oil and mild vinegar and add some walnut halves for crunch.
ROMAINE LETTUCE (Cos Lettuce)	Heads grow erect with large cross ribs. Outer leaves are dark and can be tough and bitter. Inner leaves slightly sharp and pleasing.	Discard tough ribs. Classic use is Caesar Salad. Also good in combination with spinach.
ICEBERG LETTUCE	Firm, cabbagelike head. Crisp light green leaves.	Because leaves lack flavor, this is most interesting in conjunction with other greens. Iceberg is particularly good for shredding or a chiffonade.
LOOSE LEAF LETTUCE (Simpson, Ruby Red, Salad Bowl, Oak Leaf, and hydroponic lettuce varieties)	Many of these are colorful and some have frilly leaves. Quite perishable and susceptible to bruising. Good flavor.	Toss with Bibb or Boston for an interesting color and texture effect. Use a mild dressing lightly accented with herbs.
CHICORY (loose-leaf endive, escarole)	Relatively sharp taste and unusual shapes. Frequently very sandy.	Takes well to stronger vinaigrettes, nice with croutons and grated Parmesan cheese.
SPINACH	Deep green leaves, distinct rich flavor. Can be sandy.	Sturdy green that takes well to wilting. Great in hearty salads with the addition of bacon, cubed ham, and julienned cheeses or riced hard-cooked eggs. Fruits such as oranges or apples a fine addition.

WATERCRESS	Small, deep green leaves with a decidedly sharp hot taste. Keep stems in water until ready to use.	Elegant as a single salad ingredient with a sweet-tart dressing. Wonderful in combination with mild, light green lettuces. A pretty garnish green. Good with fruits.
DANDELION	Use greens only when young. Wash well. Sharp flavor.	A surprising spring salad ingredient. Great as a wilted salad with a bacon dressing.
ARUGULA	Hot with a mustardlike flavor. Very popular in Italy.	Use in combination with milder greens for a peppery accent. A mustard vinaigrette with a few herbs heightens the flavor.
MÂCHE (Lamb's Lettuce or Corn Salad)	Another European green especially popular in France. Nutty, delicate taste.	Arrange on individual plates and top with a slice of marinated goat cheese. Also good dressed with a vinaigrette made from nut oils.
COMPLEMENTARY SALAD HERBS	Dill, basil, mint, chives, parsley, oregano, tarragon, thyme.	Either sprinkle herbs over salad, use in the dressing, or as accent.

ONIONS

NAME	DESCRIPTION	FLAVOR	COMMENTS	BEST USES
PEARL ONIONS	1 ounce, white, red, or yellow skin, white flesh.	Mild	Pearl onions are onions harvested when the bulbs are still small.	Boiled, pickled, creamed, sautéed, stews, gravies.
RED ONIONS: Red Italian Bermuda	8 to 12 ounces, purple skin, white flesh. Red purple veins. Red Italian are usually elongated.	Medium	Usually sweet and mild. Red onions come in a variety of flavors.	Very good raw in salads, or sliced paper-thin in sandwiches.
SPANISH ONIONS (also called Bermuda)	8 to 12 ounces, golden yellow skin, white flesh.	Medium	Readily available year-round. Spanish onions have a longer shelf life than mild whites or red.	Also good raw, sliced in salads and sandwiches.
VIDALIA ONIONS	4 to 12 ounces, yellow skin, white flesh.	Sweet and mild	Vidalias come only from Vidalia, Georgia, from mid-May to mid-June. Make sure they are genuine.	Excellent raw or sautéed, Vidalias have a reputation for being the sweetest onion available.
WALLA WALLA SWEET ONIONS	1½ to 2½-inch diameter, light golden yellow.	Sweet and mild	Difficult to find but worth the effort, Walla Wallas are available only from late June through August.	Good plain, sliced in salads or sandwiches.
WHITE ONIONS	8 to 12 ounces, white silvery skin, white flesh.	Medium	White onions generally don't keep as well as yellow. Best kept refrigerated.	Good all-purpose onions; sautéed, stewed.

ONIONS (continued)

NAME	DESCRIPTION	FLAVOR	COMMENTS	BEST USES
YELLOW GLOBE ONIONS	1½ to 2½ inches diameter, golden yellow.	Strong	The typical northern cooking onion, with a long storage life.	Soups, stews, casseroles, stuffing.
ELEPHANT GARLIC	6 to 16 ounces, white skin, white flesh.	Mild	Easy to peel, keeps well for six months.	Mild enough to enjoy raw in salads or with cheese. Can be sautéed and served plain.
GERMAN RED GARLIC	3 to 4 ounces, white skin, purple-red flesh.	Strong	Probably the most flavorful garlic, but a very short storage life.	Excellent rubbed into lamb or pork before roasting, good in potato pancakes, dumplings.
ITALIAN GARLIC	3 to 5 ounces, purple and white skin, white flesh.	Strong	Very aromatic, hotter than elephant; superior to garlic found in most stores.	Poultry, pasta, salads, vinaigrettes.
SUSANVILLE GARLIC	2 to 4 ounces, white skin and flesh.	Strong, distinctive	Will keep a full year in a cool, dry, dark place.	Good for general use; sauces, soups, casseroles, pasta.
WHITE GARLIC	2 to 3 ounces, white skin, creamy flesh.	Strong	This is the standard garlic everyone's familiar with. Best when fresh and seldom keeps more than a month or two.	Another strong all-purpose garlic.

ONIONS (continued)

NAME	DESCRIPTION	FLAVOR	COMMENTS	BEST USES
LEEKS	8 to 10 inches long, blue-green tops with white base and rootlets.	Mild	An excellent winter vegetable.	Good served plain or in soups, stews, or with a vinaigrette.
SCALLIONS	8 to 10 inches long, green tops with small white bulbs and rootlets.	Mild	Also called spring onions, bunching onions, and green onions.	Excellent raw, sliced in salads or stir-fries.
SHALLOTS	1 to 3 ounces, gold to purple, usually coppery skin, yellow-white flesh.	Mild	Shallots grow in cloves like garlic, but their flavor is a mild blend of garlic and onion.	Classic sauces, all French cooking, salads.
RED SHALLOTS	1 ounce, coppery skin, creamy flesh.	Mild	Widely considered finer than ordinary shallots, these are often called "French" shallots.	Classic French cooking, sauces, eggs, poultry, seafood.
CHIVES	4 to 6 inches long, blue-green, with a waxy bloom.	Mild	Chives are the round, slender tops of onion varieties grown specifically for this purpose.	Best fresh in salads or with eggs, potatoes, fish, cottage cheese, sour cream, cream cheese.
GARLIC CHIVES ("Chinese chives")	4 to 6 inches long, flat and dark green, with a waxy bloom.	Medium	The flavor of garlic chives is somewhat stronger than standard chives.	Use as regular chives; excellent in Oriental recipes.

Spring Menus

ONE day it's warm enough to eat on the terrace, the next day there's snow on the lilacs. These menus for a New England spring are all freshness and greenery—the first strawberries, the first rhubarb, the first young spinach—to be served indoors or out at the whim of the weather.

COMPANY DINNER PARTY

Most of the preparation is done before the guests arrive, allowing the well-organized host to be out on the terrace serving aperitifs, talking about trips to the Dordogne, and giving the illusion that someone else is making dinner.

MARINATED GOAT CHEESE   (*49*)

FILLETS OF SOLE WITH SPINACH   (*75*)

OLD-FASHIONED PARSLEY-BUTTERED NEW POTATOES   (*91*)

ORANGE-GINGER STRAWBERRIES   (*100*)

LEMON ICE BOX COOKIES   (*109*)

SPRING

MAKE-AHEAD MEAL

We know people who can spend the entire day in the Metropolitan Museum, get home half an hour ahead of the guests, and still serve dinner serenely. There's no secret—all they do is make everything the night before and set the table at breakfast time.

AVOCADO MOLD *(52)*
COLD MARINATED CHICKEN *(79)*
SPRING VEGETABLE SALAD *(62)*
RHUBARB CRUMBLE *(108)*

ITALIAN NIGHT

Nobody doesn't like Italian food. Here's a relaxing spring combination to serve at the end of a complicated day. Serve small plates of linguine—the liver should be the star attraction.

LINGUINE WITH GREEN VEGETABLES *(65)*
CALVES' LIVER À LA VENEZIANA *(81)*
ROMAN SPINACH *(95)*
YOGHURT WITH HONEY AND FRUIT *(111)*

FAMILY FEAST

After a week of going in different directions, it is nice for everybody to sit down at the table at the same time, celebrating a birthday, or a new job, or just being together for *once*. If each person makes one thing, it's not work.

MOZZARELLA, TOMATO, AND ROAST YELLOW PEPPER SALAD *(57)*
GRILLED LAMB WITH SAGE *(84)*
ARTICHOKE PURÉE *(86)*
BRAISED SUGARSNAPS *(93)*
HAZELNUT-STRAWBERRY MERINGUE *(100)*

LATE NIGHT SUPPER

You've been to the movies, or to a party, and it's time for something easy and light. Eggs and asparagus go well with the peppery watercress, and the orange delight is a refreshing finish.

POACHED EGGS AND ASPARAGUS   *(69)*
WATERCRESS SALAD   *(61)*
ORANGE DELIGHT   *(111)*

LUNCH FOR A FEW

Come and have lunch and sit in the sun—the apple blossoms are out, and it's too nice to stay inside!

PASTA PRIMAVERA SALAD   *(64)*
GARLIC BREAD
LIGHT STRAWBERRY MOUSSE   *(98)*

SPECIAL OCCASION LUNCH

It's somebody's birthday, or a baby shower, or a lunch for the bridesmaids. Just add fresh bread and a green salad, put narcissus and daffodils all around the house, and serve a light and sparkling white wine.

COLD ASPARAGUS CURRY SOUP   *(45)*
ARTICHOKE-CRABMEAT RAVIGOTE   *(77)*
STRAWBERRIES WITH STRAWBERRY PURÉE   *(98)*

Spring Recipes

COLD ASPARAGUS CURRY SOUP

Even people who begin the season thinking they can eat buttered asparagus at every meal welcome variety after a while, and this make-ahead cold soup is lovely on a warm spring day. Be sure to process the broth and asparagus a little at a time, so the processor doesn't overflow.

SERVES 4

1 pound fresh asparagus
3 cups well-seasoned chicken broth (see page 8)
1 cup heavy cream
2 to 2½ teaspoons Madras curry powder
Lemon juice
Salt and freshly ground black pepper to taste
2 teaspoons butter

Cut off asparagus tips in 1½-inch lengths and steam until just tender. Set aside. Chop the rest of the stems and simmer in chicken broth until very tender. Process the chopped asparagus and broth in a food processor or blender until smooth. Return purée to the saucepan and add cream, curry powder, lemon juice, and salt and pepper to taste.

Simmer for 5 minutes. Beat in butter, cool, and chill soup.

Just before serving, beat the soup with a whisk and pour into serving bowls, sherbet cups, or iced mugs. Top each bowl with several asparagus tips and serve with freshly ground pepper.

A spoonful of crème fraîche can be added to each bowl before serving, or pass a bowlful separately.

SORREL SOUP

The tangy, fresh flavor of sorrel has always been familiar in European cooking, often paired with spring veal or used to flavor soups and vegetable dishes. This version of the classic French Potage Germiny is a nice introduction for anyone who is cooking with sorrel for the first time.

SERVES 6

3 tablespoons butter
⅓ cup scallions, minced
5 cups fresh sorrel (about 1½ pounds), washed, stemmed, and cut up
Salt to taste
3 tablespoons flour
5 cups well-seasoned chicken broth (see page 8)
½ cup heavy cream
3 tablespoons butter
1 tablespoon scallions, sliced very thin

Melt 3 tablespoons butter in a saucepan. Cook scallions gently until tender. Stir in sorrel and salt. Sweat, covered, for about 5 minutes.

Sprinkle flour over the sorrel and stir well. Cook for 3 minutes. Beat in broth. Simmer 20 minutes.

Beat in the cream and simmer gently for 5 minutes longer. Beat in remaining 3 tablespoons butter, 1 tablespoon at a time. Check seasoning. Serve topped with scallion slices.

If a smoother soup is preferred, purée the broth and sorrel in a food processor or blender before beating in the cream and other ingredients.

SORREL AND POTATO SOUP

Rich and filling, this is a creamy sorrel version of vichyssoise. It can be served chilled, but if so may need a little more salt and pepper.

SERVES 6

2 tablespoons butter
2 leeks, the white part and 1 inch of green of each leek thinly sliced
1½ pounds potatoes, peeled and diced
6 cups well-seasoned chicken broth (see page 8)
1 pound sorrel leaves, washed and cut up
Lemon juice
Salt and freshly ground black pepper to taste
1 cup heavy cream
1 tablespoon butter

Heat 2 tablespoons of butter in a large saucepan and cook the leeks until they are transparent. Add potatoes and sauté for 5 minutes. Add the chicken broth and half of the sorrel. Simmer 20 minutes or until potatoes are tender. Process the mixture in a food processor until smooth.

Return purée to the saucepan. Add lemon juice, salt, and pepper to taste. Stir in the remaining sorrel and cook just until tender. Beat in cream. Beat in 1 tablespoon butter. Serve at once.

AVOCADO SOUP

This silky soup can be served warm or cold but, like the sorrel soup on page 47, may need more seasonings if it is to be served chilled—cool temperatures tend to make foods taste a bit bland.

SERVES 4

2 medium-ripe avocados, peeled, halved, seeded, and diced
1 cup heavy cream
3 cups well-seasoned chicken broth (see page 8)
3 tablespoons dry white wine or sherry
½–1 teaspoon salt
Freshly ground black pepper
1 ripe avocado, peeled and thinly sliced
Tabasco sauce to taste (optional)

Purée the diced avocado in a food processor with half of the cream. Add the rest of the cream and process briefly.

Bring broth to a boil in a large saucepan. Reduce to a simmer and stir in the avocado mixture. Stir in the wine and salt and pepper to taste. Simmer for 5 minutes. Gently stir in sliced avocado. For extra zip, add Tabasco to taste.

BARBECUED OYSTERS

Driving to the Hatteras shore for roast oysters is one of the great memories of growing up in North Carolina. They were purveyed by some of the most ramshackle eateries in the continental United States, where shuckers wearing long rubber gloves worked quickly up and down long zinc counters, popping oysters into heavy china bowls in front of customers who dipped them in melted butter or barbecue sauce and ate them as quickly as they were dispensed. Roast oysters have turned up in plusher settings since then, but somehow without the smell of the sea air, the banging of the screen door, and the crashing of the crockery on the counter, they have never tasted quite the same.

SERVES 4

1 peck fresh oysters, washed to remove mud
1 cup melted butter and/or
1 cup Barbecue Sauce (see page 160)

Spread the washed oysters on the hot charcoal grill. When the shells begin to open (usually 5 to 6 minutes), remove oysters from heat. Protecting your hands with a heavy glove, quickly open the shells and cut the oyster from the attaching muscle with a sharp knife. Dip the hot oysters into melted butter or barbecue sauce and wash down with beer, white wine, or tall glasses of iced tea.

MARINATED GOAT CHEESE

The tang of fresh goat cheese, especially the little aged rounds known as Crottins de Chavignol, is refreshing as the weather gets warmer. Thanks to the enterprise of several young East and West Coast cheesemakers, we are now able to buy it in prime condition. Even people who think that cheese can be made only in France have found American goat cheese highly acceptable.

SERVES 4

1 cup extra-fine olive oil
2 tablespoons fresh parsley leaves
2 tablespoons freshly snipped chives
1 tablespoon fresh basil leaves, minced
1 tablespoon fresh thyme leaves
1 tablespoon fresh rosemary

4 Crottins de Chavignol or 1 small goat cheese log such as Ste. Maure or
  Montrachet, sliced into rounds
1 clove garlic, sliced thin
Whole sprigs of fresh basil, thyme, or rosemary (optional)
Freshly ground black pepper

Heat the olive oil until very hot. Pour the hot oil over the herbs in a shallow pan. Let the oil cool and then transfer the oil and herbs to a crock or jar. Add goat cheese, garlic, and whole sprigs of herbs if desired. Make sure the cheese is completely covered with the oil.

Cover the crock and let it stand in a cool, dry place for several days. After 3 days the jar may be refrigerated. Remember to remove the jar from the icebox at least 4 hours before serving to allow the oil to come to room temperature and the flavor of the herbs to recover from the cold.

Remove cheese from the oil, drain, and arrange on individual plates. Season with freshly ground black pepper. Serve with toasted crusty homemade white bread.

AVOCADO WITH GARLIC

Popular in France and a nice quick beginning for a party menu, this unusual appetizer requires the finest quality avocados and extra-fresh, thick yoghurt.

SERVES 4

2 large ripe avocados, halved and stoned
½ lemon
1 cup plain yoghurt (or puréed ricotta, or a puréed mixture of yoghurt and
  ricotta)
1 teaspoon finely chopped garlic
1 tablespoon white wine vinegar
8 drops Tabasco sauce, to taste
Salt to taste
Freshly ground black pepper to taste
2 tablespoons fresh chives, chopped

Rub cut surface of avocado with lemon half.

Beat yoghurt with garlic, vinegar, and Tabasco until well mixed. Refrigerate 1 hour or more. Add the salt and pepper to taste.

Spoon the mixture into the avocado halves. Serve at once, garnished with a sprinkle of chopped chives.

Two tablespoons finely sliced scallions can be stirred into the yoghurt mixture, or 1 teaspoon freshly chopped dill or basil can be added just before serving.

SPICY GUACAMOLE

Don't just use this as a dip; it's great as a topping on a mixed vegetable salad, or as a condiment, Mexican style, with ham or lamb or roast pork.

SERVES 4 TO 6

1 small onion, very finely chopped
2 large, ripe avocados, peeled and cut up
Juice of 1 lemon
1 small fresh chile pepper, washed, seeded, and finely chopped or 1 teaspoon
  canned chopped hot chilies
4 tablespoons freshly chopped coriander
Tabasco sauce to taste

With a fork, mash together all ingredients except coriander and Tabasco. The mixture should be slightly chunky.

Stir in coriander and Tabasco to taste. Cover tightly with plastic wrap until time to serve.

Serve with unsalted tortilla chips.

One large tomato peeled, seeded, and chopped can be stirred into the purée before serving.

AVOCADO MOLD

For all their richness, avocados are light-tasting enough to go well in warm weather. This mold is a good way to start a spring dinner or enhance a party buffet; it is pretty served on a bed of lettuce and filled with shrimp salad, cherry tomato halves, or cold marinated miniature vegetables.

SERVES 8 OR MORE

½ cup boiling water
1 envelope of unflavored gelatin, softened in ½ cup cold water
1 teaspoon salt
1 tablespoon finely grated onion
½ teaspoon finely chopped garlic (optional)
2 tablespoons lemon juice
2 cups avocado purée (about 2 to 3 ripe avocados)
½ cup Homemade Mayonnaise (see page 18)
½ cup crème fraîche (see page 12), thinned with a little milk and then whipped
    until stiff, or ½ cup heavy cream, whipped stiff

Pour boiling water over softened gelatin mixture. Stir until gelatin is completely dissolved. Cool.

Add salt, onion, garlic if desired, lemon juice, and puréed avocado. (If using heavy cream, increase the lemon juice to 3 tablespoons.) Stir well. Stir over ice until thick. Gently fold mayonnaise into beaten crème fraîche or heavy cream. Then fold cream mixture into the puréed avocado. Pour at once into a 6-cup ring mold that has been lightly oiled. Chill at least 4 hours, until fully set.

Turn the mold onto a service platter lined with lettuce. Fill the center as desired. Serve with thick slices of toasted homemade bread.

ASPARAGUS WITH BACON PANCAKES AND HOLLANDAISE

Although asparagus is now a West Coast crop, our taste for it goes back to our own Connecticut Valley and beyond that to the valley of the Rhine; both have been rich asparagus sources for hundreds of years. This recipe comes originally from Germany, where the first spring asparagus is received with fanatical enthusiasm; in many regions there is even a festival called (appropriately) the Spargelfest, at which chefs vie to create the largest number of asparagus recipes and devise menus in which asparagus appears in some form in every course but dessert!

SERVES 6

8 eggs
2½ cups milk
½ teaspoon salt
1 cup flour
1 cup crumbled, crisply fried bacon
6 tablespoons butter
36 or more fresh asparagus stalks, steamed for 3 to 4 minutes, or until crisply tender, drained, and cooled slightly
1 cup Hollandaise (see page 18)
2 teaspoons lemon juice
Freshly ground black pepper

Beat eggs in a large bowl. Beat in milk just to blend, and add salt. Add flour, a little at a time, stirring constantly. Stir in bacon.

For each pancake: Melt 1 tablespoon butter in a nonstick, 10-inch frying pan. Pour in about ½ cup batter and tilt pan to spread batter evenly over bottom. Cook over moderate heat until bubbles appear in the surface and begin to break.

Flip the pancake to cook the other side, or carefully loosen the pancake and slide it out onto a plate. Invert skillet over plate and then quickly turn pancake back into the skillet. Cook just until completely set, only a moment or two longer.

Slide finished pancake onto a heated serving plate, wrapping in a kitchen towel to keep warm, and then finish remaining pancakes.

Serve pancakes hot topped with steamed asparagus and Hollandaise that has been thinned by beating in the lemon juice. Serve with freshly ground black pepper and a chilled Liebfraumilch.

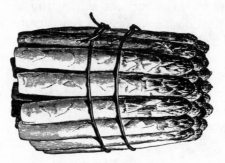

ASPARAGUS WITH HAM AND ORANGE CHANTILLY SAUCE

Simple and delicious, this asparagus recipe also originates in a German Spargelfest. The Chantilly Sauce is Hollandaise lightened with whipped cream.

SERVES 4

½ pound Westphalian or Virginia ham, sliced paper thin
1 pound pencil-thin asparagus, steamed for 3 to 4 minutes, or until crisply
  tender, drained, and cooled slightly
3 tablespoons orange juice
⅔ cup Hollandaise, at room temperature (see page 18)
⅓ cup whipped cream
Freshly ground black pepper

Arrange thin slices of ham on each plate. Top with well-drained asparagus.
Stir orange juice into Hollandaise; fold in whipped cream. Top each serving with a tablespoon of sauce and freshly ground black pepper. Pass remaining sauce in a separate dish.

FRESH PAPAYA AND WESTPHALIAN HAM

With very ripe papaya and top-quality ham, this variation on an old theme becomes truly extraordinary.

SERVES 4

1 large, ripe papaya, peeled, seeded, and cut into thin wedges
⅓ pound Westphalian ham, sliced paper thin
Grated fresh ginger
1 lime, quartered, and cut into thin, triangular slices
Freshly ground black or white pepper

Wrap each wedge of papaya in a slice of ham. Dust with a little grated ginger and top with a thin slice of lime.

Serve with freshly ground black or white pepper.

Figs, melon, fresh peaches, or pears can be substituted for papaya.

PISSALADIERE

Superb on a picnic, this onion tart is a Provençal favorite. The name is derived from the fish paste that some French recipes use instead of anchovies to counterpoint the sweet cooked onions. Use onions generously; they should form a good thick layer on the crust. Tomatoes and small French olives are not always specified, but we think they enhance the Provençal flavor.

SERVES 6

2 tablespoons olive oil
6 cups onions, peeled and sliced very thin
2 cloves garlic, minced
Salt and freshly ground black pepper to taste
Pastry for a one-crust pie (see page 105)
2 tomatoes, thinly sliced
⅓ cup (or more) small French olives
1 tablespoon olive oil

8 anchovy fillets, rinsed to remove salt and dried
½ teaspoon dried oregano

Preheat the oven to 425°F.

Heat the olive oil in a deep, heavy saucepan. Add the onions and garlic. Simmer, covered, over low heat until the onions are transparent, very tender, but not browned. This takes at least one hour. Season with salt and pepper to taste.

Roll out the pastry and fit it into a 10-inch tart pan. Crimp the edges. Spread the cooked onions over the bottom of the prepared crust. Arrange the tomato slices in a circle on top of the onions and decorate with olives. Sprinkle olive oil over the tart. Lay the anchovy fillets on the tomatoes like the spokes of a wheel. Sprinkle with oregano.

Bake at 425°F for 20 minutes. Remove from the oven. Serve hot or at room temperature.

To carry the tart on a picnic, leave it in the pan to protect it. Slide it onto a plate or a board and slice it like a pizza to serve.

RICE SALAD SUPREME

Protein-rich salads made of wheat, rice, or corn are light and nourishing additions to the spring repertoire. Serve this one for supper or for lunch outdoors on Saturday with homemade whole-grain bread and fresh fruit.

SERVES 4

1 head leaf lettuce (Boston, Bibb, or the like), washed and chilled
1 head chicory, washed and chilled
½ cup sauce vinaigrette made with tarragon vinegar (see page 392)
2½ cups cooked rice, chilled
1 small green pepper, seeded and cut into rings
2 tomatoes, quartered
2 eggs, hard-boiled, shelled, and quartered
½ cup green olives (oil-cured, if possible)
½ pound fresh asparagus tips, steamed until crisply tender
½ pound small fresh shrimp, steamed, peeled, and chilled
1 tablespoon fresh mint leaves

Arrange the lettuce and chicory on a large serving platter. Mix the vinaigrette with the rice and mound in the center of the platter. Surround the rice with green pepper rings, tomato quarters, hard-boiled egg quarters, olives, and asparagus.

Mound the shrimp on top of the rice and garnish with fresh mint leaves.

MOZZARELLA, TOMATO, AND ROAST YELLOW PEPPER SALAD

Yellow peppers add color and a nice mild flavor to all kinds of dishes; here they are roasted and then combined with mozzarella and tomatoes in a salad that goes well with spring lamb for the first spring cookout. We like buffalo mozzarella; it has more flavor and character and a less rubbery texture than the mass-produced supermarket version.

SERVES 6

2 large yellow peppers, halved and seeded
1 teaspoon extra-fine olive oil
½ pound fresh buffalo mozzarella cheese, sliced
2 large tomatoes, peeled and thickly sliced
3 tablespoons fresh basil, chopped
1 tablespoon Dijon mustard
2 tablespoons red wine vinegar
Salt and freshly ground black pepper to taste
1 tablespoon warm water
⅓ cup extra-fine olive oil
Fresh basil leaves

Broil the pepper halves on a baking sheet, watching them constantly until the skin begins to char and bubble. Drop the hot peppers into a paper or plastic bag, close, and let stand for 5 to 10 minutes. Remove peppers and peel off the skin. Slice peeled peppers thinly and toss with a teaspoon of olive oil.

Arrange the cheese, tomatoes, and peppers in an overlapping pattern on a serving platter.

Beat the basil, mustard, vinegar, salt, pepper, water and ⅓ cup olive oil together until the dressing is smooth and creamy. Pour over the cheese, to-matoes, and peppers and garnish with whole basil leaves. Serve at room temperature.

ENDIVE AND CITRUS SALAD WITH HONEY LEMON DRESSING

Serve this salad as a first course before roast lamb or pork; its tartness is a refreshing contrast to the richness of the roast meat.

SERVES 4

4 Belgian endive, washed, dried, and quartered
1 large grapefruit, peeled and sectioned
2 oranges, peeled and sectioned
2 tablespoons honey
¼ cup fresh grapefruit juice
½ teaspoon salt
½ teaspoon grated fresh ginger
1 teaspoon sesame seeds, lightly toasted

Arrange one endive on each serving plate. Divide the grapefruit and orange sections between the plates and arrange in an attractive pattern.

Mix honey, grapefruit juice, salt, ginger, and sesame seeds in a small jar. Shake well to mix thoroughly. Pour dressing over the salads and chill.

FRESH GRAPEFRUIT AND SHRIMP SALAD

We like to use Orchid Island grapefruit for this salad; its particular sweetness goes well with seafood.

SERVES 4

2 large fresh grapefruit, halved, seeded, and sectioned
1 cup cooked shrimp, preferably the tiny ones
¾ cup diced fresh celery
⅓ cup diced fresh green pepper
Salt to taste
½ cup Homemade Mayonnaise (see page 18)
1 head leaf lettuce (Bibb, Boston, or Red-Tipped), washed and dried
1 cup cherry tomatoes
¼ cup cooked whole shrimp (tiny ones) for garnish
Fresh dill

Cut grapefruit sections into small pieces and toss with 1 cup shrimp, celery, green pepper, salt, and mayonnaise. Serve on lettuce-lined plates and garnish with cherry tomatoes and whole shrimp. Garnish with a sprig of fresh dill.

SAVOY CABBAGE SLAW

The Dutch contracted the French *salade* into *slaa* (slaw), and their own *kaal* (kale) evolved into the word for cabbage, but the word *coleslaw* is used only in the United States. Wilted just a little by the hot sauce, crinkly and delicate Savoy cabbage is a nice change of pace in this make-ahead version. We like the mildness of rice wine vinegar in the sauce.

SERVES 6

1 small head Savoy cabbage, cored and thinly shredded
1 red Bermuda onion, very thinly sliced
¼ cup rice wine vinegar

1 tablespoon sweet mustard
Salt to taste
½ cup safflower oil
¼ cup pecans, chopped

Toss the cabbage and onion together well. Mix the vinegar, mustard, salt, and oil in a saucepan. Boil for 5 minutes and pour over the cabbage. Sprinkle with pecans and toss until thoroughly coated. Allow to stand at room temperature for at least 30 minutes.

ENDIVE AND WALNUT SALAD

This French salad is excellent served just before the richness of roast pork.

SERVES 4

¼ teaspoon dry mustard
1 tablespoon Dijon mustard
1 tablespoon wine vinegar
3 tablespoons olive oil
2 tablespoons heavy cream
1 tablespoon lemon juice
Salt and freshly ground black pepper to taste
3 large Belgian endive, washed, cored, and cut into 1-inch rounds
3 tablespoons coarsely chopped walnuts
¼ pound Gruyère cheese, cubed
Leaf lettuce for garnish
Walnut halves

Combine mustards with vinegar. Whisk together thoroughly and then add oil and cream. Beat in lemon juice and salt and pepper. Toss dressing with endive, walnuts, and cheese cubes.

Serve mounded on a bed of lettuce. Garnish with a few walnut halves.

WATERCRESS SALAD

Watercress, with its peppery taste, makes salads that go naturally with grilled or roasted lamb. This one would also be good with roast pork.

SERVES 4

2 tablespoons white wine vinegar
4 tablespoons olive oil
½ teaspoon dry mustard
Salt to taste
½ teaspoon freshly ground black pepper
3 cups fresh watercress, thoroughly washed, picked over, and well dried

Beat the vinegar, oil, mustard, salt, and pepper together until thoroughly mixed. Pour over watercress. Toss gently.

CALIFORNIA CHAYOTE SALAD

Chayote, or chocho, has only recently become generally available, but it has been growing in this hemisphere for centuries (see page 32). A mildly flavored tropical squash, it can be substituted in any recipe for summer squash or zucchini.

SERVES 4

2 chayotes, peeled and halved, then boiled or steamed until just tender. Cool and cut into small chunks.
1 bunch scallions, chopped (all but the green leaves)
2 tomatoes, peeled, seeded, and cut into chunks
1 teaspoon sweet mustard
3 tablespoons lime juice
¼ cup salad oil (or olive oil)
Salt and freshly ground black pepper to taste
1 head leaf lettuce, washed, dried, and chilled
¼ cup ripe olives, seeded and cut in half
2 tablespoons chopped fresh coriander

Toss together chayote chunks, scallions, and tomatoes.

Make a salad dressing with the mustard, lime juice, and salad oil. Add salt and pepper to taste.

Toss salad with dressing and pile in a lettuce-lined bowl. Garnish with olives and a sprinkling of chopped fresh coriander.

SPRING VEGETABLE SALAD

Entertaining is almost effortless when you make things ahead; you just slide the food out of the icebox when the guests arrive, and the pots and pans have long since been dealt with. This salad goes well with cold poached bass or salmon; serve it with homemade bread or muffins.

SERVES 6

2 large carrots, cut into fine julienne, steamed until just tender
1 small zucchini, cut into fine julienne, steamed 2 minutes
2 medium leeks, steamed for 5 minutes and cut into fine julienne
3 stalks celery, cut into fine julienne
1 cup whole tiny french green beans, steamed until crisply tender

¾ *cup Thick Vinaigrette (see page 389) beaten with*
  1 egg yolk
  ⅓ cup sour cream
1 head leaf lettuce (Bibb, Boston, or Red-Tipped), washed, dried, and chilled
1 pound fresh small shrimp, shelled and then steamed for 3 minutes
Fresh parsley or basil

Toss vegetables with vinaigrette and allow to marinate in the refrigerator for several hours.

Arrange vegetables on salad plates lined with lettuce. Top each serving with several cooked shrimp and garnish with fresh parsley or basil.

SPRING SALAD WITH VIDALIA VINAIGRETTE

This salad makes a wonderful appetizer; it is a celebration of Vidalia onions, which are so sweet that they can—truly—be eaten like apples.

SERVES 4

½ pound very thin green beans, tipped and steamed for 5 minutes
1 large Vidalia onion, very thinly sliced
1 bunch of scallions, thinly sliced
2 tablespoons sun-dried tomatoes, cut into thin strips
1 head leaf lettuce (Red-Tipped, chicory, Romaine, anything)
¼ pound Westphalian ham, thinly sliced and then cut into thin strips (cold roast beef, duck, chicken, or lobster can be substituted)
2 tablespoons balsamic vinegar
1 tablespoon minced Vidalia onion
1 tablespoon Dijon mustard
1 egg yolk
½ cup olive oil
Salt and freshly ground black pepper to taste
Fresh parsley, chopped

On individual plates arrange green beans, onion slices, scallions, and sun-dried tomatoes on a bed of lettuce. Top with ham or other cold meat.

Beat the vinegar, minced onion, mustard, and egg yolk together. Slowly beat in the olive oil, a little at a time, beating until the dressing is thick and creamy. Season to taste with salt and pepper.

Drizzle the dressing over each salad and sprinkle with a little chopped parsley.

ORANGE AND ONION SALAD

Mild, sweet Vidalia onions can almost be eaten out of hand; they are wonderful with oranges and other fruits.

SERVES 6

3 cups mixed salad greens, washed and dried
3 fresh seedless oranges
1 medium Vidalia onion, thinly sliced and separated into rings
3 tablespoons lemon juice
¼ cup safflower oil
1 clove garlic, very finely minced
Salt and freshly ground black pepper to taste
½ teaspoon powdered mustard
1 teaspoon sugar

Tear the salad greens into pieces and arrange in a glass salad bowl. Peel the oranges and slice. Arrange the oranges and onion rings in an attractive pattern on top of the greens.

Combine the remaining ingredients in a jar. Shake until thoroughly mixed. Dress the salad just before serving. Toss lightly.

PASTA PRIMAVERA SALAD

This superb cold salad is adapted from the classic combination of hot pasta and vegetables originally made popular by Sirio at Le Cirque in New York.

SERVES 4

1 large tomato, cut into chunks
⅓ cup olive oil
3 tablespoons wine vinegar
1 tablespoon fresh basil leaves
Salt and freshly ground black pepper to taste
4 large tomatoes, peeled, seeded, and coarsely chopped
½ pound fresh mushrooms, sliced
1 medium onion, peeled, halved, and thinly sliced
*½ pound fresh fettuccine pasta, cooked, tossed with 1 tablespoon olive oil, and
    cooled to room temperature*
2 cups broccoli, broken into small fleurettes and steamed until crisply tender
½ cup scallions, thinly sliced

Purée tomato, oil, vinegar, and basil in a food processor. Beat in salt and pepper.

Toss purée with chopped tomatoes, mushrooms, and onion slices. Toss with cooled pasta and broccoli. Sprinkle with scallion slices and serve.

LINGUINE WITH GREEN VEGETABLES

Like most of our recipes, this one assumes a supply of very fresh vegetables, but don't miss making it just because there aren't any fresh peas in the market. Frozen ones are fine.

SERVES 4

½ pound shelled peas (frozen if not available fresh)
2 tablespoons butter
2 tablespoons olive oil
*2 bunches of scallions, sliced very thinly (both white and green parts up to the
    leaves)*
1 cup broccoli, separated into tiny fleurettes
¼ cup white wine
¼ cup heavy cream
1 head lettuce, shredded
Salt to taste

Freshly ground black pepper to taste
1 pound fresh linguine
3 tablespoons freshly chopped parsley
Freshly grated Parmesan cheese

If using fresh peas, steam them for 5 to 10 minutes, or until they begin to become tender.

Melt butter and oil in a skillet. Add scallions and cook gently for 5 minutes or until transparent. Add peas, broccoli, wine, and cream. Cook 10 minutes. Add lettuce and cook 5 minutes longer. Season with salt and pepper.

Pour sauce over cooked linguine. Toss lightly. Sprinkle with fresh parsley and serve with plenty of freshly grated pepper and Parmesan cheese.

RAVIOLI WITH SPINACH

Contrary to popular belief, making ravioli is a snap, particularly if you have a ravioli mold and buy sheets of fresh pasta. This version is wonderful as an appetizer or as a main dish.

SERVES 4

1¾ pounds spinach, washed, stemmed, and shaken dry
2 tablespoons soft butter
⅓ cup Parmesan cheese
6 ounces ricotta cheese, blended to a smooth paste in the blender
3 egg yolks, well beaten
Salt and freshly ground black pepper to taste
1 pound flat fresh pasta sheets
4 tablespoons (½ stick) melted butter
6 tablespoons heavy cream

Cook the spinach in the water that clings to the leaves after washing and shaking. Drain thoroughly. Squeeze out remaining juice by wringing the spinach in your hands. Chop the spinach finely.

Mix chopped spinach with 2 tablespoons soft butter, ¼ cup Parmesan cheese, the ricotta cheese, egg yolks, and salt and pepper.

Make ravioli, using the spinach mixture as filling. (To make ravioli:

Lightly roll out sheets of pasta. Cut sheets in half. Lay one-half of the pasta sheet on the ravioli mold. Gently press with plastic insert, forming shallow hollows. Fill hollows with the spinach mixture. Brush the edges of the pasta with water. Lay the remaining half of the pasta sheet over filling. Roll with a rolling pin to seal edges and cut ravioli into squares. Let ravioli dry for 10 minutes before cooking.)

Cook the ravioli a few at a time, in boiling, salted water for 4 minutes. Melt the remaining butter and scald the cream. As the ravioli rise to the surface, remove them with a slotted spoon and arrange them in a serving dish. Sprinkle each layer with melted butter, cream, and a little of the remaining grated Parmesan cheese. Serve at once.

WHOLE WHEAT PASTA PRIMAVERA

Whole wheat pasta has a nutty, more pronounced flavor than conventional durum wheat pasta and so requires a vigorous sauce. Here prosciutto and herbs make a robust version of classic Pasta Primavera.

SERVES 4

4 tablespoons olive oil
1 medium onion, thinly sliced
¼ pound fresh mushrooms, sliced
3 small tomatoes, peeled, seeded, and cut into chunks
½ cup fresh zucchini, cut into fine julienne

¾ *cup sugarsnap or snow peas, blanched in boiling water for 2 minutes (choose the tiniest pods available)*
½ *pound thin, fresh asparagus, scraped, steamed, and cut into 1-inch chunks*
2 ounces Virginia ham, prosciutto, or salami, cut into thin strips
Salt and freshly ground black pepper to taste
1 teaspoon dried basil (or 1 tablespoon fresh basil, chopped)
1 pound whole wheat fettuccine
2 tablespoons softened butter
¾ *cup Parmesan cheese, freshly grated*

Heat the oil in a heavy skillet. Sauté the onion until transparent. Add the mushrooms and cook for 3 minutes. Add tomatoes, zucchini, peas, and asparagus. Cook for 5 minutes. Add ham and salt and pepper to taste. Add basil. Simmer 7 to 10 minutes.

Cook the pasta for 2 minutes, drain, and toss with 2 tablespoons softened butter. Pour the vegetable mixture over pasta and top with several tablespoons of Parmesan cheese. Serve remaining cheese separately.

WHOLE WHEAT FETTUCCINE WITH PROSCIUTTO AND MASCARPONE

Rich, creamy, fresh mascarpone often appears as a dessert cheese or in layered torta cheeses. Here it makes a voluptuous sauce for whole wheat pasta.

SERVES 4 TO 6

1 egg, beaten
1 egg yolk
3 ounces mascarpone cheese
8 drops Tabasco, or to taste
¼ *cup grated Parmesan cheese*
Salt to taste
⅓ *cup boiling water*
1 pound fresh whole wheat fettuccine
3 ounces prosciutto, cut into thin strips

Fiery Phoenix Wings

- ☐ 12 chicken wing drumettes
- ☐ Salt and cayenne pepper to taste
- ☐ 4 cups oil, for frying
- ☐ 1 teaspoon minced fresh ginger
- ☐ 1 small clove garlic, minced
- ☐ 1 scallion, minced
- ☐ 2 tablespoons soy sauce
- ☐ 1 teaspoon chili oil
- ☐ 1 tablespoon rice vinegar
- ☐ 1 teaspoon sugar
- ☐ 2 teaspoons sesame oil
- ☐ Freshly ground pepper to taste

Season drumettes with salt and cayenne, and deep-fry in a wok or deep-fat fryer preheated to 350 degrees until golden brown, 8 to 10 minutes. Remove and drain. Combine ginger, garlic, scallion, soy sauce, chili oil, vinegar, sugar, sesame oil and pepper for dip. Serve hot drumettes with dip. Makes four appetizer servings.

egg yolk, mascarpone cheese, Tabasco, Par- ⅓ cup boiling water.

Drain and toss immediately with egg and ve very hot with more Parmesan.

AND ASPARAGUS

ch, or for a light supper, or serve it

ES 4

1 tablespoon chopped shallots
½ cup white wine
1 pound asparagus, washed and trimmed
8 eggs
Salt and freshly ground white pepper to taste
¼ pound (1 stick) butter

Soak shallots in white wine for 2 hours—overnight, if desired. Steam asparagus until barely tender. Drain well.

Poach eggs in acidulated water (see page 7), taking care that the yolks are still liquid.

Bring white wine, shallots, and salt and pepper to a boil and reduce to about 2 tablespoons liquid. Reduce heat and add butter, a little at a time, whisking constantly. Be sure the pan does not get hot enough to melt the butter; the mixture should be light-colored and frothy. Like any mounted butter sauce, this sauce is served lukewarm.

Arrange 5 to 6 asparagus on each plate. Top with two poached eggs and spoon the sauce over all. Serve at once with buttered toast fingers.

An easy variation on this theme is Soft-Boiled Eggs with Asparagus. Prepare the asparagus as directed above. Soft-boil two eggs per person. Cut the tops off very hot eggs and serve in egg cups on a plate already containing 5 to 6 cooked asparagus. The asparagus are picked up by hand and dipped into the hot yolk, which, when seasoned with salt and pepper, serves as a sauce. The remaining egg is eaten with a spoon.

SPINACH AND RICOTTA OMELET

The filling for this omelet is adapted from the traditional filling for crêpes and shaped pastas.

SERVES 4

1 pound fresh spinach, washed, stemmed, and finely chopped
¼ pound fresh ricotta cheese
Salt, freshly ground black pepper, and nutmeg to taste
4 tablespoons butter
8 eggs, beaten with 1 tablespoon heavy cream and salt and pepper to taste
Freshly chopped parsley

Cook the spinach in 2 tablespoons water for 2 minutes. Squeeze out all moisture.

Mix spinach with ricotta cheese. Season with salt, pepper, and nutmeg to taste. Melt 1 tablespoon butter in an omelet pan. Add two beaten eggs and stir vigorously with a fork. Spoon one-quarter of the spinach mixture onto the center of the omelet. When the bottom is set, fold one edge of the omelet over the center, using a fork. Carefully roll the omelet onto a serving plate. Repeat with the other three omelets.

Serve the omelets very hot topped with a little freshly chopped parsley.

HAY DAY AVOCADO HALVES
BAKED WITH SEAFOOD

This is an elegant lunch dish the Van Rensselaers brought back from Europe. Nobody ever thinks of heating an avocado (it should just be warmed through, not really cooked), but it is heavenly. We use the same seafood mixture as a filling for crêpes—fill eight crêpes, fold them over, brush with butter, sprinkle with Parmesan, and bake—but it is just as good on toast or in a pastry shell.

SERVES 6

¼ pound bay scallops
¼ cup dry white wine
2 tablespoons butter
3 tablespoons flour
½ cup milk
1 cup heavy cream
½ teaspoon finely chopped fresh tarragon (or 1 teaspoon dried)
1 tablespoon finely chopped fresh parsley
Salt and freshly ground black pepper to taste
Dash of Tabasco
½ cup grated Gruyère cheese (or 2 tablespoons Parmesan)
¼ pound cooked, peeled, coarsely chopped deveined shrimp (approximately ½ pound raw)
¼ pound crabmeat
4 avocados, halved and brushed with lemon juice
¼ cup Gruyère or 2 tablespoons Parmesan for topping
Chicory greens
Parsley

Preheat oven to 350°F.

Poach scallops in white wine for 1 minute. Reserving the liquid, drain scallops and boil down cooking liquid by half. Set aside. Melt butter in 2½ quart saucepan. Add flour and cook for 1 minute, stirring constantly. Slowly whisk in milk, cream, reserved cooking liquid, tarragon, parsley, salt, pepper, and Tabasco. Cook, stirring and whisking until very thick. Remove from heat, fold in Gruyère (or Parmesan) and all the seafood. Taste for seasonings.

Fill 8 ripe avocado halves with mixture. Sprinkle with cheese for topping. Warm in oven for 20 minutes. Serve on bed of chicory greens with parsley.

Note: This recipe also can be used to fill 8 crêpes. Put 2 tablespoons of filling in each crêpe, roll them up and brush with butter. Sprinkle with Parmesan cheese and bake in 350°F oven until warm throughout, 10 to 15 minutes.

BELGIAN BAKED FISH

The inspiration for this dish came from Brussels, where one can eat incredibly well. Obviously, cooking time will vary with the thickness of the fish.

SERVES 4

3 tablespoons butter
1 leek (white part only), cut in rounds
1 onion, thinly sliced
⅓ cup dry white wine
2 tablespoons chives (or finely chopped green onion tops)
2 tablespoons lemon juice
4 fresh fish fillets—sole, flounder, red snapper, striped bass, bluefish—whatever is the catch of the day
Salt and pepper
2 tablespoons freshly chopped parsley
1 lemon, cut in wedges

Preheat the oven to 400°F.

Butter an ovenproof baking dish with 1 tablespoon of butter. Melt the remaining butter in a skillet and add the leek and onion. Sauté until tender. Add wine, chives, and lemon juice. Cook 1 minute.

Arrange the fish fillets in the prepared baking dish, sprinkle with salt and freshly ground black pepper and pour the hot wine mixture over them. Cover with foil and bake at 400°F for 6 to 10 minutes, depending on the thickness of the fish.

Arrange the fish on a serving dish, spooning the sauce over the fillets. Garnish with chopped parsley and serve with lemon wedges.

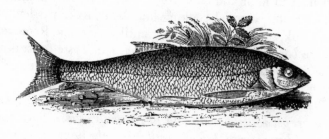

POACHED STRIPED BASS

Obviously, if striped bass is endangered in your area, seek out one of the alternatives suggested below. We always remove the gills before poaching whole fish; they can make it very bitter.

SERVES 6

1 three-pound striped bass (or red snapper, sea bass, or salmon), cleaned and
gills removed
1 quart Court Bouillon (see page 12) or 2 cups white wine and 2 cups clam
juice

Wrap fish in clean cheesecloth, leaving extra long twists at each end to lift the fish in and out of the poaching liquid. Bring the liquid to a boil.

Lower the fish into the bouillon or other liquid, cover, and allow the liquid to return to barely a simmer. Simmer 10 minutes for each inch of thickness. As soon as the cooking time is finished, remove the pan from the heat and cool the fish briefly in the liquid.

Remove the fish from liquid, drain, and allow to firm up. Remove cheesecloth. Cool to room temperature. Arrange fish on a serving platter and garnish with lemon slices or wedges, tomatoes, and cucumber salad.

Serve with Herbed Mayonnaise (see page 185).

BLUEFISH FILLETS IN LETTUCE LEAVES

This is an Americanized version of a traditional French dish. Although it isn't difficult to make, it is sophisticated enough for an elegant dinner.

SERVES 6

1 head leaf lettuce, separated into leaves
½ pound mushrooms, finely chopped
2 shallots, finely chopped
4 tablespoons butter
1 cucumber, peeled, halved, and seeded
¼ cup dry vermouth

½ cup dry white wine
1 bottle clam juice
2 pounds small bluefish fillets
½ cup sour cream, or crème fraîche
Salt and freshly ground black pepper to taste
1 lemon, cut in wedges, for garnish

Wash the lettuce well and blanch in boiling water for 1 minute. Spread leaves out carefully on a towel to dry.

Sauté mushrooms and shallots in 2 tablespoons butter just until transparent. Grate one-half of the cucumber and cut the other half into julienned strips.

Boil together the vermouth, white wine, clam juice, and grated cucumber in the bottom of a steamer. Sauté the julienned cucumber in 1 tablespoon butter just until transparent.

Spread out each lettuce leaf. Top each one with a fillet of bluefish and a small spoonful of the mushroom and shallot mixture. Wrap the lettuce around each fillet to form a tight bundle. Steam the bundles over the wine mixture for about 6 to 8 minutes, depending on the thickness of the fillets. Set aside and keep warm.

Strain the cooking liquid and beat in sour cream and 1 tablespoon softened butter. Arrange the fillets on a serving platter, top with cucumber julienne, and coat with sauce. Season with salt and pepper to taste. Serve lemon wedges and remaining sauce on the side.

COLD POACHED SALMON WITH
AVOCADO SAUCE

If you do not have a fish poacher, use a roasting pan large enough to hold the entire fish. Place the fish in the pan and pour in enough hot liquid just to cover it; cover with aluminum foil and bake at 375°F until it is just tender, approximately 10 minutes for each inch of thickness. Fish should not be cooled in broth; it becomes tough and overcooked.

SERVES 6 TO 8

1 four-pound fresh salmon (gills removed), poached in Court Bouillon (see page 12), skinned and chilled

1 head leaf lettuce, washed and dried
1 lime, cut in wedges
1 tablespoon onion, finely chopped
1 tablespoon green chilies, seeded and finely chopped (canned, if not available
  fresh)
1 very ripe avocado
⅓ cup plain yoghurt
2 tablespoons lime juice
Salt and freshly ground black pepper to taste
3 tablespoons olive oil
1 tablespoon fresh coriander

Arrange salmon on a serving platter that has been lined with curly lettuce. Garnish with lime wedges.

In a food processor, process the onion and green chilies until smooth. Add avocado and yoghurt with the lime juice and process 1 minute. Turn into a bowl and beat in salt, pepper, and olive oil a little at a time. Stir in coriander and refrigerate for ½ hour.

Serve in a sauce boat topped with a little more chopped coriander.

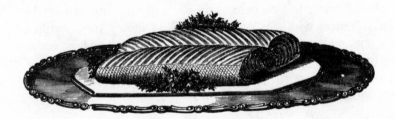

FILLETS OF SOLE WITH SPINACH

The first fresh mint of the season gives this dish a nice springtime character.

SERVES 4 TO 6

1½ pounds sole fillets, wiped and dried well
1 tablespoon fresh mint leaves
2 cloves
½ cup white wine

½ *pound fresh spinach, well washed and stemmed*
1 tablespoon olive oil
2 medium onions, chopped
2 tablespoons butter
2 tablespoons flour
Salt and freshly ground black pepper to taste
1 cup crème fraîche (see page 12), or heavy cream if crème fraîche is not
   available
1 lemon, sliced thin

Preheat oven to 425°F.

Lightly butter a flat baking dish. Arrange fillets in the bottom of the dish. Add mint and cloves and pour in white wine. Marinate 15 minutes and then poach fillets in the oven for 6 to 10 minutes, depending on their thickness. Drain and keep warm.

Steam spinach in the water that clings to the leaves after washing, just until it is wilted and tender. Drain well, squeezing juice out with your hands. Chop finely.

Heat oil in a heavy skillet and sauté the chopped onions until golden but not brown. Add the spinach, stir once, and remove from the heat.

Melt the butter in a saucepan and stir in flour. Simmer over low heat for 5 minutes. Season with salt and pepper. Add crème fraîche and cook for 6 minutes, stirring constantly. Remove the sauce from the heat and stir into the spinach mixture.

To serve, arrange the spinach on a platter. Lay the fillets of sole on top. Garnish with thinly sliced lemon.

SHRIMP SUPREME

The flavors and textures of the shrimp and the asparagus enhance each other, making this a stunning spring presentation for both of them. The dressing can be made well in advance and the shrimp and asparagus prepared ahead of time, so it works well for even a crucial dinner party. It is a good idea to vary the size of the shrimp with the thickness of the asparagus: thin asparagus, small shrimp; fat asparagus, big shrimp.

SERVES 4

½ cup Homemade Mayonnaise (see page 18)
2 tablespoons Dijon mustard
Juice of 1 lemon
½ cup white wine
1 small tomato, peeled, seeded, and chopped
1 tablespoon fresh chopped chives
2 pounds small shrimp, boiled 1 minute and cooled in cooking liquid
1 pound thin green asparagus, washed, cut into 2-inch lengths, steamed until
   just tender, and chilled
2 tablespoons fresh dill
1 small head leaf lettuce for garnish

Beat mayonnaise, mustard, lemon juice, and wine until smooth. Stir in tomato and chives. Peel shrimp and toss, along with the asparagus, in the dressing.

Arrange the salad on a bed of lettuce and garnish with fresh dill.

ARTICHOKE-CRABMEAT RAVIGOTE

Serve this for lunch, with crusty French bread and a chilled white wine.

SERVES 4

4 large artichokes, washed, trimmed, and boiled until tender in water and 2
   tablespoons lemon juice to cover, well drained
1 cup Homemade Mayonnaise (see page 18)
1 tablespoon chopped capers
2 tablespoons chopped scallions
2 cloves garlic, chopped
½ teaspoon tarragon (or ¼ teaspoon dried)
1 teaspoon dried mustard
1½ pounds lump crabmeat, well picked over
Salt and paprika to taste

Remove center leaves of the artichokes and scrape out choke with a spoon.

Gently toss together the remaining ingredients. Fill artichokes with crab mixture. Season with salt and paprika. Serve with additional mayonnaise.

HAY DAY'S TARRAGON CHICKEN SALAD WITH JICAMA

This pretty salad is incredibly easy, and with the feathery scallion strips, it's all green and white. We've sold a lot of jicama, which appears in eastern markets as an "interesting new vegetable" but has been savored in Mexico for hundreds of years. The dressing is ten times better if it's made ahead—even overnight—so the flavor of the tarragon can take hold.

SERVES 6 TO 8

4 large whole, cooked, boneless, and skinless chicken breasts, cut in large julienne strips
1½ cups jicama, peeled and cut in large julienne strips
3 scallions, tops only, cut lengthwise in long thin strips
2 eggs
4 tablespoons tarragon vinegar
2 teaspoons Dijon mustard
½ teaspoon salt
½ teaspoon white pepper
2 cups safflower oil
2 tablespoons (packed) freshly chopped tarragon

Toss chicken, jicama, and scallions together gently.
Blend eggs, vinegar, mustard, salt, and pepper in a food processor. Slowly add oil. Pulse in tarragon leaves. Fold into salad ingredients. Adjust the salt.

CHARCOAL-GRILLED ROSEMARY CHICKEN

The acidic flavor of the lime blends with the rosemary to make the chicken fragrant and flavorful. Cornish game hens are also good split, marinated, and broiled this way; thick cuts of swordfish, dolphin, or fresh tuna work well, too.

[78]

SERVES 4 TO 6

¼ cup lime juice
1 tablespoon sesame oil
4 tablespoons safflower oil
1 tablespoon balsamic vinegar
6 or more fresh sprigs of rosemary
4 boned chicken breasts and 4 boned thighs
Salt and freshly ground black pepper to taste

Blend lime juice, oils, vinegar, and rosemary. Marinate chicken in the mixture at least 4 hours. Remove chicken, pat dry, and season with salt and pepper. Grill chicken over vine cuttings, mesquite charcoal, or hickory chips. Brush chicken often with marinade, using more fresh rosemary as a brush. Grill uncovered 6 minutes to a side.

COLD MARINATED CHICKEN

Light, mild champagne vinegar will not overwhelm the flavor of the chicken, but white wine vinegar is fine.

SERVES 4 TO 6

¼ cup olive oil
1 three-pound chicken, cut up as for frying
1 cup dry white wine

½ cup dry white wine vinegar (champagne vinegar, if available)
2 onions, diced
1 carrot, peeled and sliced
1 leek, sliced into 1-inch lengths
1 stalk celery, thinly sliced
Fresh parsley
1 lemon, thinly sliced
2 cloves garlic, minced
Fresh thyme
Salt and freshly ground black pepper to taste
Lemon or lime slices

Heat the oil in a heavy skillet and brown the chicken pieces on all sides. Add wine, vinegar, vegetables, garlic, and thyme. Cover and simmer 30 minutes. Arrange the chicken, vegetables, and lemon in a deep serving dish. Season with salt and pepper. Cover with cooking liquid and chill at least 4 to 6 hours, or overnight.

Remove chicken from the icebox at least 1 hour before serving. Drain chicken pieces and serve, garnished with lemon or lime slices.

HAY DAY'S CURRIED CHUTNEY CHICKEN BREASTS

Helen Brody evolved this recipe from a suggestion in the *New York Times*; it's a nice hot dish for fall and winter, and it sells well. We use our own homemade chutney, but any brand will do as long as the pieces are cut fine enough. The shallow slits down the center of the chicken breasts make a groove for the stuffing and keep the stuffed breast from losing its shape. Toast the coconut in a 350°F oven until it is golden, or substitute toasted almonds.

SERVES 4 TO 6

4 boneless, skinless chicken breasts, halved
⅓ cup onion, chopped coarsely
⅓ cup celery, chopped coarsely
½ teaspoon medium curry powder
4 tablespoons butter

½ Granny Smith apple, skin left on, cored and coarsely chopped
¾ cup soft bread crumbs, coarsely chopped
2 tablespoons chutney
⅓ cup parsley, chopped coarsely
Salt and freshly ground black pepper to taste
3 tablespoons melted butter
1 tablespoon medium curry powder
2 cups heavy cream
Toasted almonds or coconut (optional)

Lightly pound chicken breasts and make one or two small lengthwise slits down the center of each. Sauté onion, celery, and curry powder in butter for 2 minutes. Add apple. Sauté another minute. Remove from heat, fold in bread crumbs, chutney, parsley, salt, and pepper. Put 1 to 2 tablespoons of filling on each breast. Roll up breast, tucking in sides as much as possible. Place seam side down in buttered roasting pan. Brush breasts with melted butter, cover with foil, and bake in preheated 350°F oven for 30 minutes. Remove breasts from pan and keep warm.

Pour all but 1 tablespoon fat from roasting pan; add curry powder to remaining juices and cook on top of the stove for 1 minute, stirring constantly. Whisk in cream and reduce sauce to 1½ cups. Strain over chicken breasts and serve. Garnish with toasted almonds or coconut if desired.

CALVES' LIVER À LA VENEZIANA

Tender and delicious, this is a classic Italian way of preparing liver. Liver that is gray and tough will never convert anybody; it must be treated with respect and cooked very, very lightly.

SERVES 4

1 pound very fresh calves' liver, cleaned and cut into ½-inch strips
3 tablespoons flour
2 tablespoons olive oil
2 tablespoons butter
4 medium onions, sliced very thin
2 tablespoons chopped parsley
Salt and freshly ground black pepper to taste
⅓ cup dry white wine

Dredge liver strips in flour, knocking off any excess. Set aside.

Heat the oil and butter in a heavy skillet and sauté the onions until soft and golden. Add liver, parsley, salt, and pepper. Cook over medium heat about 4 minutes, turning liver often.

Remove the liver and onions from the skillet.

Pour the wine into the skillet and cook 3 minutes over high heat. Pour the sauce over the liver and serve at once.

BELGIAN ENDIVES AND HAM

Served with a leaf lettuce salad and a loaf of crusty bread, this is a popular European Sunday night supper. It can be assembled in the morning, or even the night before, and refrigerated; it should be brought to room temperature for about an hour before baking.

SERVES 4

8 large Belgian endives, trimmed and washed
2 tablespoons fresh lemon juice
½ teaspoon salt
Water
2 tablespoons butter
2 tablespoons flour
1¼ cups milk
½ cup plus 2 tablespoons grated Swiss or Parmesan cheese
1 egg yolk
Salt and freshly ground black pepper to taste
8 slices boiled ham or prosciutto

Preheat the oven to 350°F.

In a saucepan, place the endives, lemon juice, salt, and enough water just barely to cover. Simmer over low heat about 10 minutes, or until the endives are just tender. Drain and dry well between paper towels, pressing firmly to remove all juice.

Heat the butter in a saucepan and stir in flour. Cook gently for 4 minutes. Stir in the milk all at once. Cook, stirring constantly, until the sauce is smooth and thick. Stir in the ½ cup Swiss cheese. Remove from heat and stir until the cheese is melted. Beat in the egg yolk. Season with salt and pepper.

Wrap 1 ham slice around each endive. Place seam side down, side by side, in a shallow, buttered baking dish. Pour the cheese sauce over ham rolls and sprinkle with remaining 2 tablespoons cheese. Bake at 350°F for about 15 minutes or until browned and bubbly.

VEAL WITH LIME

This recipe is an interesting variation on veal piccata.

SERVES 4

12 very thin slices of veal (about 1 pound), pounded between sheets of waxed paper
Flour
3 tablespoons peanut oil
2 tablespoons butter
3 tablespoons lime juice
½ cup white wine
Salt and freshly ground black pepper to taste
Tabasco sauce to taste
1 lime, sliced very thin

Dust the veal slices with flour. Heat the oil in a skillet. Briefly sauté the veal, 2 minutes to a side. Remove from pan and keep warm.

Pour off any remaining oil. Melt the butter in the same skillet and add lime juice and wine. Boil hard until reduced by two-thirds. Season with salt, pepper, and Tabasco and pour over veal.

Garnish with very thin slices of lime and serve very hot.

GRILLED LAMB WITH SAGE

Be sure the coals are gray and ashy on the outside before you put the meat on the fire. Lamb shrinks very quickly, and a flaming hot fire will make it shrivel and toughen. If necessary, add more charcoal after the lamb has cooked about 20 minutes.

SERVES 8

1⅓ cups whole-grain mustard
⅓ cup red wine
½ cup salad oil
¼ cup fresh sage, chopped
1 butterflied leg of lamb, the thick parts pounded to ensure even cooking
Handful of fresh sage, soaked in water

Mix together mustard, wine, oil, and chopped sage.

Brush both sides of lamb with mustard mixture and grill over charcoal about 15 to 20 minutes to a side. Brush occasionally with mustard mixture. About 10 minutes before serving, shake water from sage and toss onto charcoal under lamb.

To serve, slice lamb thin and pass remaining mustard sauce—heated, if you like.

LAMB CHOPS WITH ROSEMARY SAUCE

The cream sauce celebrates the natural affinity of lamb and rosemary; serve it with roast lamb, too.

SERVES 4

3 tablespoons butter
8 rib lamb chops
2 tablespoons flour
1 cup light cream
1 tablespoon fresh rosemary
Salt and freshly ground black pepper

Melt 1 tablespoon butter in a heavy skillet. Brown lamb chops on both sides. Sauté until done. Remove chops and keep warm.

Melt 2 tablespoons butter in the same skillet. Add flour and cook over medium heat until well browned but not burned. Watch carefully. Add cream all at once and then rosemary. Simmer until slightly thickened. Season with salt and pepper.

Serve lamb chops with a little sauce poured over them and pass the remaining sauce in a separate bowl.

ARTICHOKES ROMAN STYLE

Arrange the artichokes on lettuce leaves and serve lukewarm as a first course with a loaf of French bread and lots of sweet butter. Most of the preparation can be done ahead of time, but be sure to let the artichokes warm to room temperature for an hour if they have been refrigerated.

SERVES 4

16 to 20 tiny Italian artichokes, sharp points trimmed, hard outer leaves removed
1 tablespoon lemon juice
1 teaspoon salt
Water
3 tablespoons olive oil
⅓ cup dry white wine
½ teaspoon thyme
2 tablespoons minced parsley
2 cloves garlic, finely minced
Freshly ground black pepper to taste

Boil the artichokes gently for 20 minutes with lemon juice and salt in water to cover. Drain well and remove the chokes with a small spoon.

Heat the oil in a skillet, add the artichokes, and sauté for several minutes. Add wine and thyme. Cook 10 minutes more, until artichokes are very tender. Add parsley and garlic. Heat thoroughly. Season with freshly ground pepper.

ARTICHOKE PURÉE

This is excellent with lamb and beef.

SERVES 6

3 cups diced, fresh artichoke hearts (approximately 9 large artichokes, trimmed)
⅓ cup minced onion
2 tablespoons butter
Salt and freshly ground black pepper to taste
1 cup heavy cream (more or less)
2 tablespoons pistachios, chopped

Simmer the artichoke hearts in boiling acidulated water, until very tender—about 45 minutes.

Sauté onion in butter until transparent. Purée the artichoke hearts and onion until smooth. Cook over low heat until the purée is fairly dry. Add salt and pepper and enough cream to make a thick purée. (The amount of cream needed will depend on the size and freshness of the artichokes. Add cream a little at a time.)

Serve very hot topped with chopped pistachios.

The artichoke hearts should be boiled or steamed until very tender before proceeding with this recipe.

ASPARAGUS AND MUSHROOM SAUTÉ

For special occasions, vary this by tossing the asparagus with more exotic mushrooms like shiitake, cepes, or chanterelles.

SERVES 4

1 pound fresh asparagus, steamed 6 to 8 minutes
¼ cup cooking oil
¼ pound mushrooms, quartered
Salt and freshly ground black pepper to taste
1 teaspoon sesame seeds, toasted until golden

Cut the asparagus into 1-inch lengths. Heat oil in a skillet or wok. Stir in asparagus and mushrooms. Stir for 4 minutes. Add salt and pepper to taste and sesame seeds. Toss gently.

BROCCOLI WITH ENDIVE

Try this dish with a luncheon omelet—fines herbes is a good choice—with hot bread or hard rolls and butter.

SERVES 4

1 pound broccoli, trimmed into fleurettes, washed and steamed 5 minutes or until just tender
¼ pound endive, washed, sliced, and steamed for 5 minutes
¼ cup chopped walnuts
¼ cup crumbled Roquefort cheese
4 tablespoons olive oil
2 tablespoons walnut oil
Freshly ground black pepper to taste
1 tablespoon chopped parsley
1 tablespoon lemon juice

Arrange broccoli on a serving platter. Spread endive on top. Shake together in a jar with a tightly fitting lid the walnuts, cheese, olive oil, walnut oil, and freshly ground pepper. Pour dressing over vegetables. Sprinkle with parsley and lemon juice and serve either hot or at room temperature.

Instead of Roquefort, try crumbling ¼ cup ewe's milk Feta into the oil mixture for a tasty alternative.

BRAISED CUCUMBERS

It is high time people started thinking of serving cucumbers as cooked vegetables. Everybody uses them raw in salads or with dips, but they are also superb steamed or braised.

SERVES 4 TO 6

3 tablespoons butter
1 tablespoon sugar
Salt to taste
3 large cucumbers, peeled, cut lengthwise, seeded, and cut into 2-inch lengths
1 bunch scallions, sliced
¼ cup dry white wine
½ teaspoon oregano
½ pint cherry tomatoes, halved
3 tablespoons cream

Melt butter with sugar. Add salt, cucumbers, and scallions. Sauté briefly until the mixture begins to turn golden. Add the wine and oregano and cook 10 minutes. Add tomatoes and cream and stir gently. Cook 5 minutes.

Serve very warm.

CITRUS BRAISED ENDIVE

The flavor of this vegetable dish is sharp and clean enough to stand up to the richness of roast pork.

SERVES 6

1½ pounds Belgian endive, washed and dried
¼ cup dry white wine
Juice of 2 limes
3 tablespoons butter
2 teaspoons sugar
Salt and freshly ground black pepper to taste
2 tablespoons butter
Chopped parsley (optional)

Arrange dry endive in a heavy skillet that has a tight-fitting lid. Add wine, lime juice, 3 tablespoons butter, sugar, salt, and pepper.

Cover with a round of buttered waxed paper that has a small hole cut in the middle to allow steam to escape. Cover with skillet lid and braise (or simmer gently) for ½ hour.

Remove endive and keep warm. Add 2 tablespoons butter to the sauce and reduce to about ⅓ cup. Pour over the endive. Top with chopped parsley, if desired.

BAKED GREEN PEPPERS WITH FETA CHEESE

Served with a green salad and homemade bread, this makes a delicious light lunch. The peppers can be stuffed and arranged in the baking dish ahead of time, then set aside or kept in the icebox until time to bake and serve them. Cow's milk gradually replaced the sheep's milk that gave Feta cheese its unique fragrance, but we still prefer the original.

SERVES 4

4 green Italian frying peppers
¼ pound Feta cheese (sheep's milk, if possible)
1 egg
1 tablespoon sour cream
Salt to taste
4 tablespoons olive oil

Preheat the oven to 400°F.

Roast peppers in the oven until the skin begins to pop and turns golden brown. Reduce the oven to 375°F. Cool the peppers in a plastic bag for 10 minutes and then peel by hand or rub with a coarse towel to remove skin. Cut an opening lengthwise in each pepper and remove the seeds.

Mash the Feta cheese with a fork and then beat in the egg and sour cream. Add salt, if needed. Stuff the peppers with the cheese mixture and arrange, cut side up, in a baking dish. Drizzle with olive oil.

Bake 30 to 40 minutes at 375°F until the peppers are very tender and the cheese is puffy.

SMOTHERED LETTUCE

This is good with roast or grilled beef, lamb, or game. It can be made with regular American bacon but is better with the robust, peppery Italian pancetta.

SERVES 4

1½ pounds leaf lettuce (Boston or Bibb)
2 tablespoons vegetable oil
¼ cup scallions, thinly sliced
¼ pound pancetta, finely chopped
Salt and freshly ground black pepper to taste

Remove lettuce leaves from stem and tear them into pieces if they are too large.

Heat the oil in a skillet or wok. Add scallions and pancetta. Sauté until the scallions are transparent. Add lettuce a little at a time until wilted. Cover. Cook 1 minute. Uncover and cook 2 minutes more. Serve at once with salt and freshly ground pepper.

HAM-STUFFED ONION

Originally designed to be served as a vegetable, these are also substantial enough for a light lunch.

SERVES 6

6 small sweet onions, peeled (Vidalia if available)
2 tablespoons butter
½ pound boiled ham, ground
2 medium tomatoes, peeled, seeded, and finely chopped
2 tablespoons tomato purée
1 tablespoon fresh thyme, chopped
½ teaspoon salt
Freshly ground black pepper to taste
⅓ cup grated Monterey Jack cheese
1½ tablespoons butter
1 cup beef stock

Preheat the oven to 400°F.

Cut a slice off the top of each onion and scoop out the insides with a sharp spoon, leaving a shell about ¼ inch thick. Cook in boiling water for about 5 minutes and then remove from water and drain upside down for about ½ hour.

Chop the insides of the onion very finely and sauté in 2 tablespoons butter until transparent but not browned. Combine the onion, ham, chopped tomatoes, tomato purée, thyme, salt, and pepper.

Stuff the onion shells with the onion mixture and top with grated cheese. Dot with butter.

Place the onions in a shallow, well-buttered baking dish and pour stock around them. Bake at 400°F for about 30 minutes, occasionally basting with stock.

Serve with roast pork, chicken, or goose.

OLD-FASHIONED PARSLEY-BUTTERED NEW POTATOES

Often the time-tried recipes are the best; this one will bring back childhood memories for some people and create them for others. Peel a strip around the middle of the potatoes to keep them from bursting.

SERVES 6

2 pounds very small, red-skinned potatoes, washed
Salt
Water
¼ pound (1 stick) butter
3 tablespoons freshly chopped parsley

Peel a small strip around the middle of each potato.
Boil potatoes in salted water until tender. Drain.
Melt butter in a saucepan. Toss hot potatoes in butter and sprinkle generously with chopped parsley. Serve very hot.
For a more robust variation, mix 2 finely minced cloves of garlic with the melted butter and sauté briefly. These potatoes are sensational with lamb.

PEAS AND LETTUCE

Nika Hazelton, one of America's most knowledgeable cooks, likes her peas this classic French way.

SERVES 6

2 tablespoons butter
1 bunch scallions (white and green parts), thinly sliced
1 small head Boston or Bibb lettuce, finely shredded
3 pounds fresh peas, shelled
4 tablespoons water or chicken broth (see page 8)
Salt to taste
Freshly ground black pepper to taste
1 sprig of fresh thyme
¼ cup chopped parsley

Melt the butter in a heavy saucepan. Add scallions and lettuce. Toss to coat with butter. Add fresh peas. Stir in chicken stock. Season with salt, pepper, and thyme.
Cover and simmer 5 to 10 minutes or until the peas are tender. Serve garnished with chopped parsley.

BRAISED SUGARSNAP PEAS

Exceptionally tender sugarsnap peas have come into the market only in recent years. If you have never cooked them before, remember that they are eaten whole and merely need stringing like young green beans.

SERVES 4

1 pound sugarsnap peas, washed and strung
1 medium head leaf lettuce, washed and shredded
½ teaspoon salt
1 tablespoon sugar
4 tablespoons minced scallions
4 tablespoons butter
Water

Put all ingredients in a heavy saucepan. Add water until just visible through pea pods. Set over high heat. Simmer for 5 minutes, and then boil until liquid has evaporated. Return peas to pan, add a little more salt if necessary, and serve very hot.

CONFETTI SNOW PEAS

This dish is easy and quick to make and can be served hot or at room temperature with any meat, poultry, or fish. It is a crisp accompaniment for smoky grilled fish.

SERVES 6

1 pound snow peas, strings removed and steamed until just crisply tender
½ green pepper, seeded and thinly sliced
½ red pepper, seeded and thinly sliced
½ yellow pepper, seeded and thinly sliced (optional)
2 tablespoons sesame oil
1 tablespoon toasted sesame seeds
Salt and freshly ground black pepper to taste

Toss the hot snow peas with peppers and sesame oil. Sprinkle with sesame seeds and season to taste with salt and pepper.

SPINACH WITH GARLIC AND OIL

This Italian method of preparing fresh spinach is excellent with roast meats or chicken; it can be done ahead up to the final sautéeing of the garlic and spinach. Use the smallest spinach leaves you can find.

SERVES 4

3 tablespoons olive oil
2 cloves garlic, finely chopped
1½ pounds fresh spinach, well washed, stemmed, steamed (no more than 2 to 3
  minutes) in the water that clings to the leaves, and drained well
Salt and freshly ground white pepper to taste

Heat olive oil in a skillet. Add garlic and cook over low heat until it begins to brown slightly. Take care not to burn. Raise heat just a little and add the spinach. Cook 2 minutes, tossing spinach all the time. Add salt and pepper to taste.

Remove from skillet with a slotted spoon and serve very hot.

SPINACH SOUFFLÉ

Don't be daunted. The secret to a successful soufflé is to beat the egg whites until they are as stiff as possible. Once it has been assembled, it can be covered with plastic wrap and held at room temperature for about 30 minutes before baking in a preheated oven.

SERVES 4

3 tablespoons butter
3 tablespoons flour
1 cup milk
Pinch of salt
Pinch of nutmeg
6 egg yolks (or five, if extra large)

⅔ cup cooked spinach, squeezed very dry and chopped fine
½ teaspoon salt
1 teaspoon grated onion
6 egg whites (or five, if extra large), beaten until stiff peaks form
Freshly grated Parmesan cheese

Preheat the oven to 350°F.

Melt butter in a saucepan, add flour, and stir, cooking for 3 minutes. Add milk, salt, and nutmeg. Stir until thick. Remove from heat. Beat in egg yolks, one at a time. When thoroughly incorporated, stir in spinach, salt, and grated onion. Cool slightly.

Fold in egg whites.

Pour into a soufflé dish that has been well buttered and then dusted with grated Parmesan cheese.

Bake for about 45 minutes. Serve immediately.

ROMAN SPINACH

Although we like fresh spinach any way it comes, this is a nice alternative to the plain steamed or creamed variety. It is good with almost any main dish, especially veal; the pignoli nuts add texture and toasted nut flavor.

SERVES 4

1 tablespoon butter
2 tablespoons olive oil
½ cup pignoli nuts
3 pounds spinach, trimmed, stemmed, and washed
1 clove garlic, mashed
2 teaspoons wine vinegar
Salt and freshly ground white pepper to taste

Heat butter and olive oil in a deep skillet. Cook pignoli nuts until golden, shaking or stirring constantly. Add spinach, garlic, vinegar, salt, and pepper. Cook, covered, until just tender, about 4 to 5 minutes. Serve right away.

TOMATO COMPOTE

This crunchy relish is excellent with cold meat platters and cold poached fish or shellfish.

SERVES 6 TO 8

2 leeks, washed and thinly sliced
2 large ripe tomatoes, peeled, seeded, and chopped
1 cucumber, peeled, sliced lengthwise, seeded, and thinly sliced
1 large green pepper, seeded and finely diced
1 tablespoon chopped green chilies (canned, if not available fresh)
2 tablespoons fresh dill
Salt and freshly ground black pepper to taste
¼ cup white wine vinegar
1 tablespoon sweet mustard
¼ teaspoon salt
Freshly ground black pepper to taste
1 clove garlic, finely minced
½ cup olive oil
1 tablespoon warm water (optional)
1 tablespoon fresh parsley, chopped

Toss the leeks, tomatoes, cucumber, green pepper, chilies, and dill together in a large bowl. Season with salt and pepper.

In a small bowl beat together vinegar, mustard, salt, pepper, and garlic. Beat in the olive oil a little at a time. Add 1 tablespoon warm water, if desired. (This will keep the dressing from separating.) Pour the dressing over vegetables and allow to marinate at least 4 hours.

Serve in a bowl, sprinkled with a little chopped parsley.

GREEN PEPPER AND GRAPEFRUIT RELISH

Serve this relish with cold ham, shrimp salad, cold poached salmon, or any platter of cold cuts. Made in advance and allowed to age in the icebox for several days, it will taste even better, but be sure to take it out about an hour before serving to warm to room temperature.

MAKES APPROXIMATELY 2 CUPS

1 large green pepper, washed, seeded, and finely chopped
1 cup grapefruit sections, drained and chopped
¼ cup ripe olives, finely chopped
¼ cup sweet gherkin pickles, finely chopped
Salt and freshly ground black pepper to taste

Combine all ingredients and allow to stand for at least 30 minutes, or several hours if there is time. Serve at room temperature.

RHUBARB AND GRAPEFRUIT MARMALADE

Excellent as a spread for hot buttered toast, this can also be used to glaze roast ham, pork, or lamb. Let it stand for several days to thicken properly.

MAKES 8 HALF-PINT JARS

1½ pounds rhubarb, washed and cut into 1-inch lengths
2 grapefruit
3 cups sugar

Put the rhubarb in a glass or china bowl. Grate the grapefruit rind over the rhubarb. Halve the grapefruit and squeeze the juice. Strain the juice into the bowl with the rhubarb. Pour the sugar over all, cover, and leave overnight.

Bring the mixture to a boil in a nonaluminum saucepan (to prevent discoloring). Stir often. When the sugar has dissolved, raise the temperature and boil hard for 15 minutes. When the temperature reaches 224°F on a candy thermometer, ladle the boiling mixture into hot sterilized jars. Seal at once.

LIGHT STRAWBERRY MOUSSE

This airy confection is made with a mercifully small amount of cream and sugar, and is thus a nice light ending for a substantial meal.

SERVES 4

1 quart fresh strawberries, washed, hulled, and cut up
½ cup superfine granulated sugar
2 tablespoons lemon juice
½ cup heavy cream, whipped with 2 tablespoons Amaretto
2 egg whites, beaten until stiff peaks form
4 whole strawberries

Purée the strawberries with sugar and lemon juice. Pour the purée into a bowl and fold in whipped cream and then egg whites. Spoon the mousse into sherbet dishes and chill for at least 2 hours. Garnish each serving with one perfect, unhulled strawberry.

STRAWBERRIES WITH STRAWBERRY PURÉE

Sometimes fresh berries are so gorgeous that they need hardly any embellishment.

SERVES 4

4 cups strawberries, washed and hulled
Juice of 1 orange or ⅓ cup frozen reconstituted orange juice
3 tablespoons sweet white wine or white rum
3 tablespoons sugar

Purée one-third of the strawberries with the orange juice, sugar, and white wine or rum.

Arrange the whole berries in dessert dishes and pour purée over them. Serve with homemade cookies.

STRAWBERRIES MELBA

We celebrate the natural affinity of strawberries and raspberries with an irresistible spring dessert. Use premium ice cream, homemade if possible.

SERVES 4

1 ten-ounce carton of sweetened frozen raspberries, thawed
2 tablespoons butter
2 tablespoons light rum
1 pint vanilla ice cream (homemade, if possible—see below)
1 pint fresh strawberries, washed and hulled
½ cup whipped cream

Purée the raspberries with their syrup in a blender or food processor. Strain the purée into a saucepan and simmer for 5 minutes. Stir in butter and rum. Cool the sauce to room temperature.

Place one scoop of ice cream in each serving dish. Arrange strawberries around ice cream and top with raspberry sauce. Garnish with whipped cream.

HOMEMADE VANILLA ICE CREAM

Lydie Marshall brought this recipe with her for a cooking class at Hay Day.

1 tablespoon pure vanilla extract
1 cup half and half
2 cups heavy cream
⅔ cup sugar
6 egg yolks

Combine vanilla, half and half, heavy cream, and sugar in a saucepan. Simmer until sugar is dissolved. Beat the egg yolks with a whisk. Pour eggs into a heavy 2 quart saucepan. Whisk in the cream and sugar mixture. Simmer gently, stirring with a wooden spoon in a figure 8 until the mixture begins to thicken. Do not boil. Strain the mixture into a mixing bowl. Beat with an electric mixer for 5 minutes to cool. Chill well and freeze in an electric ice-cream freezer according to manufacturer's instructions.

ORANGE-GINGER STRAWBERRIES

Try to use top-quality fresh yoghurt; it tastes better, has a smoother, creamier texture, and is less gelatinous than the mass-produced version.

SERVES 4 TO 6

1½ cups finest quality fresh yoghurt
⅓ cup ginger marmalade, puréed in a blender with
   2 tablespoons orange juice
2 pints fresh strawberries, rinsed and hulled

Beat the marmalade mixture into the yoghurt. Arrange strawberries in glass serving dishes. Pass the gingered yoghurt.

HAZELNUT-STRAWBERRY MERINGUE

Like any meringue, this one will absorb moisture very quickly, so don't try to make it on a rainy or very humid day. It will turn a lovely golden color when it is baked. To roast the hazelnuts, spread them on a cookie sheet and roast for 15 minutes at 325°F, then cool thoroughly.

SERVES 6

3 large egg whites, beaten until stiff peaks form
1¼ cups very finely granulated sugar
½ teaspoon wine vinegar
¾ cup shelled hazelnuts, roasted, cooled, and ground

1 pint fresh strawberries, washed, topped, and cut in half
1 cup heavy cream, whipped until very stiff
Confectioners' sugar

Preheat the oven to 300°F.

Using an electric mixer, beat the egg whites until they are frothy. Beat sugar and vinegar into the egg whites a little at a time, until the egg whites shine and are very stiff. Fold ground hazelnuts gently into the egg whites.

Line two 8-inch cake pans with parchment or waxed paper. Spread meringue mixture evenly in the two pans. Swirl the top of one into an attractive pattern. Bake for 40 minutes at 300°F and then leave in closed oven until completely cool, about 1 hour.

Just before serving, fold strawberries into whipped cream. Place the plain meringue on a serving plate. Spread fruit and cream mixture over this layer and top with the one with the swirled pattern. Sprinkle with confectioners' sugar.

STRAWBERRY MERINGUE PIE

This is another version of the classic spring combination—meringue with strawberries—but it is cooked in a very slow oven so the meringue remains white. The longer meringues are left in the oven, the crisper they will remain afterward.

SERVES 6 TO 8

4 egg whites
½ teaspoon cream of tartar
1 cup sugar
1 quart strawberries, washed, hulled, and dried
3 tablespoons dark rum
1 pint heavy cream, whipped until stiff

Preheat the oven to 200°F.

Beat egg whites with cream of tartar until peaks begin to form. Gradually beat in sugar until the meringue is shiny and stiff. Pile meringue into a lightly buttered china or glass pie pan, forming a pie shell shape.

Bake at 200°F for 2 hours, then turn oven off. Meringue should be left in the oven and allowed to cool completely for at least 1 hour.

Pile clean, dry strawberries into the shell. Beat rum into the whipped cream and mound over the berries. Serve at once.

STRAWBERRY MOLD

To *macerate* fruits is to steep them in a liquid, usually wine or brandy, to enhance their flavor and soften their texture. To *marinate* foods is also to steep them in liquid, but the process more often refers to meats and vegetables and usually incorporates an oil or fat.

SERVES 6

1 quart strawberries, washed, stemmed, and half of them cut in half
Juice of 1 lemon
½ cup red currant jelly, melted
¼ cup kirsch
1 teaspoon safflower oil
3 cups water
⅓ cup uncooked rice
1⅔ cups scalded milk
2 large egg yolks
½ cup sugar
1 envelope powdered gelatin (1 tablespoon)
2 tablespoons water
2 teaspoons pure vanilla extract
1¼ cups heavy cream, whipped stiffly

Combine the cut strawberries in a bowl with the lemon juice, melted jelly, and kirsch. Macerate for 20 minutes. Lightly oil the inside of a 1-quart soufflé dish or mold.

In a heavy saucepan bring 3 cups of water to a boil. Add the rice and boil for 6 minutes. Drain. Add 1 cup hot milk and cook until the rice is tender and all the milk is absorbed. Beat the egg yolks and sugar in a small bowl until very light and creamy. Stir in ⅔ cup hot milk, beating all the time. Cook over low heat, stirring constantly, until the custard begins to thicken.

Soften the gelatin in the water. Pour into the hot custard and stir until completely dissolved. Strain the custard and gelatin mixture and add it to the cooked rice. Stir well. Add the vanilla and stir well. Chill until the mixture just begins to set. Fold in the whipped cream. Drain the strawberries, reserving the liquid.

Spread half the custard mixture in the oiled mold. Spread the berries over the custard and top with the rest of the custard. Cover with plastic wrap and chill until set. Unmold the dessert into a serving platter. Arrange whole strawberries around the edges and place the most beautiful one on top. Spoon the reserved strawberry liquid over each serving.

COEUR À LA CRÈME

In this French dessert, fresh cream cheese and cottage cheese are mixed with heavy cream to make fromage à la crème; when it is drained in a heart-shaped mold, it is called coeur à la crème. It is equally delicious with raspberries, blueberries, fresh grapes, sliced peaches, or sliced ripe pears.

SERVES 6

2 cups cottage cheese
1 cup cream cheese
1 cup heavy cream, whipped until stiff peaks form
Pinch of salt
¼ cup very finely granulated sugar
1 pint fresh strawberries

Line a heart-shaped perforated china coeur à la crème mold or basket with damp cheesecloth. Put the cottage cheese and cream cheese in the bowl of a food processor and process until smooth. Add salt and sugar and process one minute.

Fold whipped cream into cheese mixture and spoon into the mold. Cover with more dampened cheesecloth. Allow to drain on a plate in the refrigerator overnight or for several hours. Unmold onto a chilled plate and surround with the fresh strawberries.

Serve with more heavy cream and more sugar.

STRAWBERRY SAUCE

This sauce is superb with homemade vanilla ice cream, or layered with softened vanilla ice cream in parfait glasses and frozen till firm, then topped with sweetened whipped cream. Serve also with fresh fruit cup or sliced peaches, or use as a base for strawberry milk shakes—just add milk and ice cream and whirl in a blender.

MAKES APPROXIMATELY 2 CUPS

1 quart fresh strawberries, washed, hulled, and drained
1 cup superfine granulated sugar
2 tablespoons rum or cognac

Purée the berries with sugar in a blender until smooth and sugar is dissolved. Turn into a bowl and beat in rum or cognac.

HAY DAY'S STRAWBERRY-RHUBARB PIE

At Hay Day we know it's spring when the bakery starts making this pie; it was one of the first things we made for sale at the store. The recipe was adapted by the bakery crew in homage to Irma Rombauer and the *Joy of Cooking;* it's a real New England spring dessert.

MAKES ONE DEEP-DISH PIE

Pastry for a two-crust deep-dish pie (see page 105)
3 cups rhubarb
2 cups strawberries
2 tablespoons tapioca
6 tablespoons flour
Pinch of salt
1¼ cups sugar
Grated rind of 1 orange
1 tablespoon butter
1 whole egg, beaten, for glazing

Preheat the oven to 350°F.

Roll out two-thirds of the pastry and fit into 9-inch deep-dish pie plate.

Cut rhubarb into 1-inch pieces. Wash and hull the strawberries and cut them in half. Place the fruit in a large bowl and mix well.

Stir the dry ingredients together in a separate bowl and add to the cut-up fruit, mixing well. Add orange rind.

Fill unbaked pie shell with the fruit mixture. Dot fruit with butter, cut into small pieces.

Roll out the remaining pastry slightly larger than the pie, spread over top of pie, and seal it to the bottom crust by crimping it.

Glaze the crust with beaten egg. Cut slits to vent steam. Bake for 55 minutes in a 350°F oven. Remove from the oven and let cool. Serve with Home-made Vanilla Ice Cream (see page 99).

BASIC PIE PASTRY

Use this basic pastry for all the pies in the book.

MAKES 1 TWO-CRUST PIE

2 cups all-purpose unbleached flour
½ teaspoon salt
½ cup shortening (lard, butter, or a mixture), chilled
4 to 5 tablespoons ice water

Stir together the flour and salt. Cut in the shortening until the mixture resembles coarse meal. Stir in ice water. Gather the dough into a ball. Divide the dough into two parts.

STEWED RHUBARB

Serve warm or chilled, with crème fraîche, heavy cream, or vanilla ice cream.

MAKES ABOUT 3 CUPS

1½ pounds rhubarb, leaves removed and the stems cut into ½-inch pieces
¾ cup sugar

Combine rhubarb and sugar in a glass bowl. Let stand for about 30 minutes. Turn the mixture into an enamel or stainless steel saucepan. Bring to a boil and simmer, partially covered, for 20 minutes. Stir occasionally. Remove from the heat and cool.

RHUBARB COMPOTE

The grapefruit juice adds a tangy character to this New England spring classic.

SERVES 4

2 pounds rhubarb, trimmed of all leaves and cut into 1-inch lengths
⅓ cup fresh grapefruit juice
1 tablespoon lemon juice
⅔ cup sugar

Mix all ingredients together and simmer in an enamel saucepan until tender, about 20 to 30 minutes. Cool and chill. Serve with cookies or pound cake.

HAY DAY'S RHUBARB BARS

These rhubarb bars are to springtime what applesauce bars are to the fall; they're not too sweet, with a nice tart flavor, and they're great for tea or dessert.

MAKES 24 BARS

2¼ cups flour
1 cup whole wheat flour
2 teaspoons baking soda
1 teaspoon baking powder
1 teaspoon salt
2 teaspoons cinnamon
½ teaspoon nutmeg
½ teaspoon allspice
3 eggs
1 cup safflower oil
1¾ cups firmly packed brown sugar
2 teaspoons pure vanilla extract
2½ cups rhubarb diced into ½-inch pieces
¾ cup chopped walnuts

CONFECTIONERS' GLAZE

1½ cups confectioners' sugar, sifted
Pinch of salt
1 teaspoon pure vanilla extract
Grated rind of 1 orange
Half and half, enough to make spreadable

Preheat the oven to 350°F.

Butter well a 15 x 10 x 2-inch roasting pan. Sift the dry ingredients together. Beat eggs, oil, brown sugar, and vanilla in a large bowl with an electric mixer until fluffy and smooth. Fold in dry ingredients all at once just till moistened. Stir in rhubarb and walnuts. Spoon batter into the prepared pan. Bake at 350°F for 20 to 25 minutes or until firm to the touch in the middle. When coolish, glaze with confectioners' glaze. To make glaze, put sugar, salt, vanilla, and orange rind in a bowl. Add enough half and half to make a spreading consistency. Paint glaze over bars.

RHUBARB CRUMBLE

One of the great incarnations for rhubarb, this is lovely with Homemade Vanilla Ice Cream.

SERVES 6

1½ pounds rhubarb, leaves discarded, washed, peeled, and cut into 1-inch lengths
1 cup confectioners' sugar
¾ teaspoon ground ginger
1 teaspoon ground cinnamon
Juice of ½ lemon
¾ cup flour
½ cup brown sugar
½ teaspoon ground nutmeg
Pinch of salt
4 tablespoons butter, chilled
¼ cup oatmeal
Heavy cream or Homemade Vanilla Ice Cream (see page 99)

Preheat the oven to 350°F.

In a glass bowl, combine the rhubarb, sugar, ginger, cinnamon, and lemon juice. Let stand for 1 hour. Generously butter a large glass baking dish. Drain the rhubarb, discard the liquid, and pile it in the prepared dish.

In a bowl, stir together flour, brown sugar, nutmeg, and salt. Cut butter in until the mixture resembles coarse meal. Stir in oatmeal and pile mixture on top of the rhubarb.

Bake at 350°F for 1 hour or until the top is lightly browned. Serve with a small pitcher of heavy cream or Homemade Vanilla Ice Cream.

RHUBARB BISCUITS

This is an unusual way to cook with rhubarb, rather like using it instead of raisins and spices to make sweet rolls.

SERVES 6 TO 8

2 cups rhubarb, cut in ½-inch chunks
¾ cup sugar
¼ cup water
6 tablespoons butter
¼ cup sugar
1 cup flour
2 teaspoons baking powder
Pinch of salt
2 tablespoons sugar
⅓ cup milk or cream

Preheat the oven to 400°F.

In an enamel saucepan, simmer the rhubarb with ¾ cup sugar and the water until tender, about 20 minutes. Cool the mixture.

Melt 2 tablespoons butter in an 8-inch square pan. Sprinkle melted butter with ¼ cup sugar.

Stir together flour, baking powder, salt, and 2 tablespoons sugar. Cut in 2 tablespoons butter until the mixture resembles coarse meal. Stir in milk or cream. Form the dough into a ball. Turn out on a floured board and knead for 30 seconds. Roll out the dough to ¼-inch thickness. Drain the rhubarb mixture and spread the fruit over the dough. Dot with 2 tablespoons butter. Roll the dough up like a jelly roll and chill. Cut into 1-inch thick slices. Arrange cut side down in the prepared baking pan. Bake at 400°F for 30 minutes. Serve warm with Homemade Vanilla Ice Cream (see page 99), if desired.

LEMON ICE BOX COOKIES

The tang of fresh lemon juice cannot be duplicated.

MAKES ABOUT 4 DOZEN COOKIES

3 cups unbleached flour
½ teaspoon baking soda

½ *teaspoon baking powder*
Pinch of salt
1 cup sugar
¼ *pound (1 stick) butter, softened*
1 whole egg
Juice of 2 lemons
2 tablespoons grated lemon rind
Granulated sugar

Stir together flour, baking soda, baking powder, and salt. In a separate bowl, beat together sugar and butter until light. Beat in egg. Add lemon juice and rind. Add the flour mixture. Form into a roll and wrap in waxed paper. Refrigerate until firm.

Unwrap dough and slice very thin. Preheat the oven to 400°F. Sprinkle the cookies with sugar and bake on an ungreased cookie sheet at 400°F for 6 minutes. Cool on a rack.

GINGERED FRUIT

Ginger goes well with citrus; here, oranges and strawberries are steeped in a ginger syrup, a treatment that would be equally good for pears.

SERVES 4

⅓ *cup white corn syrup*
⅓ *cup water*
1 tablespoon lemon juice
3 ounces fresh ginger, cut into fine julienne
1 quart fresh strawberries, sliced
2 oranges, peeled and sliced, slices cut into quarters

Boil together corn syrup, water, and lemon juice. Add ginger and simmer for 15 minutes. Cool the hot syrup, then add strawberries and oranges. Macerate in the icebox at least 2 hours. Drain and save the syrup for another use. Serve very cold.

YOGHURT WITH HONEY AND FRUIT

A boon for counters of calories, this would be a lovely way to serve oranges, melon, or mangoes.

SERVES 4

1 pint fresh, high-quality yoghurt
3 tablespoons honey
3 tablespoons chopped toasted almonds
Fresh fruit

Beat together yoghurt and honey. Stir in almonds.
Serve in glass compote dishes, accompanied by a plate of freshly cut-up fruit.

ORANGE DELIGHT

This very light finale for a spring dinner should be made the night before.

SERVES 4

1½ cups fresh orange juice
1 cup sugar
4 large pieces of orange peel, white pith removed
2 eggs and 2 egg yolks, beaten until frothy

Preheat the oven to 300°F.
In a large saucepan stir together the orange juice, sugar, and orange peel. Simmer 5 minutes and then remove the orange peel. Skim off any froth that has formed.
With a whisk, beat the hot syrup into the eggs in a very thin stream. Pour the egg mixture into 4 individual soufflé dishes. Set the dishes in a pan of boiling water.
Bake at 300°F for about 1 hour. Cool to room temperature, cover lightly, and chill overnight.
Serve with lemon-flavored sugar cookies.

BERRY GRUNT

A grunt is an old-fashioned steamed berry pudding, probably dating from colonial times; it can be made with raspberries, blueberries, or huckleberries, and it deserves annual revival during berry season. Steaming is not difficult—the only trick is to keep the water out of the pudding and yet simmering hard all the time. If there is no covered mold available, fill a small crockery bowl with the mixture, cover it with foil, and tie the foil tightly around the bowl with string or a rubber band.

SERVES 4 TO 6

2 cups berries (raspberries, blueberries, etc.)
¾ cup water
½ cup sugar
1½ cups flour
½ teaspoon salt
2 teaspoons baking powder
1 tablespoon butter
½ cup milk

Simmer berries in water until just soft. Stir in sugar and simmer 3 minutes more. Pour into a buttered pudding mold equipped with a lid. Stir together flour, salt, and baking powder. Cut in butter. Add milk and stir. Spread dough over fruit. Cover mold tightly and place on a rack in a deep kettle. Pour in boiling water to 2 inches from the top of the mold. Steam for 1 hour. Unmold and serve hot with Homemade Vanilla Ice Cream (see page 99) or heavy cream.

HAY DAY'S HOT CROSS BUNS

We sell hundreds of these at Easter time; they are as much part of the image of spring as daffodils and baby rabbits. Hot cross buns are descended from loaves baked in medieval times from the dough used in church and distributed to the sick or the poor, but they are probably more ancient than Christianity. Loaves marked with a cross were found at Herculaneum (A.D. 79) and are illustrated even earlier.

MAKES APPROXIMATELY 20 BUNS

⅓ cup half and half
¼ pound (1 stick) unsalted butter
⅓ cup sugar
1 teaspoon salt
2 tablespoons active, dry yeast, dissolved in ½ cup warm water*
3 beaten eggs
⅔ cup currants
4 to 5 cups of flour
1 beaten egg white for glaze

FROSTING

1 cup sifted confectioners' sugar
Remaining egg whites
½ teaspoon pure vanilla extract
½ teaspoon grated lemon rind
Half and half, if needed

Heat half and half to scalding and add butter, sugar, and salt. Stir to dissolve. Set aside to cool. While half and half mixture is cooling, dissolve yeast in warm water. Let proof. When proofed, add to cooled half and half mixture. Add beaten eggs and then the currants. Add the flour gradually, 1 cup at a time, beating well after each addition. Add flour as needed to make a soft dough.

Knead just until the dough is smooth and satiny. Put dough in a buttered bowl, turning once to butter the top, and let rise in a warm place until doubled, about 1 hour. Punch down.

Flatten out dough to about ½ inch thick. Shape the dough into 2½-inch buns. Place in a well-buttered baking pan leaving a little space between each bun so they can rise. Let rise about 1 hour. Preheat oven to 350°F. If desired,

---

* When dissolving yeast, fill a 1 cup measuring cup with ½ cup of warm water. Add yeast slowly, stirring with a tiny wire whisk to help dissolve the yeast. Let it sit until you see a layer of foam on top.

snip a shallow cross in each bun with sharp scissors. Brush tops with 1 slightly beaten egg white (you'll have some left over so save it for the frosting). Bake in a 350°F oven for 20 to 25 minutes, or until golden brown. Remove from oven and cool slightly.

Mix the frosting ingredients well. Add a little half and half if it is too thick. Pipe frosting crosses on while buns are warm.

SUMMER

There is nothing that is comparable to it, as satisfactory
or as thrilling, as gathering the vegetables one has grown.
ALICE B. TOKLAS

I T begins with strawberries and ends with the last of the peaches; starts with peonies and ends with goldenrod. Summer goes faster now, but it used to be the longest of the seasons, and if you were a child marooned in the country by the war, it was endless. We measured the crawling days by sounds: the noon whistle from the firehouse, the tractor snarling in the hayfield in the hot afternoon, the thunder in the west at teatime no more ominous than the purr of a cat in the bed. We heard the first cicada in July and knew it was midsummer; gloomier interpreters heard in it the ghastly approach of school.

Events were few in those days. Somewhere life moved faster—somewhere people raced sailboats and drove to tennis lessons—but not in the green hills of Connecticut, where even after the war driving was still a luxury. You could pick blueberries and swim in the lake; you could walk up to the farm at the end of the road and let Joe Anderson squirt milk in your mouth straight from the cow, aiming down the line from you to your brother to the cats. Fourth of July was a parade in the village and firecrackers, if you were lucky. The big event was driving to town (twice a week at most) for groceries, eating an ice cream cone at the drugstore, and coming home with books from the cool, musty library.

But even then there was all the cornucopia of New England summer: strawberries and melons, peaches and blueberries, raspberries and apricots. Victory gardens grew peas and green beans, lettuce and spinach, summer squash and sweet corn. Pickling and canning went on all summer, and the procession from strawberry jam through watermelon pickles to peach preserves, wild grape jelly, and apple butter was as timeless and inevitable as the season itself.

Obviously much has changed since then, but the progression of the summer crops continues. We still buy corn and watermelons from the same farms, and still make jams and jellies from some of the same recipes that were tacked over the stove when we came roaring in at the age of seven, slamming the screen door and thundering across the porch, called in to test the wild grape jelly cooling in the kitchen.

Several farmers bring their produce to us, and we buy a good deal in markets, but every few days all through the summer one of the Hay Day trucks travels to farms in Connecticut and New Jersey and New York State, buying sweet corn and tomatoes, peaches and melons. Fairfield County is hardly the breadbasket of New England, and there aren't many large-scale growers left, but there are a few, and buying from them is often worth the extra time it takes to make a special trip.

Consider the peach. It can't develop sugars on its own, so it will never be sweeter than it is the day it's picked. Peaches bought locally, therefore, which don't need as much handling and travel time, can be picked a little later and will still have as long a shelf life as California fruit—and they'll be a lot sweeter.

We buy peaches from Dave Henry at the Blue Hill Farm in Wallingford; his family has had the orchard since 1904, and he has wonderful fruit.

Rattling up there in the truck is hardly a jaunt for pleasure; trucks can't go on the Merritt Parkway, so we have to go the long way round by New Haven on I-95. When we used to have to line up in the truck lanes at the tolls it felt like having to ride in the back of the bus. For a while, we are neck and neck with two great red tractor-trailers from Finast.

But when we leave the highway, we leave Finast, too. The houses thin out, and along the winding road we pass fields of clover and Queen Anne's lace and black-eyed Susans; you can see the peach trees in the distance, up on a hill. The crop is huge this year. Inside the old packing shed, workers are sorting and grading peaches by hand. The peaches—Red Haven, Candor, Garnet Beauty—are in classic, slightly cone-shaped baskets in the shade. They're fragile, so they can't be graded by machines like pears and apples and can't be packed tightly in cartons. Dave doesn't fill the baskets full—for every two baskets we pay for, he puts three on the truck.

The peach baskets are tippy, so one of us has to perch on the front of the forklift to hold them steady. Nothing is written down; we load the truck together, keeping count in our heads, and afterward Dave makes out an invoice leaning on an apple barrel.

"You're writing a cookbook?" he says. "My wife's up at the house—I'll get her to tell you how to make Peach Crisp. It's a nice easy recipe." (She does, and it is—just slice four or five peeled peaches into a pie tin, cover with crumbs, dot with butter, bake for 20 minutes at 350°F and serve with whipped cream. She uses graham cracker crumbs, but we liked it fine with our own butter/sugar/flour crumb topping.)

Bumping down the narrow road on the way home (could a Finast truck make it up here?) we have to go slowly because the peaches bruise easily. Our driver remembers the day a car cut him off on the highway and he had to stop short with a truckload of apples loose in crates; he ended up with the cab so full of apples they were about up to his waist. His leg muscles hurt from the effort it took to keep their weight off the accelerator. Think of that next time you cut off a truck in traffic.

We wish we could do more buying locally; there are good small farms not far away, but they can only produce a small part of what we'd like to have. At any rate, we do as much as we can, and we get a kick out of it, especially when people look at the big sign in the stores that says "We sell no day-old corn" and ask us if it's really true. Bet your boots it's true, we say, confidently. We saw it picked this morning, because we were *there*.

The Summer Market

THE first time each year that you smell the pungent perfume of a bunch of fresh *basil* is rather like taking the cap off the Coppertone—you know summer's really here. People who could hardly recognize fresh basil ten years ago are now avidly grinding it into Pesto (see page 187); stand in line behind one of them at the herb counter and you'll be lucky if there's any left for you. Basil and tomatoes are the obvious summer combination, but try it in Pistou (see page 248), or try the recipe for Tarragon Jelly on page 190 and use the opal variety for color. Basil is, of course, only one of the multitude of herbs—fresh tarragon, parsley, marjoram, and the rest—that enrich summer cooking. The chart on page 129 describes them in detail.

Sweet baby *green beans* (we still call them "string" beans, although the strings have long since been bred out of them) are one of the hardest vegetables to find really fresh in the market. If they're fresh, they'll snap when they're broken; if they're flabby, forget it. Cooked briefly enough to retain their snap and color, they are one of the treasures of summer.

Buy beans of a uniform size so they'll cook evenly. Wash, trim off the ends, and cook quickly, uncovered, in enough rapidly boiling water to keep them moving in the pot. When their color becomes more intense, they are just tender. Drain, then plunge in cold water to stop cooking, and serve cold with a vinaigrette or reheat gently in butter. Yellow wax beans are cooked exactly the same way. Fresh green beans keep well in a bowl of water in the icebox, or just rinsed and stored in a plastic bag.

We used to hate *lima beans* as much as we hated parsnips, probably because our grandmothers boiled them down to a chalky mush. We know now that if they're cooked like glazed carrots in half butter and half water, or cooked in a lot of boiling water till they're just tender—somewhere between ten and twenty minutes—and drained and tossed with butter, they are excellent.

Beets are much better baked or steamed to retain flavor and nutrients than they are boiled or cooked in a pressure cooker. (In Europe beets are traditionally sold precooked; it used to be that the greengrocer would pile them in the baker's ovens as they cooled down, but today it is done commercially.) The trick is to keep them from bleeding, so after washing leave the roots intact and cut off all but two inches of stalk at the top, then bake, covered or wrapped in foil, in a slow oven (300°F) for at least an hour, depending on their size. They can be baked at a higher temperature if necessary, but in that case it's a good idea to add a little water to the pan. Beets are done when their skins loosen, or when they can be pierced easily with a fork. Young and tender *beet greens* are delicious, too. Wash and wilt them with a little butter, just as you would spinach.

All year long we get a steady supply of *broccoli* from California, but the crop from local farms is abundant in July. Broccoli is a good source of vitamin A (there's a lot in the leaves, too, so cook them along with it). The fleurettes should be tightly bunched and the stalks firm and green. Cook the broccoli until it's crunchy, plunging it immediately in cold water to keep it from overcooking. Blanching broccoli or any green vegetable in large volumes of boiling water keeps it green but accelerates the loss of vitamins. Steaming is harder to control but may retain more nutrients. It's a trade-off.

We don't need to say much about *carrots*, except that when you buy fresh summer ones with their feathery tops still on you know you're getting them one or two days out of the garden. (Take the tops off when you get home, though, because the green leaves will draw moisture from the roots.) Carrots that come topless and in cellophane bags may be up to six weeks old and are almost always treated with a fungicide to prolong shelf life.

One summer herb that deserves special mention is *coriander*, also called cilantro or Chinese parsley. Popular all over the world (it is widely used in Mexican, Chinese, and Indian cooking), it has been slow to catch on in this country, and some people still regard it with deep suspicion. It usually turns up as a garnish for flavoring, rather than being used in the actual cooking process. Coriander is a bit more fragile than parsley, but if you buy it with its roots still attached and keep them moist, it keeps well in the icebox. Don't wash it until just before it is to be used.

Like peas, *sweet corn* turns its sugars to starch very quickly, which is the reason both should go straight from the plant to the pot. Place husked corn in a large amount of boiling water and cook for three to four minutes after the water comes back to the boil, or until a test kernel is just tender. If you're cooking outdoors, try dipping the corn whole in water, husks and all, and then roasting it with the silk removed for about fifteen minutes on the charcoal grill.

Look for green, fresh husks and fresh cornsilk; you will develop an instinct for ears that have been around for a while. Peel the husks back to check for worms, and look for glossy, plump kernels that are fairly close together. Produce buyers at Hay Day test corn by pulling back the husks and biting into the raw kernels—you can taste the freshness—but that's a little awkward if you're a customer. Another test for fresh corn is to poke a kernel with a thumbnail: if the juice is thin and watery it's fresh, but if it is milky and thick the corn has already turned starchy.

Magnificent *eggplants* are in season now. Buy them very firm, and don't worry about size, big eggplants are just as tender as little ones. Many recipes specify salting larger eggplants, peeled or unpeeled, and although this sounds like makework, it is actually a good idea. It extrudes the liquid in the flesh, gets rid of any bitterness (although with the newer hybrids this is less of a problem), and most of all reduces the amount of oil that a raw eggplant will absorb. Sprinkle salt on eggplant slices and leave them for thirty minutes in a colander; be sure to pat them dry afterward. Most recipes call for sautéeing eggplant slices, but we've found that they will absorb less oil if they are broiled instead; just brush them lightly with oil and broil (watching them carefully) till golden brown, turning once.

We've also discovered that the technique for peeling peppers works beautifully with eggplant, too. Split an eggplant in half and put it flesh side down close to the flame in a preheated broiler for about ten minutes or until the skin starts to bubble. If the skins do not immediately come off easily, put the halves in a paper or plastic bag for ten minutes and try peeling them again. By sweating some of the liquid out of the eggplant, this technique also reduces the amount of oil it will absorb.

Nasturtiums and squash blossoms are finding their way into markets these days; home gardeners have known for years that they are superb in summer cooking. The leaves of nasturtiums, a member of the cress family, are often eaten in salads, but the fun is to add the brilliant color and peppery flavor of the flowers to salads, sandwiches, and hors d'oeuvres. Squash blossoms (zucchini and yellow squash, for example) can be treated the same way or stuffed, deep-fried, or sautéed.

People are rarely neutral about *okra*. Even at Hay Day people either love or hate it. But this southern classic is excellent in stews and, of course, gumbos, in which its unique taste and natural thickening properties greatly improve the character of the sauce. Okra goes well in summer casseroles with tomatoes, eggplant, bacon, and ham; it is excellent with fish and shellfish. Its partisans like it plain—steamed, sautéed, or deep-fried—but even flinty New Englanders like it with a mixture of other textures. Buy it as young and green as possible— the pods should be no more than two or three inches long, with no trace of brown—and don't keep it in the icebox more than a day or two. Although its flavor will withstand simmering in a stew, it should never be overcooked (it gets a little slimy) if it is served on its own. Steam or sauté till it is just tender but still green.

Green and yellow *summer squash* and *zucchini* need scant mention here.

They should be picked when very small—from four to six inches in length—and should be glossy and crisply firm. Gardeners who come home from a trip to find themselves hip-deep in giant squashes can grate them or use them for stuffing, but they are not very rewarding. *Pattypan* squashes for steaming should be no more than two and a half inches across, although larger ones are fine for stuffing. We think we may have started something by featuring tiny zucchini and yellow and pattypan squashes picked in infancy (only one or two inches long) and serving them in the store with a dip.

We've said elsewhere that you can buy anything at any time if you pay enough and know where to look, but *tomatoes* are the exception. Hydroponic varieties in the spring come close, and some of the imports from Holland and Israel aren't bad, but a resplendent New England summer tomato cannot be duplicated at any other season. Baby tomatoes are good for serving with dips, and they also work well in salads and are excellent broiled. Yellow tomatoes are sweet and delicate and much less acid than red ones, but one word of caution: if you're canning tomatoes of any color, remember that they are all now being bred with less acid and are thus no longer naturally equipped to retard the growth of bacteria. Add a teaspoon of lemon juice or vinegar to each quart jar.

Many recipes call for tomatoes "peeled, seeded, and juiced," which makes them less watery and often more digestible, but we found out not long ago that the highest concentration of vitamin C in a tomato is in the watery jelly that surrounds the seeds—it's confusing, isn't it? To peel a tomato, dip it in boiling water for ten seconds and the skin will slip off easily.

Unjustly maligned *turnips* can be eaten raw; they're wonderful sliced thin and served like radishes with dips and other crudités. Buy them as young as you can—you can tell by the greens, which are usually sold with them—and serve steamed, boiled, baked, in stews, or cut in slices or julienned strips for stir-fry. Tiny new turnips are excellent sautéed with their greens.

Like peaches, *apricots* are natives of China that came to Europe through Persia about two thousand years ago, and some of their exotic quality still remains. Apricots are often picked green, and they can be hard as bullets; don't buy them unless they are a tiny bit soft and very brightly colored—the stronger the color, the riper they are. Eating them fresh from the tree is glorious, though most people use them in jams, tarts, glazes, and stuffings.

One of our best summer memories is picking wild, high-bush *blueberries* on the east end of Nantucket Island, where clusters of berries grew so thick they seemed to pour into our hands. Wild blueberries rarely reach our wholesale markets, so we often send a truck to Maine to bring some down for Hay Day. They are rare because they are both fragile and difficult to clean; growers find it easier to freeze them immediately so they can withstand cleaning, then send them straight on to be processed into jam. The best market blueberries come from Vineland, New Jersey, and there are now so many varieties that the season starts in May and keeps going through early August. Like cranberries, blueberries can easily be frozen at home in the plastic basket or in freezer containers. Once frozen, blueberries are soft and good only for cooking, but who can argue with blueberry pie in November?

The season for *cherries* starts in mid-May with early varieties from southern California, then moves north along the coast as the bright red Bings ripen during June, reaching their peak in early July. In mid-June, watch for the New York State crop from the orchards of the Hudson Valley; their season is short, but since they are picked ripe and shipped from close by, their flavor is wonderful. We love the magnificent, perishable sweet black cherries from the shores of Lake Michigan, but they're hard to find in eastern markets; during late July we have to fly them in specially. We like cooking with sweet cherries and don't bother with the sour ones; a cherry pie made with sweet Michigan Blacks will knock your socks off.

Don't wash cherries until they're about to be used or eaten. When you are served cherries for dessert in France, a bowl of water is put on the table with them. They are like strawberries or any other perishable fruit, and once their protective bloom has been removed with washing, they spoil more rapidly.

It takes some people years to catch on that ripe *figs* are magnificent as hors d'oeuvres with prosciutto, or as dessert with heavy cream or crème fraîche, or just eaten plain out of the bowl. A procession of varieties comes in season from early June till frost; most prominent are the Green Mission, Black Mission, Kadota, and Calimyrna. How can you tell when figs are ripe? Wait till they're plump, fresh smelling, and soft to the touch. Sometimes the blossom end opens up very slightly and a little color is visible inside.

It is hard to imagine summer picnics without Thompson *seedless grapes* and the newer Red Flame seedless, but many of them, as author Jane Grigson says, are "bought without enthusiasm and eaten without surprise." Wild grapes tumbled over a stone wall give off an unforgettable fragrance and make gorgeous jelly, but they almost never turn up in the market. We eat seedless grapes all summer, like everybody else, but the table grapes with the most character are the Calmerias, the black Ribiers, the red Tokays, and the blue Concords (all of them have seeds); our favorites are the tiny Black Corinth or "champagne" grapes (they should not be confused with real champagne grapes, which are the Pinot Noir and Chardonnay varieties).

Mangoes are a treat now. Their deep-orange, sweet flesh enhances desserts (friends in the Philippines say mango meringue pie is incredible), but they're also good eaten plain. Green mangoes are chopped up and made into chutney. Mangoes have an enormous pit, firmly embedded in the flesh; to cut, stand the fruit on end and make a vertical slice on each side of the center, producing two manageable sections. The fruit that still clings to the pit can be scraped off. (The process is a little messy, but the effort is worth while.) Like avocados, mangoes should be slightly soft to the touch and should be refrigerated only when they're ripe. They should be green with splashes of red when you buy them, and they will ripen at room temperature in a brown paper bag.

Our definition of bedlam is the day Paul Newman bought part of a watermelon. We had a hard time separating the people who wanted the rest of it. *Melons* are sweetest and juiciest in the summertime—they're not the same at any other season. Don't go by softness in choosing a melon; like pears, they ripen from the inside, and a melon that's soft on the outside may well be rotten at the core. Ripe ones will be heavy with juice; compare two that are the same size, and choose the heavier one. The best melons are picked "full slip," meaning that they've been allowed to ripen on the vine until only a gentle pressure of the thumb will slip them free of the stem. (The actual—and less romantic—truth is that the pickers save stooping by kicking all the melons very gently—the ripe ones will roll off the vines.) The chart on page 130 lists the characteristics of all the summer melons, but if the opportunity arises, don't miss trying a rich, juicy Hand melon from upstate New York, or one of the extra-sweet old-fashioned muskmelons from our friends on nearby Connecticut farms.

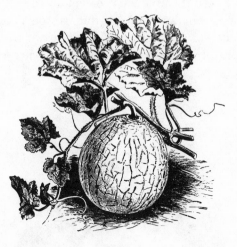

The sweetest *peaches* are the ones that have developed their sugars by being left the longest to ripen on the tree. How do you find them? Look for fuzz. Peaches that are picked green can stand washing, brushing, grading, and packing, but they lose their fuzz in the process, and many of them will never ripen properly. Try to buy fuzzy peaches from local orchards; they are more likely to ripen properly in a day or two. White peaches, with their delicate flesh and luminous pink and green overtones, are our favorite—a must for making Peach Melba. *Nectarines* are not peaches crossed with plums, as many people think; they are simply a fuzzless variety of peach, with a sharper, richer flavor.

The *plum*, the cousin of the peach and the apricot, comes into the market in a rainbow of colors from July to September, starting with red Santa Rosas and ending with the blue-black Italian prune plums. We play a game each summer to see how many varieties we can have in the store on the same day. The record is nineteen. Plums are all rich and sweet, and they give color and sweetness to a vast range of salads and desserts. They will ripen easily at home; don't eat them till they are very soft.

Like peaches and melons and other summer delights, *raspberries* can now be imported almost any time of year, but flying these fragile beauties halfway round the world makes them horribly expensive; we tend to side with other frugal New Englanders who think the price is scandalous. (Just because we offer them in February at $7 a half pint doesn't necessarily mean we think people should buy them!) At any rate, raspberries flourish locally in the summer, and if you can't pick them yourself or get an earnest child to do it, then buy them as close to home as you can—they're too delicate to travel well. Raspberries or blackberries are best served with heavy cream or crème fraîche the day they're picked; they are superb combined with white peaches. They are rich in vitamins C and B_1.

HERBS

CHOICE OF HERBS

BEEF	Oregano, parsley, rosemary
VEAL	Oregano, tarragon
PORK	Basil, marjoram, oregano, rosemary, sage
LAMB	Basil, marjoram, mint, oregano, rosemary
CHICKEN	Basil, oregano, rosemary, sage, tarragon
FISH	Basil, dill (with salmon), marjoram, oregano, sage, tarragon, thyme, parsley
EGGS	Basil, marjoram, chives
SHELLFISH	Dill, oregano
SALADS	Basil, dill, mint, oregano, rosemary, chives
SOUP	Mint (with yoghurt), oregano (with vegetables), chives (cold soups)
BEANS	Basil, dill, marjoram
CARROTS	Marjoram, mint
PEAS	Basil, marjoram, mint
EGGPLANT	Basil, oregano, thyme
TOMATO	Basil, marjoram, oregano, parsley, tarragon, thyme, chives

BEST USES

BASIL	All tomato dishes, pesto, salads, stews, and sauces for chicken and fish
CHIVES	Cold soups, dips, spreads, omelets, salads
CORIANDER	Tex-Mex foods, chili, omelets, meat loaf
DILL	Dips, eggs, cold or hot fish, cucumbers, marinades, shellfish, salads
MARJORAM	Omelets, cheese casseroles, string beans, bean pots, carrots, peas, tomatoes, fish, lamb, pork
MINT	Carrots, peas, salads, lamb, fruit, drinks, mint sauce
OREGANO	Tomatoes, eggplant, salads, shellfish, chicken, pork, veal, beef, sauces
PARSLEY	Tomatoes, fish, cream sauces, garnishes
ROSEMARY	On meat before roasting, chicken, salads, breads
SAGE	Turkey, chicken, fish, squash, eggplant
TARRAGON	Veal, chicken, fish, tomatoes, Béarnaise and other sauces
THYME	Fish, poultry, tomatoes, and sauces

MELONS

TYPE OF MELON	SEASON	FLESH COLOR	COMMENTS	HOW TO CHOOSE WHEN RIPE
CANTALOUPE	Year-round	Light orange	Usually picked at hard-ripe stage and will ripen at home in a brown paper bag at room temperature. Rich, musky-sweet flavor with a touch of tartness. An excellent melon available almost year-round.	Skin color should be warm yellow-brown. Has slight yield to pressure. Sweet, strong aroma. Seeds may rattle.
CASABA	July–November	White	A difficult melon to ship. Should be picked ripe and usually is not. Very juicy with a subtle sweetness but usually lacks flavor.	Color should be golden yellow all over. Slight softness at blossom end. Has no aroma. Best ones are found at farm stands where grown.
CRANSHAW	July–October	Salmon	Usually picked 4 or 5 days before peak of ripeness. Very perishable. Bruises easily. Refrigerate ripe melons. Juicy sweet flavor with mildly spicy aroma. An excellent choice.	Bright buttercup yellow when fully ripe and slightly soft at blossom end. Skin should have a tacky texture. High sweet aroma at blossom end. If very green it will never ripen. If slightly yellow, it will ripen quickly at room temperature.
GALIA	January–May	Pale green	Imported from Israel, this excellent melon has brightened our winters. Small, round, very sweet, and juicy with a nectarlike flavor and powerful aroma.	When this melon turns a warm brown-green color and is slightly soft at blossom end it is ready to eat. Galias will ripen nicely at home at room temperature and have a very noticeable pleasant melon aroma when ready.

MELONS (continued)

TYPE OF MELON	SEASON	FLESH COLOR	COMMENTS	HOW TO CHOOSE WHEN RIPE
HAND	August	Deep orange	This is our favorite. Grown in upstate New York near Saratoga. Very large fruits, 7 to 10 inches diameter, thick, sweet, juicy flesh. From the muskmelon family but larger and sweeter.	We have found all Hand melons to be ripe when they arrive because they are always picked "full slip," when the fruit separates from the stem with gentle pressure. Keep refrigerated and serve soon.
HONEYDEW	June–October	Pale green	The sweetest, juiciest, and finest-textured melon is a vine-ripened honeydew, but because they are not grown in the East, they are often picked unripe for shipment. A large, round melon with honeylike sweetness and firm crisp flesh. The best come from central California in late August.	When rock hard and color is chalky white, a pale green, or canary yellow, they will never ripen. If color is that of creamery butter and the skin feels velvety, slightly tacky like a nervous hand, and the honeydew aroma is pronounced, you have found the perfect fruit.
JAUNE CANARI	July–November	Pale yellow	Not an outstanding melon in our book. Lacks flavor when cut too early and when allowed to ripen flesh becomes mushy even though rind remains hard.	Turns completely bright golden yellow like a canary when ripe. Rind will not yield to the touch but continues to be hard.
MUSKMELON Connecticut-grown	August–September	Orange-red	Another of our favorites when grown on Connecticut farms and picked full slip (completely ripe). Very sweet, high musky cantaloupe flavor and a very high flesh content.	Creamy-brown skin often markedly ridged. Very strong melon aroma. Slight yield to pressure. Seeds may rattle.

MELONS (continued)

TYPE OF MELON	SEASON	FLESH COLOR	COMMENTS	HOW TO CHOOSE WHEN RIPE
ORANGE FLESH HONEYDEW	June–October	Orange	Smaller than the green honeydews. Have a lot of cantaloupe bred into them. Flesh color, flavor, and fragrance are similar to cantaloupe.	A creamy, light orange rind color changing from pale white signals ripeness. Skin should be tacky or slightly waxy like the green honeydew.
PERSIAN	June–October	Deep orange	This is a hard melon to find in our part of the country. If vine-ripened they are sensational.	Rind turns from gray to bronze under a fine netting. Usually picked too immature because they are hard to ship when ripe. Good quality is hard to find in the East and flesh is often rubbery.
SANTA CLAUS	August–December	Yellow-green	Looks like a large football with broad stripes of dark green and yellow. Named because it was the only melon available at Christmastime. Crisp flesh, not as sweet as most melons. Good with Italian prosciutto or smoked hams.	Yellow stripes become brighter and green stripes turn darker as this melon ripens. The hard, thick rind will not soften. Larger sizes, over 4 to 5 pounds, often have better flavor.
SHARLYN	July–September	Creamy white	Looks like a Persian on the outside but is creamy white inside. Flesh has a sweet perfumy fragrance and can be eaten to the rind. A much better choice than the Persian.	Ripe when completely rusty-orange under its loose, irregular netting. We prefer them less sweet—about 75 percent rusty-orange and 25 percent green-brown. As long as some orange is showing, the Sharlyn will ripen at home. If seeds rattle, it's probably too ripe.

EARLY APPLES

APPLE	ORIGIN	HARVEST DATES*	DESCRIPTION	BEST USES
Jerseymac	Introduced by Rutgers University, 1973. July Red x N.J. 24.	August 15	A medium large red apple similar to McIntosh, but 1 month earlier.	A good all-purpose apple. Keeps well for about 2 weeks refrigerated.
Tydeman's Red	A cross between the Worcester Pearmain and the McIntosh by the Department of Agriculture in England in 1964.	August 25	Brilliant scarlet color, hard, snappy, sweet-tart, and juicy.	One of the best eating early apples. Excellent for snacks, salads, and cooking. Not a good keeper.
Paulared	Another McIntosh-type apple. Grows well in the New England area.	August 25	A crisp, hard, mildly tart flavorful apple.	Another excellent eating early apple. Good for snacks, salads, and cooking. Not a good keeper.
Jonamac	A cross between McIntosh and Jonathan, developed at the Geneva, New York, Experiment Station in 1972.	August 25	Medium-sized fruit with a very red blush. Mildly tart, crisp and hard.	Good all-purpose early apple for snacks, salads, and cooking. Not a good keeper.

EARLY APPLES (continued)

APPLE	ORIGIN	HARVEST DATES*	DESCRIPTION	BEST USES
Gravenstein	Germany 1800's.	September 1	A large firm apple striped with red. Tart, spicy, juicy.	A flavorful apple unexcelled for cooking during its season. Good eaten raw, with nuts, or in salads. Excellent pies and sauce.
Mollie's Delicious	New Jersey, 1966. A cross of [Golden Delicious x Edgewood] x [Gravenstein x Close].	September 1	A very large, shapely fruit that is half red, half yellow. Yellow flesh, sweet flavor.	Just right for anyone who enjoys a sweeter apple.
Lobo	Ottawa, Canada, 1910. A McIntosh descendant.	September 1	Bright purple-red, thick skin, fine, white, juicy flesh, similar to McIntosh.	Good for eating fresh, fair for sauce and salads.
Burgundy	New York State Experiment Station. 1974. Monroe x [Macoun x Antonovka].	September 1	Large, round, and thoroughly dark red, with crisp, white, slightly tart, juicy flesh.	Very attractive and very good quality for eating out of hand.
Opalescent	Ohio, 1899.	September 5	A very large, glossy yellow apple with a splash of scarlet. Firm, sweet-tart, yellow flesh.	Very good for eating fresh, pies, sauce, and baking whole. Keeps well if refrigerated.

* These dates apply to the New England growing region. Even under refrigeration, early apples don't keep more than a week or two.

Summer Menus

SUMMER means long, golden evenings, a blue haze over the Berkshires, and picnics on the lawn at Tanglewood or Music Mountain. We savor the abundance of summer gardens and the relaxed pleasure of eating outdoors.

AT HOME

When guests come for the weekend you want to be free for expeditions, not tied to the stove. Make the corn chowder early in the morning; the rest is quickly assembled, even after spending the entire day on the boat.

CORN CHOWDER (*139*)

CHARCOAL-BAKED CORNISH HEN (*162*)

GREEN TINT PERSILLADE (*176*)

OLD-FASHIONED TOMATO SALAD (*151*)

MINTED PEARS (*196*)

FOURTH OF JULY

This meal is portable, so if somebody proposes watching fireworks from the beach, dinner goes in the back of the car with the grill. The tomato casserole is baked in the morning and reheated at the edge of the fire; the ribs are started at home and finished over charcoal as the sun goes down. Everything else comes out of the cooler.

ZUCCHINI SOUP *(143)*

MESQUITE-BARBECUED RIBS *(161)*

TOMATO-ONION-CHEESE BAKE *(169)*

SUMMER SQUASH SALAD *(153)*

STRAWBERRY FOOL *(195)*

ELEGANT BARBECUE

Put white peaches in a Venetian glass bowl and set it on an outdoor table with a view of the hills. This civilized midsummer dinner can be assembled ahead and cooked quickly at suppertime.

TOMATO GRANITA *(145)*

LIME-GRILLED CORNISH GAME HENS *(163)*

CORN SOUFFLÉ EN TOMATE *(181)*

ZUCCHINI WITH DILL *(176)*

APRICOT MOUSSE *(195)*

SUNDAY SUPPER

Stretch out the weekend—nobody wants to go back to town yet. None of these dishes requires much time in the kitchen, and there are very few pots to do afterward.

HERBED TOASTS *(145)*

SUMMER LINGUINE *(155)*

ZUCCHINI AND TOMATO SALAD *(149)*

HAY DAY'S DEEP DISH CHERRY PIE *(212)*

COMPANY COOKOUTS

Except for the salad and the dessert, which take less time to make than they do to describe, this entire meal can be cooked on the grill. It's a natural for an August evening.

MESQUITE-BARBECUED BRISKET (*159*)
CORN ON THE COB WITH HERBS (*180*)
GRILLED EGGPLANT (*179*)
CALIFORNIA TOMATO SALAD (*151*)
INSTANT BLUEBERRY GRANITA (*209*)

VEGETARIAN VARIATIONS

Vegetables are so beautiful now, why serve anything else? Add some French bread and the first crop of peach jam, and this hot weather menu could be lunch or a light supper.

EGGPLANT SALAD (*153*)
SKILLET TOMATOES (*173*)
SUMMER MARINADE (*183*)
MUSHROOM SALAD (*152*)
CANTALOUPE IN BLUEBERRY HONEY (*197*)

LUNCH FOR A BUNCH

Take everything out of the icebox when the group assembles; this midsummer combination of chicken, tomatoes, and basil is a casual paper-plate lunch that the host will enjoy as much as the guests.

TOMATO SOUP WITH BASIL (*143*)
SAVORY CHICKEN SALAD (*164*)
PIÑA COLADA ICE CREAM (*214*)

BRUNCH

Sunday brunch can go on all day, if you ask us. Pick all the zinnias and stow them in a pottery jug, and serve this celebration of summer flavors—peaches, tomatoes, blueberries, and watermelon.

PEACH SOUP *(142)*

TOMATO BAKED EGGS *(155)*

CUCUMBERS IN YOGHURT *(147)*

BLUEBERRY MUFFINS *(216)*

WATERMELON SORBET *(214)*

Summer Recipes

CORN CHOWDER

Here's what you do with corn when you bought a dozen ears too many, or when you're looking for a new variation on an old theme. It is good cold, too, but in that case substitute heavy cream for the milk and, because cold tends to deaden flavors, increase the seasonings by about half, according to taste.

SERVES 4 TO 6

3 tablespoons butter
¼ cup onion, chopped
1½ cups well-seasoned chicken broth (see page 8)
½ cup dry white wine
2 large potatoes, washed and diced, but not peeled
Salt and freshly ground black pepper to taste
1 teaspoon fresh thyme
4 cups corn, freshly cut from the cob (about 12 ears)
3 cups milk

Melt butter in a heavy kettle. Add onion and cook until transparent but not brown. Add broth and wine. Add potatoes and simmer, uncovered, until they are fork tender, about 20 minutes. Season with salt and pepper to taste. Stir in thyme. Stir in corn and milk and heat about 5 minutes, or until very hot. Do not boil.

Serve at once.

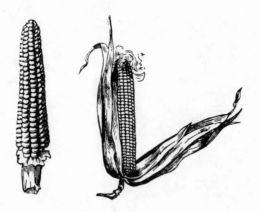

PESTO SOUP

With a little Italian magic, pesto sauce becomes Pesto Soup. It makes a good first course for a special dinner, but it's also great on its own for lunch with a fresh green salad on the side.

SERVES 6

1 cup fresh basil leaves
2 cloves minced garlic
1 tablespoon pine nuts
2 tablespoons grated Parmesan cheese
1 tablespoon grated Romano cheese
About ⅓ cup olive oil
6 cups chicken broth (see page 8)
4 ounces fresh egg noodles, cut into 1-inch pieces
1 very small zucchini, thinly sliced
1 very small summer squash, thinly sliced
Salt and freshly ground black pepper to taste
Parmesan cheese for garnish

Purée the basil, garlic, pine nuts, both cheeses, and 3 tablespoons of the oil in a food processor or blender. Add enough oil to make a smooth, thick paste. Set aside.

In a large kettle, bring the broth to a boil. Add the pasta, zucchini, and summer squash and cook about 3 minutes until the pasta is done and the vegetables are crisp and tender. Season with salt and pepper and whisk in the pesto paste.

Ladle into soup bowls and serve with extra Parmesan cheese.

GAZPACHO

Our version of the famous Spanish "salad in a bowl" is easy and very light. When you serve the soup, put bowls of croutons, finely chopped onions, diced green peppers, and finely chopped tomatoes on the table so guests can create their own combinations.

SERVES 4

1 clove garlic
¼ teaspoon salt
2 tablespoons olive oil
5 ripe tomatoes, peeled and sliced
1 onion, sliced
½ teaspoon salt
Freshly ground black pepper to taste
¼ teaspoon paprika
1½ tablespoons vinegar
1 cup cold water
1 cucumber, peeled, seeded, and chopped
4 slices firm white bread, torn into pieces

Chop the garlic very finely with a little salt. Stir in the oil to form a paste. Add the tomatoes, onion, salt, pepper, paprika, vinegar, and water. Let the mixture stand for ½ hour. Before serving, add the chopped cucumber, bread, and half a dozen ice cubes. Garnish with croutons or a sprig of watercress.

PEACH SOUP

Begin a summer dinner with this elegant cold soup, made with the first peaches of the season.

SERVES 6

4 cups peeled and pitted ripe peaches, diced
2 cups sweet white wine
2 cups water
⅓ cup sugar
1 cinnamon stick
2 tablespoons lemon juice
¼ teaspoon almond extract
Fresh mint leaves

Combine peaches, wine, water, sugar, and cinnamon stick in a large saucepan. Bring to a boil. Cover and reduce heat. Simmer for 30 minutes, stirring occasionally. Remove and discard the cinnamon stick. Stir in lemon juice and almond extract. Pour half the mixture into the container of an electric blender or food processor. Process until smooth. Pour into a serving bowl or individual compotes. Repeat with the remaining mixture. Cover bowls and chill for several hours. Stir well and garnish with fresh mint leaves.

TOMATO SOUP WITH BASIL

This soup blends two of summer's richest flavors—fresh basil and tomatoes.

SERVES 4 TO 6

1 medium onion, thinly sliced
1 carrot, finely chopped
2 tablespoons butter
2 cups beef stock
2 slices raw bacon, chopped
Salt and freshly ground black pepper to taste
1 pound fresh tomatoes, peeled, seeded, and coarsely chopped
Pinch of sugar
1 sprig thyme
3 tablespoons fresh basil, finely chopped
½ teaspoon paprika
4 tablespoons heavy cream
Fresh basil leaves for garnish

Sauté the onion and carrot in butter until limp, about 10 minutes. Add stock, bacon, salt and pepper to taste, tomatoes, sugar, herbs, and paprika. Cover and simmer for 30 minutes. Remove thyme. Place soup mixture in a blender or food processor and purée. Return to the saucepan.

Bring to a boil and add cream. Simmer for 5 minutes. Serve immediately, garnished with fresh basil leaves.

ZUCCHINI SOUP

This creamy midsummer soup should be in the repertoire of everyone who lives within range of a prolific garden. It freezes well, too, but in that case leave out the cream and add it later when the soup is reheated.

SERVES 4

2 tablespoons butter
1 tablespoon olive oil
1 medium onion, finely chopped
1 pound small zucchini, thinly sliced
1 quart well-seasoned chicken broth (see page 8)
¼ cup grated Parmesan cheese
3 tablespoons fresh oregano
2 tablespoons chopped parsley
¼ cup heavy cream

Melt butter and olive oil in a large kettle. Sauté the onion and zucchini in the hot oil for 5 to 6 minutes. Add chicken broth and simmer for 15 minutes. Pour the soup into the bowl of a food processor (it may take two batches) and process with Parmesan cheese, oregano, and parsley. Stir in the cream, heat thoroughly, and serve at once.

CHERRY SOUP

Made with firm, ripe (not soft) sweet cherries—Bing, if possible—this hot soup can be served either as an appetizer or a dessert. If it is to be served as a first course, add a tablespoon of sour cream to each bowl just before bringing to the table.

SERVES 6

4 cups red wine
1 pound sweet dark cherries, washed and pitted; reserve pits
3 tablespoons sugar
Zest of 1 lemon
1 stick cinnamon

In a small saucepan boil one cup of the wine and the cherry pits, uncovered, for 10 minutes, until reduced to about 3 tablespoons. Put cherries, sugar, lemon zest, remaining wine, and cinnamon in a heavy saucepan. Simmer for 10 minutes, then transfer to serving bowl. Discard cinnamon stick and strain reduced wine over cherry mixture.

Serve the soup hot in compote cups.

HERBED TOASTS

Serve these sandwiches with Tomato Baked Eggs (see page 155) for a good quick Saturday lunch. Start the eggs first, then 5 minutes before they're done, run the sandwiches under the broiler.

SERVES 4

8 slices bread, lightly toasted on both sides
4 tablespoons melted butter
8 slices cooked Virginia ham
1 cup grated Monterey Jack cheese
1 tablespoon fresh tarragon, chopped
2 tablespoons Homemade Mayonnaise (see page 18)

Brush each slice of bread with melted butter. Top with a slice of ham. Toss together cheese, tarragon, and mayonnaise. Spread bread with cheese mixture. Broil until cheese is golden and bubbly.

For a more pronounced tarragon taste, toss the ham, tarragon, and cheese together several hours before broiling. Refrigerate and then spread on ham-covered toast and broil. For quick hors d'oeuvres, increase the mayonnaise to ⅓ cup and spread mixture on toast rounds. Broil until puffy.

TOMATO GRANITA

Serve Tomato Granita as an unusual and delicate hot-weather appetizer or to clear palates between courses. Be sure the tomatoes have been peeled and seeded before stewing.

SERVES 8

2 cups water
⅓ cup white wine vinegar
1 tablespoon sugar
½ cup coriander leaves
1½ cups stewed fresh tomatoes, puréed (see page 172)
Fresh coriander for garnish

In a large nonaluminum saucepan, combine the water, vinegar, sugar, and coriander leaves. Bring to a boil and simmer until the liquid is reduced by half. Strain through cheesecloth or a fine sieve.

Stir in the puréed tomatoes and pour into a 9-inch-square freezer dish.

Freeze until nearly solid. Break into chunks and process briefly in a food processor until mixture is slushy. Refreeze.

To serve, scrape ice into balls and serve in individual serving dishes. Garnish with fresh coriander.

The granita can be frozen in an ice cream freezer until slushy. Spread slush in a 9-inch-square dish and place in freezer for 1 hour.

GREEN BEAN AND TOMATO SALAD

Farmers often wait to pick green beans till they're tough, heavy, and middle-aged, and young ones are rare in many markets. Use the smallest, crispest beans you can find.

SERVES 4

1 pound fresh whole green beans, the freshest and thinnest available
1 teaspoon salt
3 tablespoons tarragon or other herb vinegar
1 tablespoon hazelnut oil
½ cup fine olive oil
2 teaspoons grated onion
Pinch of salt
Freshly ground black pepper to taste
1 head leaf lettuce, washed, dried thoroughly, and torn into large pieces
2 large, ripe tomatoes, sliced
1 tablespoon finely chopped coriander

Steam beans over salted water for 8 to 10 minutes, or until still crisp but tender. Refresh in cold water. Beat vinegar, oils, onion, salt, and pepper until well mixed. Pour over the green beans and marinate for ½ hour.

To serve, line the serving platter with salad greens. Arrange tomato slices in an overlapping pattern around the edge of the platter. Fill center with green beans and sprinkle coriander over all.

POTATO AND GREEN BEAN SALAD

For a variation, try using small, unpeeled, red-skinned potatoes to add vitamins, minerals, and eye appeal.

SERVES 4

1 pound green beans, boiled until crisply tender and cut into 2-inch lengths
5 large potatoes, cooked, peeled, and cubed
1 bunch scallions, cut into thin slices
4 tablespoons wine vinegar
1 clove garlic
1 tablespoon fresh oregano, chopped
1 tablespoon fresh thyme
Salt and freshly ground black pepper to taste
½ cup olive oil
1 head leaf lettuce, washed and diced
Tomato wedges
1 small red onion, very thinly sliced
1 small green pepper, seeded and sliced into thin rings

Place beans, potatoes, and scallions in a bowl. Mix together vinegar, garlic, herbs, and salt and pepper. Beat in olive oil. Pour this vinaigrette over the warm vegetables. Toss gently and chill. Serve on a bed of lettuce garnished with tomato wedges, sliced red onion, and green pepper rings.

CUCUMBERS IN YOGHURT

Yoghurt, an excellent hot-weather food in itself, goes well with crisp, cool, sliced cucumbers. Serve with lamb curry or with cold poached salmon.

SERVES 6 TO 8

3 large cucumbers, peeled, halved, seeded, and thinly sliced
2 teaspoons salt

½ to ⅔ cup plain yoghurt
2 tablespoons Dijon-style mustard
1 tablespoon freshly chopped parsley
Tabasco to taste
Salt to taste

Sprinkle cucumber slices with salt. Let stand 1 hour. Rinse well, drain cucumber, and dry in a towel.

Beat together yoghurt, mustard, and parsley. Season to taste with Tabasco and salt. Toss with cucumber. Mix well and chill ½ hour. Serve in a glass dish.

HONEYDEW AND GREEN GRAPE SALAD

Classic summer fruits make a cooling combination.

SERVES 4

½ medium honeydew melon, seeded and peeled
1½ cups seedless green grapes, halved
2 tablespoons olive oil
1 tablespoon lime juice
Pinch of sugar
Pinch of salt
Freshly ground black pepper to taste

Cut the melon into thin slices. Divide slices between 4 serving plates. Sprinkle the grapes evenly over the melon.

Combine all remaining ingredients in a small jar. Shake well. Spoon 2 teaspoons of the dressing over each salad. Let stand at room temperature for 30 minutes before serving.

ZUCCHINI AND TOMATO SALAD

A superb variation for these standbys in the summer garden.

SERVES 6

3 tablespoons red wine vinegar
1 tablespoon minced shallots
1 teaspoon Dijon mustard
2 tablespoons minced fresh basil
Salt and freshly ground black pepper to taste
½ cup olive oil
4 large tomatoes, cut in wedges
4 small zucchini, washed, cut into julienne strips, steamed 3 minutes, and chilled
1 tablespoon freshly chopped parsley
1 bunch scallions, thinly sliced, including 1 inch of green
1 head leaf lettuce, washed and dried

Beat together vinegar, shallots, mustard, basil, salt and pepper. Beat in olive oil.

Toss tomatoes and zucchini together with dressing. Garnish with parsley and scallion slices and serve on a bed of lettuce.

MOZZARELLA AND TOMATO SALAD

This traditional salad is perhaps the ultimate summer first course in Italy, where it is known as Insalata Caprese. For a spicy variation, try using smoked mozzarella or alternating slices of fried peppers or prosciutto with the cheese and tomatoes.

SERVES 4

½ pound fresh buffalo milk mozzarella cheese, sliced thickly
2 very red ripe tomatoes, sliced
¼ cup fine-quality olive oil

¼ teaspoon balsamic vinegar
1 tablespoon chopped basil leaves
¼ cup fresh basil leaves
Freshly ground black pepper

Arrange cheese slices on a platter alternately with tomato slices. Beat olive oil, vinegar, and chopped basil leaves together until well mixed. Pour dressing over cheese and tomato slices. Arrange whole basil leaves over all and serve with freshly ground black pepper.

ANCHOVY-TOMATO SALAD

The salty anchovies are a rich contrast to the sweetness of ripe summer tomatoes.

SERVES 4 TO 6

4 large ripe tomatoes
6 anchovy fillets
⅓ cup fine olive oil
3 tablespoons wine vinegar
1 teaspoon fresh oregano, chopped
Freshly ground black pepper
Greek olives (optional)

Peel tomatoes and cut into thick slices. Arrange slices on a serving platter. Wash and drain anchovy fillets and mash them in a bowl. Beat in oil, vinegar, oregano, and pepper. Spoon over sliced tomatoes. Garnish with Greek olives, if desired.

OLD-FASHIONED TOMATO SALAD

A light dusting of sugar accentuates the sweetness of ripe tomatoes; we even put it in tomato sauce to bring out the flavor.

SERVES 4

3 large tomatoes, peeled and sliced
2 tablespoons sugar
Pinch of salt
3 tablespoons finely chopped coriander or 1 tablespoon chopped fresh thyme, or lemon thyme
Freshly ground black pepper

Slice tomatoes and arrange in a shallow dish. Sprinkle sugar and salt over the slices. Dust with freshly chopped herbs and ground pepper. Allow to stand at room temperature for at least 15 minutes.

CALIFORNIA TOMATO SALAD

This summer salad with a slight Mexican accent is excellent served with warm flour tortillas or pita bread.

SERVES 4

2 ripe avocados
Salt and freshly ground black pepper to taste
2 tablespoons lemon juice
2 tablespoons olive oil

1 teaspoon balsamic vinegar
2 slices cooked ham, chopped fine
Tabasco to taste
5 large lettuce leaves
4 medium-sized tomatoes, sliced

Halve the avocados and remove the flesh from the shell. Mash the flesh in a small bowl with salt, pepper, lemon juice, oil, and vinegar. Stir in ham. Season with Tabasco to taste.

Arrange lettuce on a serving plate and top with slices of tomato arranged in a circle. Fill the center with the avocado mixture.

MUSHROOM SALAD

Mushrooms are just as good in salads as they are in hot dishes; here a combination of herbs accentuates their delicate flavor.

SERVES 6

1 pound mushrooms, wiped, dried, and thinly sliced
3 tablespoons lemon juice
1 bunch scallions, thinly sliced
1 tablespoon fresh parsley, chopped
1 tablespoon fresh tarragon leaves, chopped
½ cup vinaigrette (see page 389)
⅓ cup sliced stuffed green olives
Salt and freshly ground black pepper to taste
1 tablespoon Dijon mustard
Leaf lettuce

Toss the sliced mushrooms in a large bowl with lemon juice, scallions, parsley, and tarragon. Refrigerate, covered, for 1 hour.

Combine vinaigrette, olive slices, salt, pepper, and mustard. Stir to mix well. Refrigerate.

Toss mushrooms with dressing. Arrange on a bed of leaf lettuce and serve.

SUMMER SQUASH SALAD

For a variation, add thinly sliced unpeeled cucumber to give this salad a very different character.

SERVES 6

4 small yellow squash, washed and sliced very thin, steamed 1 or 2 minutes
1 cup yoghurt
1 small onion, very thinly sliced
1 clove garlic, crushed
3 tablespoons finely chopped fresh mint
Salt and freshly ground black pepper to taste
Fresh mint leaves

Drain squash, dry, and chill. Blend yoghurt with onion, garlic, and mint. Add salt and pepper to taste. Chill.

Just before serving, combine squash and yoghurt mixture. Toss gently. Serve in a glass bowl with a sprinkling of chopped fresh mint and freshly ground black pepper.

EGGPLANT SALAD

This unusual eggplant salad can complement other main-dish salads and goes exceptionally well with grilled fish.

SERVES 4

2 large eggplant
2 large ripe tomatoes, seeded and cut in wedges
1 bunch scallions, the white part thinly sliced
¼ cup diced green pepper
½ cup cucumber, seeded and diced
¼ cup fresh parsley, chopped
2 tablespoons fresh coriander, chopped
1 clove garlic

3 tablespoons red wine vinegar
Salt and freshly ground black pepper to taste
Tabasco to taste
½ cup olive oil

Preheat the oven to 350°F.

Bake the eggplant whole at 350°F for 1 hour. Cool. Halve and seed. Cut the pulp into small chunks and press out as much moisture as possible. Turn into a salad bowl. Add tomato wedges, scallions, green pepper, cucumber, parsley, and coriander.

Make a vinaigrette by beating together the garlic, vinegar, and seasonings. Beat in olive oil. Pour over salad and toss. Chill 1 hour or longer. Taste and add more salt or pepper, if necessary.

TABOULEH

Refreshing Middle Eastern dishes are good in hot weather. Tabouleh variations come from all over the eastern Mediterranean. We like it for cookouts and family meals as well as company dinners.

SERVES 6

½ cup bulghur wheat
Cold water
3 tomatoes, peeled, seeded, and chopped
¾ cup freshly chopped parsley
2 bunches scallions, very finely sliced
Juice of 2 lemons
Salt to taste
⅓ cup fine-quality olive oil
3 tablespoons freshly chopped mint
1 head leaf lettuce, washed and dried

Place wheat in a bowl. Cover with cold water and let stand 10 to 15 minutes. Drain in a colander, pressing to remove all excess water. (The wheat can be wrapped in a towel and wrung out to remove water.)

Place the wheat in a clean bowl. Toss with tomatoes, parsley, and scallions. Beat together lemon juice, salt, and olive oil. Pour over wheat mixture and toss well. Refrigerate several hours. Before serving, bring the salad to room temperature and toss with freshly chopped mint. Serve on a bed of lettuce.

SUMMER LINGUINE

This recipe provides a quick way to serve pasta, the year-round favorite, with some of the abundance of the summer garden.

SERVES 6

3 tablespoons high-quality olive oil
1 large onion, thinly sliced
2 cloves garlic, minced
4 large, very ripe tomatoes, peeled, seeded, and coarsely chopped
3 tablespoons fresh basil, chopped
Salt and freshly ground black pepper to taste
6 small zucchini, cut into fine julienne
1 pound fresh linguine
Freshly grated Parmesan cheese

Heat olive oil in a medium skillet. Add onion and garlic. Simmer gently until transparent. Add tomatoes and basil. Simmer for 10 minutes. Add salt and pepper to taste.

Add zucchini to tomato mixture and simmer for 5 minutes. Cook pasta. Drain well and stir into the zucchini mixture.

Serve with freshly grated Parmesan cheese.

TOMATO BAKED EGGS

Many people find yellow tomatoes milder and easier to digest than red ones. We use them in this colorful dish, but ripe red tomatoes will do just as well.

SERVES 4

4 large, firm yellow tomatoes
Salt and freshly ground black pepper to taste
1 clove garlic, finely chopped
4 eggs
3 tablespoons tomato purée
3 tablespoons heavy cream
1 teaspoon dried thyme, or 1 tablespoon fresh thyme
2 tablespoons freshly grated Parmesan cheese
4 slices bread
Freshly chopped parsley for garnish

Wash the tomatoes. Slice off stem end and scoop out insides. Sprinkle shells with salt and pepper and turn them upside down to drain for 30 minutes.

Preheat the oven to 350°F.

When drained, dry shells inside and out. Sprinkle a little chopped garlic in each shell. Break one egg into each tomato. Beat together tomato purée, cream, and thyme. Spoon evenly over the eggs. Sprinkle with cheese and arrange the tomatoes in a buttered ovenproof dish. Bake at 350°F for 30 minutes, or longer, until eggs are set.

While eggs are cooking, cut bread into rounds. Toast and lightly butter each round. Once the eggs are set, arrange one tomato on each toast round. Sprinkle with chopped parsley and serve at once.

FILLETS OF SOLE WITH ZUCCHINI

Quick and easy, yet elegant enough for a party, this summer fish dish combines some of the zest of a ratatouille with the delicate flavor of fresh sole.

SERVES 4

¼ cup olive oil
1 small onion, sliced thin
4 small zucchini, sliced thin
½ pound fresh tomatoes, peeled, seeded, and chopped

2 tablespoons fresh basil, chopped, or 1 teaspoon dried basil
Salt and freshly ground black pepper to taste
Tabasco to taste
4 fillets of sole
2 tablespoons freshly grated Parmesan cheese
2 tablespoons butter

Heat oil in a skillet. Add onion and sauté until just transparent. Add zucchini and sauté 3 minutes. Add tomatoes and basil. Simmer 5 minutes. Season with salt, pepper, and Tabasco.

Dredge sole fillets in cheese. Knock off excess cheese. Brown in melted butter just until flaky—no more than 3 or 4 minutes—turning once.

Arrange zucchini mixture in the bottom of a serving platter. Top with fish. Serve very hot.

SALMON WITH MINT BUTTER SAUCE

Henri Charvet, well-known Parisian chef, gave us this terrific summer recipe. The sauce can also be flavored with parsley, dill, or basil, or with a little orange juice or raspberry vinegar. It goes well with any fish or shellfish.

SERVES 4

2 shallots, minced
¼ cup white wine
1 teaspoon vinegar
¼ pound (1 stick) butter, cut into pieces
Salt and freshly ground black pepper to taste
1 cup fresh mint leaves
1 tablespoon butter
4 slices fresh salmon, cut very thin
Whole mint leaves

Place shallots, white wine, and vinegar in a saucepan. Reduce over medium heat until only 1 or 2 tablespoons of liquid remain. Beat in the butter, a little at a time, with a whisk. The bottom of the saucepan should never become hot;

it should remain cool enough to touch with the hand. The butter must never melt but must emulsify into a frothy, pale yellow sauce. Whisk constantly until all the butter is incorporated. Season with salt and pepper. Set aside to keep warm *but not hot* in a warm water bath.

Chop the mint finely. Beat into the butter just before serving.

Sauté the salmon in 1 tablespoon butter just until cooked, only 1 or 2 minutes in all. Keep warm.

To serve, put a spoonful of the sauce on a serving plate and top with a slice of salmon. Garnish with a whole mint leaf. Serve any extra sauce in a separate bowl.

SCAMPI

This version of the Italian classic is for garlic lovers; don't use less than called for unless you cannot tolerate it at all, in which case increase the basil to 3 teaspoons and add a teaspoon of fresh thyme.

SERVES 6

1 pound fresh shrimp, peeled, deveined, tails left on
2 tablespoons fresh parsley, chopped
1 teaspoon fresh basil
2 teaspoons fresh thyme, chopped
2 cloves garlic, minced
¼ pound (1 stick) butter
⅓ cup olive oil
3 tablespoons lemon juice
Salt and freshly ground black pepper to taste

Preheat the oven to 475°F.

Arrange shrimp in a baking dish. Chop herbs and garlic together. Melt the butter and oil in a saucepan. Add herbs, garlic, and lemon juice and bring to a boil. Pour over shrimp. Season with salt and pepper.

Bake at 475°F for 3 to 5 minutes. Turn on broiler and broil for 2 to 3 minutes. Do not burn.

To grill the shrimp over charcoal, marinate them in the herb mixture for an hour and then thread them on skewers, leaving the shells on. Grill for 3 to 4 minutes on each side and serve them very hot, with rice.

HAY DAY'S SHRIMP AND PASTA SALAD WITH CHAMPAGNE VINAIGRETTE

One of our big summer sellers, this recipe evolved from Shrimp with Pesto one night when the pesto ran out. We like to cut the shrimp in half lengthwise to make it go further. Shelled shrimp dry out quickly, so cook your own, if possible—there is a big difference in flavor. The vinaigrette makes a good dip for shrimp if you add a few more green crushed peppercorns with a little of the brine; we like the flavor of champagne vinegar, but white wine vinegar can easily be substituted. Serve the salad at room temperature.

SERVES 6 TO 8

1 egg
2 tablespoons champagne vinegar
3 tablespoons green peppercorns in brine, drained and crushed
½ teaspoon salt
½ cup olive oil
½ cup safflower oil
1 pound cooked shrimp, peeled, deveined, and cut in half lengthwise (1½ pounds raw)
½ pint cherry tomatoes, cut in half
¼ pound thinly sliced mushrooms
1 medium-sized zucchini, cut in half lengthwise and sliced in ¼-inch half-moons
1 pound egg linguine, cooked
Fresh spinach greens, for serving
½ tablespoon drained green peppercorns for garnish

In a food processor, blend egg, vinegar, 2 teaspoons of the crushed peppercorns, and salt. Slowly add oils. Mix with remaining peppercorns and other salad ingredients, serve on a bed of spinach greens, and sprinkle with ½ tablespoon green peppercorns.

MESQUITE-BARBECUED BRISKET

This is a good party dish. If you have a covered grill and a slow fire you can skip the parboiling of the brisket. Just allow the coals to burn down to a dull gray before cooking, cover, and grill for 1 hour on a side, adding more charcoal as necessary.

SERVES 12

1 twelve-ounce can of beer
1½ quarts of water, or enough to cover the meat entirely
1 onion, sliced
2 cloves garlic, crushed
1 six-pound piece of beef brisket
2½ cups Barbecue Sauce (see below)

Combine all the ingredients except barbecue sauce in a kettle or Dutch oven just large enough to hold the meat. Cover and simmer gently about 3 to 4 hours until the meat is just fork tender. Let cool to lukewarm in the cooking liquid. Drain and dry the meat. Place meat in a bowl and cover with 1 cup of the barbecue sauce. Turn to coat the meat with the sauce. Cover and refrigerate overnight. Bring to room temperature before grilling.

Grill meat over a mesquite charcoal fire about 15 minutes on each side, basting frequently with the remaining barbecue sauce. Slice across the grain to serve. Pass remaining sauce in a separate dish.

BARBECUE SAUCE

This is so thick it is almost a condiment; to use it as a basting sauce, dilute it with one part olive oil to two parts sauce. Fabulous with chicken or any grilled meats, it will be a mainstay for cookouts all summer.

MAKES ABOUT 5 CUPS

4 cloves garlic
1 tablespoon salt
½ cup malt vinegar
1 cup olive oil
3 small onions, chopped
1 green pepper, chopped
2 tablespoons chili peppers, chopped
10 large tomatoes, peeled, seeded, and chopped
1 teaspoon oregano (dried), or 1 tablespoon fresh oregano
½ cup tomato purée
2 tablespoons dry mustard
1 teaspoon dried coriander, or 1 tablespoon fresh coriander

Chop the garlic with the salt. Heat the vinegar and oil in a heavy saucepan. Add the garlic, onions, pepper, chili peppers, and chopped tomatoes. Add the oregano and tomato purée. Stir well. Stir in the mustard and coriander. Simmer everything until thick, about 2 hours. Cool.

MESQUITE-BARBECUED RIBS

One of the secrets of tender home-grilled ribs is parboiling them ahead of time, which can be done in the morning or even the night before. The longer the ribs remain in the barbecue sauce, the more flavor they will take on. If there is no mesquite available, any hardwood charcoal is fine.

SERVES 4 TO 6

5 to 6 pounds pork spareribs
Water to cover
Salt
1½ or 2 cups Barbecue Sauce (see above)

Place ribs in a large kettle or Dutch oven and cover with salted water. Bring to a boil. Cover and reduce heat. Simmer about 25 minutes. Remove from liquid and place in a large shallow dish. Coat both sides with about two-thirds of the barbecue sauce. Cover and chill 12 hours or overnight.

Remove ribs from the sauce. Place over a mesquite charcoal fire and baste with the barbecue sauce from the marinating pan. Cook 15 minutes on each side, basting frequently with more sauce. Serve any remaining sauce in a separate dish.

CHARCOAL BAKED CORNISH HEN

Baking over charcoal keeps meats moist and tender; it is easy as long as the coals are not too hot. Use heavyweight aluminum foil to retain all the good juices.

SERVES 4

2 Cornish game hens, halved
2 large leeks, the white part cut into 2-inch julienne strips
1 clove garlic, chopped (optional)
Olive oil
4 sprigs fresh rosemary
Salt and freshly ground black pepper to taste

Arrange each Cornish hen half on a large square of heavy duty aluminum foil. Top with one-quarter of the leek strips and a little chopped garlic, if desired. Brush with olive oil. Add a sprig of rosemary to each package. Salt and pepper to taste. Make each foil square into a neat package and arrange them on a grill. Turn packages every 10 minutes for approximately 40 minutes.

GRILLED CORN

Corn cooked on a grill can be dry and leathery, but not in this version. If the ears are soaked in generous amounts of water, they will literally steam inside their husks.

SERVES 4

6 to 8 ears fresh corn

To grill, pull down the husks (do not tear off) and remove the silk. Replace the husk. Soak corn, in the husk, in cold water for ½ hour. Arrange ears on the grill. Turn often for approximately 20 minutes. Pull off husk and serve very hot with melted butter.

LIME-GRILLED CORNISH GAME HEN

Summer grills are obviously excellent for more than just steaks and hamburgers. This is a tart and delicious version of an old favorite.

SERVES 4

⅓ cup mustard, English, Dijon, or Chinese if a hot flavor is desired
1 large shallot, minced
¼ cup fresh lime juice
2 teaspoons honey
Freshly ground black pepper to taste
4 tablespoons olive oil (or 4 tablespoons butter, melted)
2 Cornish game hens, halved

Beat together all the ingredients but the game hens. Marinate the game hen halves in the sauce for at least 1 hour. Grill hens over open charcoal for 30 minutes, turning once and basting often with the marinade.

These hens can be broiled 5 minutes on each side and then baked at 450°F for 30 minutes, basting often.

HERB-ROASTED CHICKEN

This variation on a Middle Eastern favorite is a godsend when guests are expected for dinner and time is short.

SERVES 6

⅔ cup olive oil
⅓ cup lime juice
1 teaspoon salt
Freshly ground black pepper to taste
1 five- to seven-pound roasting chicken
1 large bunch each rosemary and thyme
⅓ cup dry white wine

Preheat the oven to 425°F.

Combine olive oil, lime juice, salt, and pepper. Brush sauce over chicken. Tie the herbs on the breast of the chicken with string. Roast in a hot (425°F) oven or in a closed covered grill with dripping pan for 1 hour and 45 minutes, or until the chicken is done. Baste every 20 minutes with the oil and lime juice mixture.

Remove herbs and allow chicken to rest for several minutes before carving.

Drain most of the pan juices. Place the roasting pan on a low flame. Deglaze the pan with the white wine, stirring to scrape up all the browned bits in the bottom of the pan. Pour in any remaining oil and lime juice mixture. Bring to a boil. Serve in a separate bowl.

SAVORY CHICKEN SALAD

Make this salad in the morning, with tabouleh and cucumbers marinated in yoghurt, and have a cool summer dinner all ready in the icebox—just add good hot bread and something cold for dessert.

SERVES 6

1 whole frying chicken, simmered in well-seasoned chicken broth (see page 8) until tender and cooled in the broth
½ cup sour cream
1 large onion, peeled and sliced very thinly
¾ cup fresh Homemade Mayonnaise (see page 18)
2 tablespoons Dijon mustard
Salt and freshly ground black pepper to taste
6 tablespoons fresh basil, chopped
1 large avocado, peeled and cut into chunks
Fresh tomatoes and whole basil leaves for garnish

Remove the chicken from the broth. Skin. Tear, do not cut, the meat into small pieces. Mix sour cream, onion, mayonnaise, mustard, salt, and pepper with the basil until well combined. Pour over chicken and toss gently just until coated with sauce. Gently stir in avocado. Allow to rest in the icebox about 2 hours or longer. Garnish with fresh tomatoes and whole basil leaves.

HAY DAY'S SPICY CHICKEN SALAD

The combination of sesame oil and tahini paste gives this summer pasta salad an Oriental flavor. Tahini, a nut butter made from sesame seeds, is used in many Middle Eastern and South American recipes and sold in health food stores and Oriental markets; many people use it like peanut butter. Stir it before using to be sure the oils are well mixed. Tamari is a thicker Japanese version of soy sauce with a more intense flavor and a higher concentration of sodium and other minerals. Tamari and hot oil also are readily available in Oriental markets.

We blanch the snow peas so they are no longer raw but keep their brilliant color; if the spaghettini is fresh, it will cook in boiling water in about a minute. Don't add butter to the sesame seeds; they are oily enough to be tossed in a frying pan by themselves or baked in a 350°F oven until they are golden brown.

SERVES 6

¼ *teaspoon minced garlic*
3 *tablespoons tahini paste*
3 *tablespoons sesame oil*
4 *tablespoons soy sauce*
1 *tablespoon red wine vinegar*
1 *tablespoon tamari*
1 *tablespoon hot oil*
¾ *cup safflower oil*
2 *whole cooked boneless and skinless chicken breasts, cut in strips*
1 *pound spaghettini, cooked*
⅓ *cup toasted sesame seeds*
¼ *pound snow peas, trimmed and blanched*
Fresh Romaine lettuce, washed and dried
2 *tablespoons toasted sesame seeds (for garnish)*

Whisk garlic, tahini, sesame oil, soy sauce, vinegar, tamari, and hot oil together. Slowly blend in the safflower oil.

Mix with salad ingredients. Serve on a bed of Romaine lettuce. Sprinkle with toasted sesame seeds for garnish.

HAY DAY'S CHICKEN CHÈVRE

Helen Brody evolved this recipe as a cold entrée for summer dinner parties that would be more glamorous than salads but just as pretty. It can be served warm, too, but should be heated very gently so the cheese won't burst out. It has been through a number of evolutions at Hay Day, and you will invent your own variations. Forget the sauce, for example, and have a great chicken dish for a picnic, or try fresh basil instead of the rosemary and thyme, or use any creamy goat cheese, if you can't get Boucheron (you can use Feta, too, if it is mixed with enough cream cheese not to be crumbly). We served it as an appetizer at the "Great Chefs" benefit in Greenwich by rolling the filling in a pounded chicken breast that was then sliced crosswise and served in the sauce.

Sun-dried tomatoes are produced in this country and are no longer exclusively imported and expensive, but they still have to be bought at specialty food shops.

SERVES 4 TO 6

4 boneless, skinless chicken breasts, halved and trimmed
3 ounces cream cheese, softened
3 ounces Boucheron Chèvre cheese, softened
2 tablespoons fresh parsley, chopped
1 teaspoon fresh thyme, chopped
½ teaspoon fresh rosemary, chopped
2 eggs, lightly beaten
1 cup flour
¾ cup safflower oil
2 tablespoons butter
½ cup chopped shallots
1 cup dry white wine
2 cups chicken broth (see page 8)
4 sun-dried tomatoes, halved

With a thin boning knife, cut a pocket lengthwise in each half breast without cutting through to the surface. Make the filling by beating together the cream cheese, Boucheron, parsley, thyme, and rosemary. Put the mixture in a pastry bag. Pipe approximately 1 tablespoon of the filling into each half breast, making sure it fills the entire cavity. Close the cavity so the filling is totally enclosed and refrigerate the breasts for 40 minutes.

Preheat oven to 350°F.

Dip breasts in egg, then coat lightly with flour. Sauté breasts in oil and butter until lightly golden. Save drippings in pan. Transfer breasts to a shallow baking pan and bake for 15 minutes.

Pour off the drippings in the pan except for ½ cup. Sauté shallots in this residue for 5 minutes. Deglaze with wine. Reduce by half, add broth, and reduce by half again. Serve the chicken breasts on a platter with one sun-dried tomato half on each and pour sauce around the breasts. Cool to room temperature, or serve warm.

HAY DAY'S CURRIED PEACH AND SMOKED TURKEY SALAD

This popular summer salad is easy and quick to make. Peel the peaches or nectarines by dipping them in simmering water for 15 to

30 seconds (the time will vary depending on how ripe they are), and the skins will slip off with just a little help from a knife.

SERVES 4 TO 6

2 tablespoons sugar
½ teaspoon salt
1 teaspoon medium curry powder
2 tablespoons white wine vinegar
1 teaspoon lemon juice
½ cup sour cream
3 cups smoked turkey or chicken, skin and fat removed, cut in 1-inch cubes
3 medium-sized peaches or nectarines, peeled and thickly sliced
1½ cups red grapes or sweet cherries, cut in half and seeded
1½ cups thinly sliced celery
1 tablespoon scallion tops cut in thin rings
½ cup unsalted peanuts

Whisk sugar, salt, curry powder, white wine vinegar, and lemon juice into the sour cream. Fold into salad ingredients.

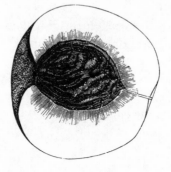

HAY DAY PASTIES

Served for a picnic, or lunch at the office, or tailgating, these are one of the best things we make; we could sell hundreds if we had time to make them. The idea comes from Cornwall, in England, where lunch for a tin miner was a small envelope of pastry filled with various meats, designed to be carried in the pocket. The saying is, "only a true Cornish woman can make a proper pasty" (rhymes with nasty), but ours come close.

SERVES 6

2½ cups grated Gruyère cheese
¾ cup coarsely chopped ham
¾ cup coarsely chopped cooked broccoli
¾ cup sliced sautéed mushrooms
¾ cup cooked spinach
2½ tablespoons herbes de Provence
3 nine-inch pastry tops
1 egg beaten with 1 teaspoon water for glaze

Preheat oven to 400°F.

Mix together the cheese, ham, broccoli, mushrooms, spinach, and herbs. Cut each pie top in half. Put ¾ cup of filling on one end of each half of the pastry. Brush edges with egg glaze. Fold pasty in half to make a quarter moon shape. Press edges together to seal. Prick with a fork and brush pasties with egg glaze. Bake on a cookie sheet in a 400°F oven for 20 to 30 minutes.

TOMATO-ONION-CHEESE BAKE

This classic American summer casserole is substantial and can be made head of time. Serve it with bread and salad, and it becomes lunch. A good aged cheddar is great with summer tomatoes.

SERVES 4 TO 6

3 cups thinly sliced onion
1 cup fresh bread crumbs
1 teaspoon salt
Freshly ground black pepper

4 large ripe tomatoes (try yellow ones if they are in the market), peeled and
  sliced
3 tablespoons freshly chopped chives
1½ cups (more or less) grated sharp cheddar cheese
Salt and freshly ground black pepper to taste
3 tablespoons butter, melted

Preheat the oven to 375°F.

Lightly butter a 2-quart casserole. Blanch sliced onion in boiling water to cover for 5 minutes. Drain. Stir together bread crumbs, salt, and pepper.

Layer half the tomatoes in the buttered casserole, top with half the cooked onions, half the bread crumbs, half the chives, and half the cheese. Season with salt and pepper. Repeat the layers, ending with the rest of the cheese. Drizzle with the butter. Bake, uncovered, in a 375°F oven about 45 minutes until cheese is golden brown and bubbling.

CREAMED TOMATOES

Excellent with grilled fish, this dish can even be served over toast with a tossed green salad for a light summer lunch.

SERVES 4

3 tablespoons butter
4 large ripe tomatoes, peeled, seeded, and cut in wedges
3 tablespoons dry white wine
⅓ cup crème fraîche (see page 12) or very heavy cream
2 tablespoons freshly chopped basil, or 1 tablespoon fresh thyme
Salt to taste
Freshly ground black pepper to taste
Whole basil leaves for garnish

Melt the butter in a skillet. Add tomatoes. Sauté 1 or 2 minutes, stirring gently. Add wine, crème fraîche, and basil and simmer for 2 minutes.

Remove tomatoes and keep warm. Reduce cream mixture until only about ½ cup remains. Strain and pour over drained tomatoes. Season with salt and pepper and garnish with whole basil leaves.

GRATIN OF SLICED TOMATOES

Another make-ahead, to be baked at the last minute for company appetizers. It's also a good beginning for a classic charcoal steak dinner.

SERVES 4

4 large, firm tomatoes, peeled and thickly sliced
4 teaspoons white wine
3 tablespoons fresh basil, chopped
Salt and freshly ground black pepper to taste
¼ cup heavy cream
⅔ cup grated cheddar cheese
1 tablespoon fresh parsley, chopped

Preheat the oven to 350°F.

Arrange one whole sliced tomato in each of four gratin or shirred egg dishes. Sprinkle a teaspoon of wine over each dish. Top with basil and season with salt and pepper. Bake at 350°F for 10 minutes. Remove from the oven and pour a tablespoon or two of cream over each dish. Spread cheese over tomatoes. Raise temperature to 400°F and bake for 10 minutes, or until cheese is melted and bubbly. Garnish with chopped parsley. Serve with bread for dipping in juices.

STEWED TOMATOES WITH CHEESE DUMPLINGS

Floods of tomatoes in August and September challenge everyone's ingenuity. This recipe is a natural served with grilled meat or cold meat salads; if you have an enameled casserole it can finish cooking on the charcoal grill. Start the tomatoes on top of the stove in the kitchen, then add the dumplings and move it outdoors.

SERVES 6

3 tablespoons butter
½ small red or green pepper, chopped
1 small onion, chopped
1 clove garlic, minced (or more, to taste)
2 tablespoons flour
3 pounds tomatoes, peeled, seeded, chopped, and sautéed in 2 tablespoons olive
    oil until soft, about 10 minutes
Pinch of sugar
Salt and freshly ground black pepper to taste

Melt the butter in a large heat-proof, covered casserole and sauté the pepper, onion, and garlic until tender. Blend in the flour and stir until smooth. Add the sautéed tomatoes, sugar, salt, and pepper. Bring to a boil and simmer 5 minutes.

DUMPLINGS
1 cup flour
2 teaspoons baking powder
Pinch of salt
2 tablespoons cold butter
½ cup grated cheddar cheese
2 tablespoons chopped parsley
½ cup milk

Preheat the oven to 375°F.
Stir flour, baking powder, and salt together. Cut in butter until the mixture resembles coarse meal. Stir in cheese and parsley. Add milk and stir just until the mixture is moistened. Drop by spoonfuls onto the hot tomato mixture. Cover tightly and cook for 20 minutes in a 375°F oven. Serve immediately.

BASIL MARINATED TOMATOES

This dish is fragrant, summery, and excellent with cold roast chicken, cold roast beef, or cold poached fish—a classic for picnics or outdoor dinners.

SERVES 4 TO 6

4 large tomatoes, peeled and thickly sliced
⅓ cup extra-virgin olive oil
1 tablespoon lemon or lime juice, or 1 tablespoon flavored vinegar
1 clove garlic, finely minced (optional)
Salt to taste
3 tablespoons chopped fresh basil
Chopped parsley
Freshly ground black pepper

Arrange the sliced tomatoes in a serving dish. Combine the oil, lemon juice, garlic, salt, and basil. Pour over tomatoes. Chill, covered, for about 2 hours. Garnish with chopped parsley and freshly ground black pepper.

SKILLET TOMATOES

Nobody wants to be stuck in the kitchen, especially on warm summer evenings; here's another side dish that can be finished outdoors on the grill. Assemble it ahead of time and start cooking it over the charcoal about 25 minutes before the meat is finished.

SERVES 4

4 large, ripe tomatoes, halved
Salt and freshly ground black pepper to taste
4 tablespoons olive oil
2 tablespoons freshly chopped basil
2 tablespoons freshly chopped parsley
¼ cup dry white wine

Arrange tomato halves, cut side up, in a single layer in a skillet. Sprinkle with salt, pepper, olive oil, and herbs. Pour in wine.

Cook over low heat for about 5 minutes. Cover and cook until tender. For garlic lovers, sprinkle one or two cloves of finely minced garlic over the tomatoes before cooking.

CURRIED TOMATOES

This dish may be served hot or at room temperature.

SERVES 6

3 tablespoons extra-virgin olive oil
2 large yellow onions, thinly sliced
1 clove garlic, minced (optional)
1 teaspoon salt
2 teaspoons medium curry powder
4 large, ripe tomatoes, cored, seeded, and quartered
¼ cup dry white wine

Heat oil in a skillet, add onions, and sauté until just transparent and tender. Mix in garlic, salt, and curry powder. Add tomatoes and wine. Simmer gently for 10 minutes.

WESTERN MARINATED TOMATOES

Herbs grown in very hot climates are much stronger and more aromatic than ours; try to find Mexican oregano, which will give a much more intense flavor.

SERVES 6

¾ cup olive oil
¾ cup salad oil
1 cup red wine vinegar
¼ cup sugar

1 tablespoon hot mustard
2 tablespoons fresh oregano, chopped
Pinch of salt
Freshly ground black pepper to taste
4 tomatoes, seeded and finely chopped
1 bunch scallions, finely sliced
1 six-ounce jar green chile salsa
1 or more cloves garlic, minced (to taste)
6 large tomatoes, quartered
1 head leaf lettuce, washed and dried
1 tablespoon fresh coriander leaves

Combine oils, vinegar, sugar, mustard, oregano, and salt and pepper. Whisk until thoroughly mixed. Stir in chopped tomatoes and scallions. Stir in salsa and garlic. Pour over quartered tomatoes and toss gently. Cover and marinate at least 2 hours.

Remove tomatoes from the marinade and arrange on a lettuce-lined platter. Sprinkle with fresh coriander.

The same marinade can be used for lightly steamed green beans, broccoli fleurettes, zucchini strips, or any other summer vegetable. Pour marinade over warm vegetables and then cover and refrigerate at least 2 hours.

SOUTH OF THE BORDER ZUCCHINI

This recipe is probably derived from an Oriental dish, but we like its Mexican accent.

SERVES 4

3 tablespoons olive oil
1 pound very small zucchini, thinly sliced
1 onion, thinly sliced
3 cloves garlic, very finely minced
3 mild green chilies, roasted, peeled, seeded, and cut into thin strips (or 1 can whole green chilies, drained and cut into thin strips)
Salt to taste
Fresh coriander leaves

Heat oil in a heavy skillet or wok until hot. Add all the other ingredients, except coriander, and sauté, stirring, until just tender. Do not overcook—about 10 minutes is sufficient. Serve at once, garnished with fresh coriander leaves.

ZUCCHINI WITH DILL

Here's a way of dealing with the last of the zucchini. If it is still coming in small and tender, cut it in quarter-inch slices; if it is a little more *fin de saison*, seed it and cut into thin julienne. It is a natural accompaniment for roast lamb.

SERVES 4

4 very small, or 2 medium, zucchini, cleaned, but not peeled
⅓ cup sour cream
1 teaspoon chopped fresh dill
Salt and freshly ground black pepper to taste

Cut zucchini into slices or julienne. Steam over boiling water until just tender, 3 to 4 minutes. Drain well and turn into a skillet. Add sour cream and heat through, but *do not boil*. Remove from the heat and season with dill and salt and pepper to taste. Serve at once.

GREEN TINT PERSILLADE

Pattypan, including the new yellow variety, are largely unsung members of the squash family—the tiny, sweet Green Tint variety is perfect for this recipe. Don't try it if you're not a garlic fancier, though; the garlic is essential.

SERVES 4 TO 6

1 pound tiny pattypan squash, washed and thinly sliced
4 tablespoons butter or fine-quality olive oil
4 cloves garlic, chopped with ½ cup cleaned parsley leaves

Blanch pattypan slices in boiling water for 1 minute. Drain. Heat the butter or oil in a heavy sauté pan with sloping sides. Sauté the squash briefly, until just tender. Add the parsley and garlic mixture and toss several times. Sauté 2 to 3 minutes longer, tossing occasionally. Serve very hot.

SESAME VEGETABLES

This recipe makes a nice combination of crunchy vegetables and velvety sauce. The vegetables can be steamed early in the day and refrigerated, then brought to room temperature and reheated in the sauce for 5 minutes at 400°F, then sprinkled with cheese and broiled.

SERVES 6 TO 8

1 cup mushrooms, sliced
1 cup zucchini, thinly sliced
1 cup cauliflower, cut into fleurettes
1 cup fresh green beans, sliced
1 tablespoon green chilies, minced
1 tablespoon butter
2 tablespoons flour
½ cup chicken broth (see page 8)
½ cup dry white wine
2 tablespoons Dijon mustard
Salt to taste
2 tablespoons toasted sesame seeds
Freshly grated Parmesan cheese

Steam each vegetable separately until just crisply tender. Set aside and keep warm.

Melt the butter, add the flour, and stir until smooth. Add the broth and wine and stir over medium heat until thick. Cook over low heat for 5 minutes. Stir in mustard, salt to taste, and sesame seeds.

Preheat the broiler.

Arrange the hot, well-drained vegetables in an ovenproof serving dish. Spoon some of the sauce over them and sprinkle generously with Parmesan cheese. Broil 1 minute until golden brown. Serve at once with the remaining sauce in a separate dish.

GARDEN EGGPLANT

A summer standby, Garden Eggplant is almost effortless. It can be baked ahead and served at room temperature, or assembled in the morning and baked at suppertime. It goes well with grilled meats, poultry, or fish.

SERVES 4

2 medium eggplant, unpeeled, washed, trimmed, and cut into ½-inch slices
  lengthwise
1 tablespoon salt
3 tablespoons olive oil
2 tablespoons fresh thyme
2 tablespoons fresh rosemary
1 clove garlic, finely minced (optional)
Salt and freshly ground black pepper to taste
¼ cup freshly grated Parmesan cheese

Preheat the oven to 400°F.

Sprinkle the eggplant with salt and arrange in a glass dish. Drain after 30 minutes and dry on absorbent paper. Lightly butter a flat baking dish. Arrange the eggplant slices in the dish and brush well with olive oil. Sprinkle with herbs, garlic, if desired, salt, and pepper.

Bake at 400°F for about 20 minutes. Sprinkle with cheese and bake 5 minutes longer.

CAPONATA

Italian menus invariably include caponata on any cold antipasto platter. Making it with young, fresh vegetables is one of the great pleasures of summer cooking. Plan ahead; it should be made the day before serving.

SERVES 8

4 very small eggplant, cubed, with the skin on
1 tablespoon salt
⅓ cup olive oil
1 cup celery, chopped, leaves and all
1 small onion, sliced very thin
3 large tomatoes, peeled, seeded, and chopped
2 tablespoons tomato paste
½ cup red wine vinegar
2 tablespoons sugar
1 tablespoon capers
½ cup broken black olives, drained
Freshly ground black pepper, or Tabasco sauce to taste
Salt to taste

Sprinkle the eggplant cubes with salt. Drain after 1 hour. Dry well on absorbent paper.

Heat the oil in a heavy skillet. Sauté the eggplant, celery, and onion until the onion and celery are transparent and tender. Stir in tomatoes and tomato paste. Simmer for 5 minutes.

Remove pan from the heat. Stir in the vinegar, sugar, capers, olives, and seasonings. Cool to room temperature and then refrigerate at least overnight. Serve at room temperature.

GRILLED EGGPLANT

While the coals are still hot after barbecuing meat, fish, or oysters, the time is right for grilling fresh eggplant.

SERVES 4

1 whole unpeeled eggplant, washed, stemmed, and cut into ¼-inch slices
½ cup Barbecue Sauce (see page 160)
2 large ripe tomatoes, cored, cut into thick slices, and warmed to room
    temperature
3 to 4 tablespoons freshly chopped oregano
Salt and freshly ground black pepper to taste

Oil the grill thoroughly. Lay out the eggplant slices and brush liberally with barbecue sauce. Grill 10 minutes on one side, turn, and grill 10 minutes on the other side. Brush often with sauce.

To serve, arrange eggplant on a serving platter, top with tomato slices, and garnish with chopped oregano. Season to taste with salt and pepper. Serve hot.

CORN ON THE COB WITH HERBS

Freshness does make a difference; the sugars in sweet corn turn to starch very quickly. If you're a vegetable gardener, you can pick corn minutes before cooking it. Otherwise, buy it from a reputable supplier, as close to home as possible. Here is a nice midsummer variation.

SERVES 4

8 ears fresh sweet corn, shucked
3 tablespoons butter
1 tablespoon lemon juice
2 tablespoons dry white wine
1 tablespoon each fresh thyme and rosemary
Salt and freshly ground black pepper to taste

Plunge corn into boiling water and cook for 3 minutes after water returns to the boil. Drain well. Arrange ears in a shallow dish. Melt the butter in a saucepan. Whisk in lemon juice, wine, herbs, and seasonings. Whisk until light and creamy. Pour over hot corn, turning ears to coat thoroughly. Serve very hot.

CORN SOUFFLÉ EN TOMATE

Excellent on its own, this soufflé is especially pretty baked in hollow tomato shells.

SERVES 6

6 large, firm, ripe tomatoes, hollowed out, pulp saved for another dish
Salt and freshly ground black pepper
2 tablespoons butter
3 tablespoons flour
1 cup milk
1 teaspoon Dijon mustard
Salt and freshly ground black pepper to taste
½ cup Monterey Jack cheese, grated
4 egg yolks
2 tablespoons chopped chives
1 cup cooked corn, cut from the cob
3 slices bacon, cooked crisp and crumbled
5 egg whites, beaten until stiff peaks form
Chopped parsley

Preheat the oven to 375°F.

Drain the tomato shells and sprinkle the insides with salt and pepper. Set aside, upside down, to drain.

In a medium saucepan, melt the butter and stir in the flour. Cook, stirring, over medium heat for several minutes. Do not brown. Add the milk all at once, whisking constantly. Stir in the mustard, salt, and pepper. Cook over medium heat until the mixture is thick. Stir in the cheese. Stir until melted. Remove from the heat. Beat in the egg yolks, one at a time. Let cool several minutes and stir in the chives, corn, and bacon.

Gently fold in beaten egg whites and spoon soufflé mixture into tomato shells. (Spoon any remaining soufflé mixture into a small soufflé dish that has been buttered and dusted with freshly grated Parmesan cheese.) Arrange the filled tomatoes in a buttered baking dish and bake at 375°F until puffed and golden, about 15 to 20 minutes. Serve garnished with chopped parsley. (Bake the rest of the soufflé 20 to 25 minutes.)

CORN PUDDING

This southern specialty is generally made with leftover cooked sweet corn.

SERVES 4

2 cups corn kernels cut from the cob (6 to 7 ears)
¼ cup flour
2 tablespoons sugar
1 teaspoon salt
2 cups milk
2 eggs, beaten
2 tablespoons melted butter

Preheat the oven to 350°F.

Combine the corn, flour, sugar, and salt. Mix well. Beat together milk, eggs, and melted butter. Stir into the corn mixture. Butter a 1½-quart casserole or glass soufflé dish. Pour in the corn mixture. Bake for 20 minutes, stir to bring the corn kernels up from the bottom of the dish, and continue to bake for 40 minutes longer.

Serve very hot.

MIXED SUMMER VEGETABLES

Be vigilant when you cook tiny vegetables—they must be just tender but still crisp. If you take them out just before you think they're cooked, they're probably about right. The steam-and-reheat method is great for summer cooking because all the vegetables can be steamed separately and refrigerated, then tossed in hot oil or butter just to heat through at serving time. Be sure to let vegetables warm to room temperature before heating.

SERVES 6

1 cup cherry tomatoes, washed
3 very small yellow squash, thickly sliced
1 bunch scallions, cut into ½-inch lengths
3 tablespoons butter
3 tablespoons fresh oregano, chopped
Salt and freshly ground black pepper to taste

Steam each vegetable separately until it is crisply tender. (If reheating later, arrange on a cookie sheet, cover, and refrigerate until 30 minutes before reheating. Be sure vegetables are at room temperature before reheating, or they will overcook before they get completely heated.)

Melt butter in a skillet. Toss vegetables in the skillet with oregano until they are very hot. Season to taste and serve at once.

SUMMER MARINADE

Great for entertaining because it is prepared well ahead of time, this melange of summer vegetables can be made with any combination, but try to keep the colors as brilliant as they are here.

SERVES 6

1 red pepper, seeded and cut into strips
1 yellow pepper, seeded and cut into strips
1 cup each, broccoli and cauliflower fleurettes
½ pound fresh green beans
½ pound whole baby carrots
½ pint cherry tomatoes
1 tablespoon tarragon mustard
1 tablespoon lime juice
1 tablespoon fresh basil, finely chopped
1 egg yolk
¼ cup white wine
Salt and freshly ground black pepper to taste
1 cup fine-quality salad oil, or ½ cup extra-fine olive oil and ½ cup safflower oil

Steam each vegetable separately just until each is tender but crisp. Cool to room temperature.

Beat together mustard, lime juice, basil, egg yolk, and white wine. Season with salt and pepper. Beat in oil a little at a time until thick.

Marinate all the vegetables in the sauce (separately, if desired) and refrigerate several hours or overnight. Drain the vegetables, reserving liquid. Arrange the vegetables on a serving plate and drizzle a little of the marinade over them. Pass the remaining marinade in a separate sauce boat.

SAVORY BRAISED LETTUCE

Most people are so used to thinking of lettuce in salads that they can't imagine it cooked, but like endive, it is excellent. Try to choose heads of uniform size so they will cook evenly.

SERVES 6

6 small heads Bibb or Boston lettuce, blanched for 1 minute in boiling water
3 tablespoons butter
1 small carrot, sliced
1 leek, thinly sliced
Fresh thyme
½ cup well-seasoned chicken broth (see page 8)
½ cup dry white wine
Salt and freshly ground black pepper to taste

Cut blanched heads of lettuce in half lengthwise. Squeeze out all the liquid. Melt butter in a skillet and sauté carrot, leek, and thyme until just tender. Arrange lettuce, cut side down, on top of vegetables. Pour in broth and wine. Cover and braise for 20 minutes. Remove lettuce to a hot serving platter. Reduce liquid until very thick. Taste for seasonings. Strain the sauce over the lettuce and serve very hot.

HERBED MAYONNAISE

Serve this mayonnaise with cold poached fish, cold roast chicken, or any cold salad.

MAKES ABOUT 1 CUP

½ cup oil
1 cup Homemade Mayonnaise (see page 18)
Salt and freshly ground black pepper to taste
5 spinach leaves, finely chopped
1 tablespoon chopped fresh tarragon
1 tablespoon fresh basil
2 tablespoons chopped fresh parsley
1 clove garlic, minced

Beat by hand ½ cup oil into the standard mayonnaise to stiffen it for piping. Rectify salt and pepper.
Beat together all ingredients. Chill several hours to "marry" flavors.

YOGHURT DRESSING FOR FRUIT SALAD

This is a lovely sauce for apples, peaches, melons, and pears, but don't use it on pineapple or papaya—their enzymes will curdle the yoghurt.

MAKES 1 CUP

1 cup plain yoghurt
2 tablespoons Homemade Mayonnaise (see page 18)
2 tablespoons honey
1 tablespoon rice wine vinegar
½ teaspoon salt

Beat all ingredients together thoroughly and refrigerate for at least 1 hour. Arrange fresh fruit salad in a glass serving bowl. Pour dressing over the top. Serve immediately.

MARINARA SAUCE

This basic sauce enhances fish, rice, spaghetti, even steak—and it freezes beautifully. Make it in August and put some away for the winter; in the middle of February it will bring back all the fragrance of summer.

MAKES ABOUT 1 QUART

½ cup olive oil
3 medium onions, thinly sliced
2 stalks celery, finely chopped
1 tablespoon fresh oregano, chopped (or use 1 teaspoon dried)
1 tablespoon fresh basil, chopped
1 tablespoon fresh thyme, chopped
8 large, ripe tomatoes, stemmed and quartered
Salt and freshly ground black pepper to taste
Pinch of sugar

½ cup tomato paste
¼ pound fresh mushrooms, thinly sliced
⅓ cup dry white wine

Heat the olive oil in a heavy skillet.
Sauté the onions gently until tender and transparent, about 10 minutes.
Add celery and herbs and cook for 5 minutes.
Add tomatoes. Stir in salt, pepper, sugar, and tomato paste. Bring to a boil and stir. Simmer for 35 minutes, stirring occasionally. Add the mushrooms and white wine. Continue to cook until sauce is thick, about 15 to 20 minutes.

PASTA AL PESTO

Pesto, a heady and rich basil sauce, adds instant flavor to soups, pastas, and stews; it has been a staple of Italian cooking for generations. Made in the summer when basil is plentiful, pesto will keep in the icebox or the freezer well into the fall. Purée the basil leaves with the garlic, oil, and pine nuts and store in the freezer or in a jar in the icebox topped with a layer of olive oil to keep it airtight. Add the salt, pepper, and Parmesan at serving time.

SERVES 4

2½ cups fresh basil leaves
2 cloves garlic, peeled
Salt and freshly ground black pepper to taste
3 tablespoons pine nuts
⅓ to ½ cup olive oil
½ cup freshly grated Parmesan cheese
1 tablespoon butter, softened
12 ounces hot, cooked, fresh pasta, lightly buttered

In a food processor or blender, purée the basil, garlic, salt, pepper, and nuts. With the machine running, pour in enough oil to make a smooth, thick paste. Blend in the cheese and butter. Toss pasta gently with the pesto to coat it. Serve immediately.

FRESH VEGETABLE RELISH

This fresh summer relish will enhance any hot or cold meat, but we like it with cold roast veal.

SERVES 6

1 large cucumber, peeled, seeded, and very thinly sliced
2 large, ripe tomatoes, peeled, seeded, and coarsely chopped
1 bunch scallions, the white part sliced thin
½ cup vinaigrette made with 1 egg yolk (see page 389)
3 tablespoons fresh mint, chopped
Salt and freshly ground black pepper to taste

Mix all ingredients thoroughly and chill several hours or overnight. Serve in a colorful bowl.

PLUM KETCHUP

Make this ketchup in the summer when fresh plums are abundant, and put it away to serve in the fall with game, or cold roast pork, or even Thanksgiving turkey.

5 pounds purple plums, halved and pitted, skins left on
3 tart green apples, quartered but not cored or peeled
2 cups malt or cider vinegar
4 cups dark brown sugar
3 tablespoons cinnamon
2 teaspoons ground cloves
2 teaspoons salt
½ teaspoon mace

Put the fruit and vinegar in a heavy, nonaluminum kettle. Simmer until very tender. Purée the cooked fruit and liquid in a food processor. Strain. Return the purée to the kettle. Add the brown sugar and spices and simmer until thick, about 1½ to 2 hours, stirring occasionally so the mixture does not stick to the bottom of the pan.

Pour the boiling ketchup into hot sterilized jars and seal immediately.

BLUEBERRY SAUCE

One summer, we rented a house in Nantucket near a field where high-bush blueberries were growing wild in a protective jungle of poison ivy in such abundance that a brave forager could bring home enough for a pie in less than half an hour. If you are blessed with a similar supply, try this rich dessert sauce.

MAKES ABOUT 2 CUPS

4 cups blueberries
¼ cup water
1 stick cinnamon
½ teaspoon whole cloves
Pinch of salt
Peel of 1 lemon
1 cup sugar
Juice of ½ lemon
1 tablespoon butter

In a heavy saucepan, simmer 2 cups of the berries with the water, cinnamon, cloves, salt, and lemon peel for about 15 minutes. Mash the berries with a spoon from time to time. Strain the juice. There should be about 1 cup of juice.

Return the juice to the saucepan and add the sugar and lemon juice. Simmer, stirring often, until slightly thickened, about 10 minutes. Beat in the butter and then gently stir in the remaining 2 cups of berries.

PEAR COMPOTE

A delicate variation on applesauce, pear compote should be seasoned with ginger or cinnamon to give it a bright flavor.

MAKES ABOUT 2 CUPS

1½ pounds Comice pears, peeled, cored, and sliced
½ cup water
1 teaspoon vanilla extract
½ cup sugar
1 teaspoon grated fresh ginger
1 tablespoon butter

Place sliced pears in a saucepan with water, vanilla, sugar, ginger, and butter. Simmer gently until pears are very tender, about 40 minutes. Mash with a fork to break up pears. Simmer until most of the excess liquid has evaporated, about 5 minutes, stirring from time to time.

TARRAGON JELLY

A welcome addition to summer menus, this jelly goes well with cold meats and fish. Try making it with other herbs from the garden, too; basil works well, for example, and the jelly turns an even prettier color if a leaf or two of the opal variety is added. It's a great make-ahead Christmas present.

M A K E S 3 H A L F - P I N T J A R S

6 tablespoons fresh tarragon leaves, finely chopped
1½ cups boiling water
⅓ cup tarragon vinegar
3½ cups sugar
1 three-ounce package liquid pectin

Place tarragon leaves in a saucepan. Pour boiling water over tarragon and let steep for 15 minutes. Strain liquid, discarding tarragon. Return the liquid to the saucepan. Add the vinegar and sugar. Bring to a boil and boil hard for 2 minutes. Stir in the pectin and boil hard for 1 minute. Remove from heat. Skim.

Pour boiling jelly into hot sterilized half-pint jars and seal immediately. Allow to set for several days before using.

OLD-FASHIONED PEACH PRESERVES

Make this when peaches are plentiful and put it away in the cupboard. Every jar you open in the winter makes the sun come out.

M A K E S A B O U T 8 O N E - P I N T J A R S

10 pounds fresh peaches, washed, peeled, pitted, and sliced
Sugar

3 tablespoons lemon juice
3 sticks cinnamon
1 teaspoon whole cloves

Measure the prepared fruit. Mix an equal quantity, cup for cup, of sugar with the fruit. Let stand overnight. In a nonaluminum pan, simmer the peaches and sugar, along with the lemon juice, cinnamon sticks, and cloves until the fruit is transparent and the syrup is thick.

Ladle into hot sterilized jars and seal immediately.

CRABAPPLE JELLY

No other jelly has the delicate flavor and pink color of crabapple. If you can't find crabapples at the farm stand or the grocery store, find a friend with a tree and see if you can't swap jelly for apples—they're easy to pick.

MAKES ABOUT 3 HALF-PINT JARS

8 cups crabapples, washed, stemmed (but not cored), and cut in quarters
About 1 quart water
3½ cups sugar (or more)

Place cut-up apples, cores and skins included, in a nonaluminum kettle. Add water until it is barely visible through the top layer of apples. Simmer gently for 15 to 20 minutes, until the apples are soft and juice begins to turn pink.

Pour fruit into a wet jelly bag or strainer lined with wet cheesecloth suspended over a bowl. Allow to drip several hours or overnight. For maximum jelly, squeeze bag to obtain all the juice possible. For crystal-clear jelly, *do not squeeze* the bag.

When all the juice has drained, measure 4 cups into a kettle and bring to a boil. Add 3½ cups of sugar and simmer until the juice falls in sheets off a spoon. This may take 20 to 30 minutes. Do not boil hard.

Once the jell point has been reached, ladle into hot sterilized jars and seal immediately.

Do not make jelly in batches larger than 4 cups at a time. The results of cooking in large batches without pectin are often not very satisfactory.

PEACH BUTTER

This spread is good on pancakes or hot buttered biscuits or poured over still-warm gingerbread.

MAKES ABOUT 3 HALF-PINT JARS

5 to 6 pounds fresh ripe peaches, peeled, pitted, and cut up
½ to 1 cup water
1 cup honey
1 teaspoon cinnamon

Preheat the oven to 300°F.

Place peaches in a heavy kettle. Add water just to cover the bottom of the pan to keep the fruit from sticking at first. Simmer until the fruit is soft, about 15 to 20 minutes. Purée fruit in a food processor.

Measure 4 cups of purée. Mix honey and cinnamon with the purée.

Pour the mixture into a flat baking pan and bake at 300°F, stirring from time to time, until very thick. The time will vary according to the amount of liquid in the fruit, but it will take several hours, as many as 10. The butter will be a rich brown color. When thick, pour the boiling hot purée into hot sterilized jars and seal immediately.

Any jar that does not seal should be refrigerated and used immediately.

MIXED FRUIT CRISP

This is inspired by a classic Girl Scout recipe. Practically foolproof, it was one of the first things that fledgling scouts were taught to make; it is equally good hot in the kitchen, warm in the backyard, or cold on a picnic. The original was made with apples and cinnamon, but this version uses summer fruits. It can be assembled ahead of time, baked at the last minute, and served piping hot with heavy cream or homemade vanilla ice cream.

SERVES 8

1 cup fresh raspberries
1 cup sweet cherries, pitted

2 large peaches, peeled, pitted, and sliced
1 cup sugar
¾ cup flour
1 teaspoon cinnamon
6 tablespoons cold butter
¼ cup oatmeal

Preheat the oven to 400°F.

Generously butter a baking dish. Toss the fruit with ½ cup sugar and pile it into the dish. Stir together remaining sugar, flour, and cinnamon. Cut in cold butter until the mixture resembles coarse meal. Stir in oatmeal. Spread the mixture over the fruit.

Bake at 400°F for 30 minutes, until the topping is golden.

MANGO MOUSSE

A light, golden dessert that does wonders for jaded summer appetites.

SERVES 6

3 large, ripe mangoes
Juice of 1 orange, strained
Juice of 1 lime, strained
¾ cup sugar
1⅓ cups heavy cream, very cold
¾ cup pecans, finely chopped
6 whole pecan halves

Peel mangoes and cut into cubes. Put mango cubes, fruit juice, and ½ cup of the sugar into the bowl of a food processor. Process until smooth.

Beat the cream with the rest of the sugar until stiff peaks form. Delicately fold the mango purée into the cream. Fold in pecans.

Spoon the mousse into individual dishes, or into a serving dish, and chill in the icebox for at least 4 hours. Top each serving with a whole pecan half.

APRICOT MOUSSE

This makes a refreshing and delicious early summer dessert.

SERVES 4 TO 6

1½ pounds fresh apricots, peeled and pitted
½ cup sugar
¼ cup white port wine
Juice of ½ lemon
2 cups heavy cream, whipped with
    ⅓ cup sugar and 1 teaspoon vanilla
10 small, crisp macaroons, crushed (or use sugar cookies if macaroons are
    unavailable)

Simmer the apricots with sugar, white port, and lemon juice for 10 to 15 minutes, or until soft. Purée the apricots in a food processor and drain well in a sieve. Chill.

Just before serving, fold drained apricots into sweetened, flavored whipped cream. Fold in crushed macaroons. Spoon into individual serving dishes.

STRAWBERRY FOOL

It is hard to say where the name fool comes from. The word could be an anglicized version of the French *fouler*, meaning to crush, or it may be a close cousin to a trifle, in that any fool can make a dessert as simple as this!

SERVES 6

1 cup heavy cream
2 tablespoons confectioners' sugar
1 pint strawberries, washed, stemmed, and lightly mashed
6 large, whole berries, stems left on

Whip the cream with confectioners' sugar. Just before serving, fold mashed berries into the whipped cream. Spoon into champagne coupes and top each serving with one whole perfect berry.

MINTED PEARS

This is a pretty and refreshing end to a summer meal, and nearly all of it can be prepared ahead of time. Children love it, too, although for them you might substitute the minted sugar syrup found in specialty food shops.

SERVES 4

4 large Bartlett pears, firm but ripe, peeled
½ cup sugar
2 cups water
¼ cup fresh mint leaves
Homemade Vanilla Ice Cream (see page 99)
¼ cup green crème de menthe, or mint-flavored syrup

Very carefully, using an apple corer, remove the blossom end and core the pears, leaving the stem intact. Stir the sugar into the water and bring to a boil. Simmer for 10 minutes. Add pears and mint leaves. Simmer just until the pears are barely fork tender, no longer. Cool the pears in the syrup.

To serve, spoon a bed of vanilla ice cream in the bottom of each serving dish. Set a drained pear upright in each dish. Pour a little crème de menthe over each pear. Garnish with fresh mint leaves. Serve with chocolate cookies.

MELON IN STRAWBERRY SAUCE

An easily made, low-calorie celebration of summer melons; we've specified cantaloupe, but Cranshaw, Persian, or casaba would be lovely, too.

SERVES 4

2 pints fresh strawberries, washed and hulled
½ cup superfine granulated sugar
¼ cup light rum
1 large cantaloupe, seeded, cut into balls
4 large strawberries, stems left on

In a food processor, process strawberries with sugar. Stir in rum. Arrange melon balls in a glass serving bowl and pour strawberry purée over melon. Garnish with whole strawberries.

CANTALOUPE IN BLUEBERRY HONEY

Every honey has a different character. Blueberry honey is subtle and fruity, and goes well with melon and berries.

SERVES 4 TO 6

2 large cantaloupes, seeded and cut into balls
1 large lime, zest and juice
¼ cup honey, preferably wild blueberry honey
1 tablespoon dark rum
1 cup fresh blueberries

Put melon balls in a mixing bowl. Add the lime zest and juice and the honey, tossing gently to coat the melon balls. Chill for about 1 hour. Stir in the rum.
Serve in individual dishes and toss with blueberries.

EARLY SUMMER PUDDING

This is a classic English nursery dish; anyone who grew up with a nanny probably knows it well. It can be made with any red or blue berries, as long as the fruit is juicy enough to give the bread the proper color. Serve more sugar on the side, and pass a jug of thick cream.

SERVES 6

1½ quarts mixed berries (raspberries, blueberries, red currants, or similar berries)
½ cup sugar
¼ cup sweet white wine
1 teaspoon lemon juice
1 loaf thinly sliced white bread, crusts removed
Softened butter

In a saucepan, simmer the fruit, sugar, and wine with the lemon juice for 5 minutes. Cool the fruit in the liquid. Cut the bread into shapes that will line a well-greased 1-quart mixing bowl or pudding basin. Lightly butter the slices on one side with softened butter. Line the bowl with the bread, buttered side out, slightly overlapping the slices. Pour in the fruit, juice and all. Top with a layer of bread and then a saucer that just fits inside the rim of the bowl. Weight the saucer with a two-pound weight, or a large can of baked beans. Place the bowl on a plate and refrigerate overnight, or longer.

Dip the bowl in hot water, dry, and then turn the pudding out onto a serving plate. Serve with whipped cream or Homemade Vanilla Ice Cream (see page 99).

CHERRY PUDDING

Cherries are as versatile as blueberries in summer menus; they can be made into compotes or a multitude of main courses or desserts. We like sweet cherries for cooking, as long as they're not soft, especially firm Bing cherries and sweet Michigan Blacks. This old-fashioned Connecticut recipe works equally well with blueberries, blackberries, and raspberries.

SERVES 6

2 pounds fresh sweet cherries, washed and pitted
3 tablespoons flour
½ cup dark brown sugar
Juice of 1 lemon
2 cups plain dry bread crumbs, or stale cake crumbs
2 cups milk, scalded
2 eggs, lightly beaten
2 tablespoons butter, cut up

Preheat the oven to 350°F.

Place the cherries in a mixing bowl and sprinkle with flour, sugar, and lemon juice. Toss and let stand for 30 minutes. Turn mixture into a heavily buttered baking dish.

Put two-thirds of the bread crumbs in a bowl. Add hot milk and beaten eggs. Stir well. Pour over cherries and stir gently to mix well. Spread remaining crumbs over cherry mixture and dot with butter.

Bake at 350°F for about 45 minutes. Serve with Homemade Vanilla Ice Cream (see page 99).

CLAFOUTIS

This delicately flavored French summer dessert originates in the Limousin region, where cherries are a major crop and every farmhouse has a different variation. Although the flavor is supposed to be very mild, you could try adding a dash of kirsch or mirabelle for a variation.

SERVES 6 TO 8

3 cups pitted fresh sweet cherries
⅓ cup sugar
1¼ cups milk
⅓ cup sugar
3 eggs, well beaten
Pinch of salt
⅔ cup flour

Preheat the oven to 350°F.

In a mixing bowl, toss the cherries with ⅓ cup sugar. In a blender, blend the milk, ⅓ cup sugar, eggs, salt, and flour until smooth.

Pour a thin layer of batter into a well-buttered ovenproof baking dish. Spread sugared cherries in an even layer on top of the batter. Pour the rest of the batter over the cherries and smooth the top with a wooden spoon.

Bake at 350°F for 1 hour until puffed and golden brown. The crust will fall when the dish is removed from the oven. Serve the clafoutis warm with a pitcher of thick cream.

FRESH FRUIT SALAD WITH LEMON SORBET

The inspiration for this recipe is a refreshing Swiss lemon ice dessert called a Colonel, which is lemon sorbet with a little iced vodka poured over it. We've added fruit salad, but we urge you to consider other variations as well.

SERVES 4

2 cups fresh fruit salad
1½ cups homemade lemon sorbet
¼ cup chilled vodka, or ¾ cup chilled sparkling white wine

Arrange fruit salad in individual dishes. Top each with a scoop of lemon sorbet. Pour vodka or wine over and serve with homemade cookies.

ROSY PEACHES

Peaches fresh and ripe from the orchard inspire all kinds of summer desserts. This one is simple, cool, and refreshing, and much of it can be assembled ahead of time.

SERVES 6

6 large, ripe peaches, peeled, halved, and pitted
1 bottle hearty red wine
1 teaspoon cinnamon
½ cup sugar
¼ pound (1 stick) butter
¾ cup red currant jelly
3 tablespoons brandy
1 pint peach ice cream
⅓ cup chopped almonds, toasted until golden

In a saucepan, poach peach halves in red wine, cinnamon, and sugar for 10 minutes, or until just tender when pierced with a knife. Cool the peaches in the syrup. In another saucepan, melt the butter and add the jelly and brandy. Whisk constantly until butter and jelly are melted and well mixed.

Drain the peaches. Spoon ice cream into dessert dishes. Arrange two peach halves in each dish on top of ice cream. Pour hot jelly mixture over the peaches and sprinkle with chopped, freshly toasted almonds.

PEACHES AND CREAM

Here is a fast and easy American classic that is as good for a party as it is for family suppertime.

SERVES 6 TO 8

1 cup brown sugar
1 cup sour cream
1 cup heavy cream, whipped

6 to 8 large fresh, very ripe peaches, peeled and thinly sliced
⅓ cup sugar cookie crumbs

Mix the brown sugar and sour cream together until the sugar is dissolved. Fold in the whipped cream. Carefully fold in the peaches just before serving and top with cookie crumbs.

GINGERED PEACHES

A classic, easy way to serve peaches.

SERVES 4

¼ cup sugar
½ cup water
2 tablespoons chopped crystallized ginger
½ teaspoon lemon juice
4 large peaches, peeled, pitted, and sliced

In a small saucepan, combine sugar, water, and ginger. Bring to a boil and simmer, covered, for 5 minutes. Remove from the heat and add lemon juice. Chill well. Pour the chilled syrup over the peaches, toss gently, and refrigerate for 1 hour.

Serve in glass dessert dishes.

PEACH MELBA

There's not much doubt that Escoffier created this classic dessert for soprano Nellie Melba, but what year it was, or what role she sang, or whether she dined at the Savoy or the Ritz-Carlton, has long since faded away. Like the original, this quick modern version should ideally be made with white peaches; the intent—probably apocryphal—was to approximate as closely as possible Dame Nellie's exquisite complexion.

SERVES 6

1 pint fresh raspberries
3 tablespoons superfine granulated sugar
3 tablespoons raspberry liqueur
6 fresh, ripe peaches, peeled, pitted, and quartered
1 quart Homemade Vanilla Ice Cream (see page 99)
Fresh mint leaves

Purée raspberries with the sugar in the work bowl of a food processor. Add raspberry liqueur.

Arrange 4 peach quarters in the bottom of each dessert dish. Top with a scoop of ice cream. Spoon raspberry purée over the top. Garnish with fresh mint leaves.

SOUSED PEACHES

The peaches—and presumably not the cook—are steeped in brandy to the eyebrows.

SERVES 6

6 tablespoons butter
¾ cup sugar
⅓ cup water
6 fresh, ripe peaches, peeled, cut in half, and seeded
⅓ cup brandy
Whipped cream or Homemade Vanilla Ice Cream (see page 99), optional

Melt butter in a frying pan or electric skillet. Add sugar and cook until melted. When the sugar is melted, add water and stir to blend. Add peach halves and simmer, turning them several times, for about 25 minutes. Pour the brandy over the peaches, ignite, and when the flame dies, serve two halves along with some of the syrup in individual dessert dishes. A little freshly whipped cream or vanilla ice cream is a delicious addition.

PEACH BAVARIAN

This elegant dessert can be prepared early in the day. We like to serve it with our own Lemon Ice Box Cookies (see page 109).

SERVES 6

2 cups fresh peaches, peeled, pitted, and chopped
Juice of 1 lemon
½ cup sugar
1 envelope granulated gelatin softened in
 ½ cup water
1 teaspoon almond extract
1½ cups heavy cream, whipped
Whipped cream for garnish

Stir the peaches, lemon juice, and sugar together in a bowl. Refrigerate 1 hour. Purée in a food processor.

Put softened gelatin and water in a bowl over hot water and stir until just dissolved. Stir melted gelatin into peach purée. Refrigerate until the mixture just begins to set.

Beat the almond extract into the whipped cream, then fold into the peach mixture. Spoon into 6 wine glasses and chill until firm. Decorate with more whipped cream.

PEACHES IN STRAWBERRY CREAM

We offer this dessert with strawberries, but with raspberries it makes a quick variation on Peach Melba.

SERVES 6

8 large, ripe peaches, peeled, pitted, and sliced
Juice of 1 lemon
3 tablespoons water
⅔ cup brown sugar

1 quart fresh strawberries, or 1 pint fresh raspberries
⅓ cup superfine granulated sugar
2 tablespoons dark rum
⅔ cup heavy cream, whipped stiff

Toss the peaches with the lemon juice. Boil water and brown sugar until sugar dissolves. Pour hot syrup over the sliced peaches. Let the peaches cool in the syrup. Purée the berries in a food processor with sugar and rum. Fold into the whipped cream and refrigerate 2 hours or more.

Arrange drained peaches in a serving dish. Spoon strawberry cream over them and serve at once.

PEACH CRUMBLE

This easy southern favorite makes any humdrum dinner into an event.

SERVES 6 TO 8

½ cup flour
½ cup sugar
½ teaspoon nutmeg
1 teaspoon cinnamon
Pinch of salt
4 tablespoons chilled butter
5 large peaches, peeled and sliced
Homemade Vanilla Ice Cream (see page 99)

Preheat the oven to 350°F.

Stir together the flour, sugar, nutmeg, cinnamon, and salt. Cut in chilled butter until the mixture is coarse and crumbly.

Butter and sugar a 1 quart, square glass baking dish. Arrange sliced peaches in one layer in the bottom of the dish. Cover with the crumble mixture.

Bake at 350°F, uncovered, for 25 minutes. Serve very hot with a scoop of vanilla ice cream on each serving.

SAUTÉED PEACHES

We like the combination of the hot, sugary fruit with the chill of ice cream.

SERVES 6

¼ pound (1 stick) butter
½ cup brown sugar
3 tablespoons rum
6 large fresh peaches, peeled, pitted, and cut in half
Homemade Vanilla Ice Cream (see page 99)

Melt butter and brown sugar in a heavy skillet. Add rum. Add peaches and cook, covered, until peaches are just tender. Uncover and cook 5 minutes longer, turning the peaches 3 or 4 times to coat well with the heavy syrup.

Arrange 2 peach halves in each serving dish. Top with a scoop of Homemade Vanilla Ice Cream and spoon syrup over all.

Bananas are also delicious this way.

PEACH CUSTARD ICE CREAM

This ice cream recipe calls for peaches that are puréed, not sliced or chopped; we don't think anybody likes to bite down on chunks of frozen peach in ice cream.

MAKES 1 ½ QUARTS

3 cups half and half
¾ cup superfine granulated sugar
3 egg yolks
1 cup heavy cream
1 teaspoon pure vanilla extract
1 teaspoon almond extract
6 very ripe peaches, peeled, pitted, and puréed

Beat the half and half, sugar, and egg yolks together in the top of a double boiler. Stir in cream. Cook over simmering water until thick. Remove from heat and cool. Beat in flavorings.

When the mixture is cold, pour it into the container of an ice cream freezer. When ice cream is beginning to thicken but is not yet frozen, add peach purée. Continue freezing until the ice cream is hard. Transfer to the freezer compartment of the icebox and let flavor develop for 1 to 2 hours before serving.

EASY PEACH SUNDAE

If there are to be no children in the group, add a teaspoon of almond extract or several tablespoons of Amaretto or light rum to the peaches before spooning them over the ice cream.

SERVES 4

4 large, ripe peaches, peeled, pitted, and crushed
⅓ cup sugar
1 pint Homemade Vanilla Ice Cream (see page 99)
Chopped toasted almonds (optional)

Sprinkle the crushed peaches with sugar. Let stand at room temperature for 15 to 20 minutes.

Spoon ice cream into serving dishes. Top with fresh peach mixture and sprinkle with almonds, if desired.

BLUEBERRY SPICE CAKE

A superb variation on one of the great summer themes. Golden Syrup is a cane-based syrup, popular in England and now available in specialty stores everywhere.

SERVES 6 TO 8

¼ *pound (1 stick) butter*
1 cup sugar
1 egg
3 tablespoons Golden Syrup
2 cups flour
2 teaspoons pumpkin pie spice (or ½ teaspoon each ground cloves, cinnamon,
  nutmeg, allspice, and mace)
Pinch of salt
1 teaspoon baking soda
1 cup buttermilk
1½ cups fresh blueberries, tossed with flour to coat
1 cup heavy cream, whipped with
  2 tablespoons dark rum

Preheat the oven to 350°F.

Cream the butter and sugar until they are light and fluffy. Beat in the egg and the syrup. Stir together the flour, spices, salt, and baking soda. Add the flour mixture to the creamed butter and sugar, alternating with the buttermilk. Stir in the blueberries.

Pour batter into a buttered and floured 9-inch square pan, sprinkle with sugar, and bake at 350°F for 1 hour. Serve warm with rum-flavored whipped cream.

MAINE BLUEBERRY CAKE

The flour on the blueberries keeps them from sinking to the bottom of this tasty tea- or coffeecake.

SERVES 6

⅔ *stick butter*
1 cup sugar
2 eggs

1 cup crème fraîche (see page 12)
2 cups flour
½ teaspoon baking soda
1 tablespoon baking powder
1 teaspoon nutmeg
Pinch of salt
1½ cups blueberries, tossed with flour to coat

Preheat the oven to 350°F.

Cream together butter and sugar until light and fluffy. Add eggs, one at a time, and beat well after each addition. Add crème fraîche. Stir together flour, soda, baking powder, nutmeg, and salt. Stir into the cream mixture. Stir until just combined. Fold in blueberries.

Pour batter into a greased and floured 9-inch square pan. Bake at 350°F for 50 minutes. Serve warm.

INSTANT BLUEBERRY GRANITA

A young French chef showed us this refreshingly easy dessert. A chunky frozen fruit concoction, full of the essence of fresh fruit, it can also be made with raspberries, blackberries, red currants, or any other ripe berries. Any unused frozen berries can be kept sealed in a plastic bag for unexpected guests and special desserts.

SERVES 4 TO 6

2 pints fresh blueberries, washed, stemmed, and spread in one layer on a cookie sheet. Freeze for 3 hours, until very hard.
½ to ¾ cup superfine granulated sugar (depending on the sweetness of the berries)
1 teaspoon lemon juice

Put frozen berries, sugar, and lemon juice in a food processor. Process until nearly smooth, about 1 minute. Serve at once in dessert glasses. Pass Lemon Ice Box Cookies (see page 109).

PLUM DUMPLINGS

The shortcake dough for this apple dumpling variation is fragile and a bit tricky but eminently worth doing.

SERVES 6

2 cups flour
2 teaspoons baking powder
Pinch of salt
1 tablespoon sugar
4 tablespoons butter
About ¾ cup milk
1 pound dark purple plums, cut in half and pitted but not peeled
½ cup light brown sugar, mixed with
  1 tablespoon cinnamon
¼ cup butter, cut into small pieces

Preheat the oven to 350°F.

Stir together flour, baking powder, salt, and sugar. Cut in the butter until the mixture resembles coarse meal. Stir in milk, a little at a time, until the pastry holds together but does not become too sticky. It may not take all of the milk. Turn the pastry out onto a floured board and roll or pat out to ¼-inch thickness. Cut into 6 four-inch squares.

Place several plum halves on each pastry square. Sprinkle with 1 to 2 tablespoons of the brown sugar and cinnamon mixture and dot with butter. Draw the corners of the pastry together up over the fruit. Pinch the edges well and prick all over with a fork. Bake on a greased baking sheet at 350°F for about 30 minutes, or until golden brown.

Serve warm.

SWEET PLUM PIE

Serve it for tea or for dessert, and substitute vanilla if you don't like almond extract.

SERVES 6 TO 8

1 pound plums, pitted and cut into quarters
½ cup sugar
2 tablespoons water
¼ pound (1 stick) butter
1 cup sugar
8 egg yolks, beaten
1 teaspoon almond extract
4 egg whites, beaten with 1 tablespoon sugar until stiff peaks form

Preheat the oven to 350°F.

Place the plums, ½ cup sugar, and water in a heavy, nonaluminum saucepan. Cook over low heat until the fruit is soft and syrup is thick.

Drain the plums carefully and spoon into the pie shell. Cream butter and 1 cup sugar, then add beaten egg yolks. Beat well. Add almond extract. Fold in the egg whites. Spread mixture over the plums. Bake at 350°F for 30 minutes, or until the custard is set.

Cool completely and serve cold.

PLUM AND WALNUT PIE

The skins of the plums are left on to keep them from turning mushy and to give the pie a nice color.

SERVES 6 TO 8

Pastry for a two-crust pie
1½ pounds plums, pitted and chopped
⅔ cup sugar
2 tablespoons flour
1 cup chopped walnuts
2 teaspoons cinnamon
3 tablespoons brandy
4 tablespoons butter
1 whole egg, beaten, for glaze (optional)

Preheat the oven to 375°F.
Roll out half of the pastry and line a 9-inch pie plate. Mix plums, sugar, flour, walnuts, cinnamon, brandy, and butter. Pile into pie shell. Roll out the remaining pastry and place over the filling. Flute the crust. Glaze, if desired. Bake at 375°F for 35 to 40 minutes.

HAY DAY'S DEEP-DISH CHERRY PIE

Alex and Sallie Van Rensselaer brought back magnificent, sweet Michigan Black cherries from the shores of Lake Michigan, and this recipe was the result. We make it in midsummer, and people don't seem to be able to get enough of it.

SERVES 8

Pastry for two-crust deep-dish pie
6 tablespoons sugar
2 tablespoons flour
¼ teaspoon cinnamon

1 quart fresh sweet cherries, pitted
¼ cup dark rum
2 tablespoons cold butter
1 whole egg, beaten, for glaze

Preheat the oven to 350°F.

Roll out two-thirds of the pastry and line a 9-inch deep-dish pie plate.

Mix the dry ingredients together and toss them with the cherries. Add the rum and toss well to coat the cherries.

Pour the prepared fruit mixture into the pie shell and dot with small pieces of the cold butter. Roll out remaining pastry and place the top crust on the pie. Crimp the edges, glaze with beaten egg, and cut a steam vent in the top.

Bake for 55 to 60 minutes in a 350°F oven. Cool slightly and serve with vanilla ice cream.

FROZEN CANTALOUPE SLUSH

This dessert makes a superb light finale to a menu of grilled meat or fish.

SERVES 6

½ cup water
½ cup sugar
⅓ cup freshly squeezed orange juice
1 small, ripe cantaloupe, peeled, seeded, and cubed
1 tablespoon orange liqueur
½ cup heavy cream, whipped until stiff
Grated orange rind

Combine water, sugar, and orange juice in a small saucepan. Bring to a boil and simmer for 5 minutes. Cool.

Purée the cantaloupe cubes in a food processor. Stir in the sugar syrup and add the orange liqueur. Fold in the whipped cream.

Freeze in an ice cream freezer until slushy. Spoon into champagne coupes and serve immediately, garnished with grated orange rind.

PIÑA COLADA ICE CREAM

Ice cream freezers are now so readily available that homemade ice cream can be made almost any time. Here's a way to visit the Bahamas without ever leaving the kitchen. Piña Colada Ice Cream is easy to freeze—a Waring Ice Cream Parlor will do it in 40 minutes and a Simac II Gelataio in 25 or less—and shouldn't be allowed to get too hard. Serve it with coconut cookies.

SERVES 8

1 cup coconut cream
1 cup crushed pineapple with its juice (natural pack, not syrup pack)
⅓ cup sugar
2 cups heavy cream
¼ cup dark rum

Mix coconut cream, pineapple, sugar, heavy cream, and rum. Allow to stand for 15 minutes. Stir well and freeze in an ice cream freezer. Serve topped with grated coconut.
If using fresh pineapple, simmer in water just to cover for 10 minutes. Drain well and chop. Cool completely before adding to the mixture.

WATERMELON SORBET

Try serving a scoop of this refreshing sorbet in a circle of melon balls. You don't taste the rum—the alcohol only accentuates the flavor of the watermelon.

SERVES 6

3 cups watermelon, seeded and cut into chunks
¼ cup sugar syrup, made of equal parts of sugar and water
½ cup water
1 teaspoon lemon juice
3 tablespoons rum

Purée watermelon chunks in a blender or food processor. Add syrup, water, lemon juice, and rum. Freeze in an ice cream freezer according to the manufacturer's directions.

Make a sugar syrup by boiling together ½ cup granulated sugar and ½ cup water for 5 minutes. Cool and store in a tightly covered container.

PEACH TEA CAKE

When we originally published this recipe in an early copy of the *Hay Day Rural Times*, the quantity of butter was misprinted as 4 cups instead of ¼ cup. One of our customers was such a staunch friend that she tried it three times before she finally called us to suggest gently that we had made a mistake. It's a wonderful quick bread, and it freezes well. (Remember, that's ¼ cup!)

MAKES 1 STANDARD LOAF OR 2 SMALL LOAVES

4 tablespoons (¼ cup) butter, softened
1 cup sugar
3 eggs
2¾ cups all-purpose flour
1½ teaspoons baking powder
1 teaspoon salt
½ teaspoon baking soda
2 teaspoons ground cinnamon
4 large peaches, peeled and thinly sliced
3 tablespoons fresh orange juice
1 tablespoon orange extract
1 teaspoon pure vanilla extract

Preheat the oven to 350°F.

Cream the butter and sugar. Add eggs, one at a time, beating well after each addition. Stir together flour, baking powder, salt, soda, and cinnamon. Add flour to creamed mixture alternately with the peach slices, beginning and ending with the flour. Stir in juice, orange extract, and vanilla.

Pour into a greased and floured standard loaf pan (or 2 small loaf pans) and bake at 350°F for 1 hour, or until a wooden pick comes out clean. Cool in the pan 10 minutes and then turn out. Cool completely or serve hot, topped with freshly made vanilla ice cream.

SPICY PEACH MUFFINS

Fruit breads are quick and easy ways to take advantage of burgeoning summer crops; they are good for breakfast or with cold dishes at suppertime. These freeze well, too.

MAKES ABOUT 20 MUFFINS

2 cups sour cream
⅓ cup melted butter
2 eggs
4 cups flour
⅔ cup packed light brown sugar
2 tablespoons baking powder
1 teaspoon salt
½ teaspoon baking soda
¼ teaspoon each allspice, cinnamon, and nutmeg, or
   1 teaspoon pumpkin pie spice
3 medium peaches, peeled, seeded, and chopped

Preheat the oven to 400°F.

Beat together the sour cream and butter. Beat in the eggs, one at a time. In a separate bowl, stir together the flour, brown sugar, baking powder, salt, soda, and spices. Combine the egg mixture and the flour. Stir just until all the ingredients are moistened; the batter should be lumpy. Fold in the peaches. Spoon into 20 paper-lined muffin cups, filling each about two-thirds full. Sprinkle the top of each muffin with a little granulated sugar.

Bake the muffins at 400°F for 20 to 25 minutes, or until the tops are golden brown. These are best served warm.

BLUEBERRY MUFFINS

Fresh blueberries are so versatile they can go anywhere in a menu from appetizer to dessert, but one of the best things to do with them is stir them into muffin batter. If you like spicy muffins, add half a teaspoon of cinnamon.

MAKES 12 MUFFINS

1 egg, beaten
¾ cup milk
3 tablespoons melted butter
1⅔ cups flour
¼ cup sugar
2½ teaspoons baking powder
Pinch of salt
1 cup fresh blueberries, washed, stemmed, and tossed with flour to coat

Preheat the oven to 400°F.

Combine egg, milk, and butter. In a larger bowl, stir together the flour, sugar, baking powder, and salt. Add the egg mixture, stirring just until moistened. Gently fold in blueberries.

Fill buttered muffin pans two-thirds full and bake at 400°F for about 20 to 25 minutes, or until the tops are puffed and golden brown.

CORN CAKES

These are small, crispy skillet cakes, a variation on the johnny (journey) cakes that were staples in New England and on the road west in the nineteenth century. Then, as part of breaking camp or setting out on a journey, what remained of the cornmeal mush was fried into a hard cake to be carried in the pocket and eaten en route. Now, we add whole sweet corn kernels and eat these like corn cakes with casseroles or grilled meats.

SERVES 4

1 large egg
½ cup milk
1 cup flour
1 teaspoon baking powder
¼ teaspoon salt
1 tablespoon melted butter
¾ cup whole-kernel corn

Beat the egg slightly in a mixing bowl. Add the milk. In a separate bowl, stir together the flour, baking powder, and salt. Add to the egg and milk mixture. Stir in the butter and corn. Beat until well mixed.

Grease a griddle or heavy skillet. Drop batter by tablespoonfuls onto the hot griddle. As soon as the cakes are browned on one side, turn them over. Cook 1 minute longer. Keep warm until all the cakes are finished.

Serve wrapped in a napkin.

FALL

"You can't go havin' a whole yearful of October."
"Why not? It's a perty month . . . we could have Octo-
ber, Christmas, the Fourth of July, an' my birthday and
let the other months go. . . . Christmas comes on the
86th of October, the first of the year falls on October
ninety-third . . . one good month all year long."

WALT KELLY

T HIS is our time of year. Goldenrod and katydids may mean gloom for the people who are still slogging through their summer reading, but they bring nothing but jubilation to Hay Day. Walk through any of the beautiful orchards around here with the sun on your shoulders and the bees working in the goldenrod, and you're about as close as you can get to the Promised Land.

The peach crop ends in the first part of September, and the tractors begin hauling down great bins of early apples—Tydeman's Red, Paulared, Jonamac, Spartan, and McIntosh. The cider press down the road, which can produce a thousand gallons a day at the peak of the season, starts pressing a couple of times a week, and pretty soon it's going just about every day. Trucks begin bringing in acorn squash and pattypan, spaghetti squash and pumpkins (when you think that Hay Day will sell twenty tons of pumpkins by Thanksgiving, you can imagine the size of the crop across the country). Local cauliflower, cabbage, broccoli, Brussels sprouts, and potatoes pour into the market, and mushrooms bring the cool, mossy scent of the forest floor into the stores with

[221]

them. The pear harvest starts (we sell pear cider, too), and it's prime time for quinces and persimmons. This is the season for making grape jelly and pear chutney; a bouquet of sage and juniper on the hall table scents the whole house. And the gorgeous parade of apple varieties keeps coming—Cortland, Wealthy, Macoun, Stayman, Empire, Winesap, Jonathan—with Mutsu, Idared, and Golden Russet (the oldest, the homeliest, and perhaps the greatest of all the apples) coming in last.

Summer gets a reprieve for a while as the katydids keep going into the warm nights of October, but fall gets down to business eventually. All of a sudden it's Halloween, and it's cold, and you lose an hour, and summer—even the pretense of it—is over.

Cooking at this season is a real pleasure. The kitchen in the early dark is once again the heart of the house, and making an apple pie for dinner, or soup for a tailgate picnic, or mincemeat for Thanksgiving with a couple of children or a couple of friends seems like the most wonderful thing in the world to be doing at the end of the day.

It has to be the weather. As soon as daylight saving time is over and the nights are long and cold, many of Hay Day's customers head for cooking classes.

We planned our Greenwich kitchen to accommodate a class of ten, and it does, but ten people armed with knives? One need look no farther for nerves of steel than at Lydie Marshall, small, elegant, French, and the personification of calm, surrounded by ten eager cooks not only chopping and slicing, but all asking questions at once and making emphatic gestures with carbon steel knives.

Lydie has written a wonderful country French cookbook, writes for food magazines, and runs a well-known cooking school in New York called À La

Bonne Cocotte; she has given many classes at Hay Day. She divides the students into teams, assigning each one part of the menu (Terrine of Scallops with Red Pepper Sauce, Magrets of Duck with Roasted Shallots, Gratin Potatoes with Sorrel, Lemon Bavarois with Raspberry Sauce, Puff Pastry Tart with Apples). Afterward everyone eats together, drinking Muscadet, talking about France, and congratulating themselves on the astonishing quality of what they have whipped up in an hour and a half.

But whether it's Lydie or any of the other superb cooks who have taught here, and whether it's participation for ten or a demonstration for forty, the classes are a circus. It's not just that even experienced cooks are inspired by bins of beautiful fresh herbs, wild mushrooms, and shallots the size of plums, or liberated by the chance to use professional equipment—mixers and processors and huge French copper bowls—but students are encouraged to take risks they'd never take at home. Would you hold a huge copper bowl of beaten egg whites upside down over your head? Of course you wouldn't—but with Lydie's encouragement it's easy. It's her way of proving the egg whites are beaten stiffly enough.

Paula Wolfert kept her demonstration class spellbound, not only with the quality and elegance of Moroccan cuisine but with her description of daily life in Tangier. Since Moroccans eat with their hands (specifically, with the first three fingers of the right hand), it is important that sauces be silky and smooth; foods must be malleable and are therefore often overcooked. Bread is used as a scoop, so it is heavy and dense. When they make Bisteeya, a rich, special-occasion dish of chicken or pigeon with eggs in phyllo, the Moroccans leave the bones in the birds and throw them on the table as they eat; when the meal is finished, they literally pick up the entire table and clear it away.

Most classes, of course, yield less exotic culinary wisdom: roasting pans have low sides so that steam and juices will evaporate, but if the pan is too big for the meat they will evaporate too fast. Blanching vegetables (always save the cooking water for stock) seals in vitamins. It's OK to stuff a Cornish hen ahead of time, if both hen and stuffing are well chilled. Puff pastry is as easy as turning on a processor. Individual mousselines (soufflés made with flour) for a dinner party can be cooked in the morning, or even the night before, and reheated at dinnertime. Always use the best quality of everything; you will taste the difference.

For the Hay Day staff backstage, preparing for a cooking class is no mean feat. Do we have saffron threads? Is there enough sorrel, and is it really fresh? Has anybody ever heard of harissa, and how do we get it? Do we have a couscousière? Every participant in a class needs mixers and processors at different times, but they're much too busy cooking to do dishes, so the staff often spends most of the class in suds to the elbows.

Still, there are few scenes more entertaining. Out of the bedlam of cutting and pounding and crashing pots come wonderful smells and fabulous dinners. Students see expert teachers getting excited about food, sharing their expertise and their enthusiasm. Timid souls come away with the courage to whack up a chicken with single strokes of a cleaver, and people for whom dinner till now has meant pushing "Defrost" on a microwave realize—yes—the joy of cooking.

And we learn a lot, ourselves.

The Fall Market

NOW is the time to savor the incredible differences in varieties of *apples*. After November the markets will offer only Delicious, McIntosh, Granny Smith, and a few others, but now the range is almost infinite (see chart on page 238). Later on they'll come from cold storage, and then from CA (Controlled Atmosphere) storage, meaning that they've been kept in carbon dioxide to slow down their respiration and, in effect, put them to sleep. CA storage is a boon, but it produces apples with a softer texture, which must be refrigerated and rarely are. For this reason, keep all apples in the icebox. Most of the vitamins in apples are contained in the skin, so peel them only if you have to.

Cider is the unadulterated juice of apples squeezed in a press. If the juice is filtered until it's clear and heated to stop the natural fermenting process that turns sugar into alcohol, it's apple juice. Let the alcohol develop, and it's hard cider. Let sweet cider stand in an open container for 4 to 5 weeks at room temperature, and it will turn to vinegar. We find it hard to imagine drinking anything else for breakfast at this season; why buy a cardboard box of reconstituted orange juice in a supermarket, when you can enjoy the juice of your own neighborhood apples, often for much less money? Almost all cider is pressed from a mixture of apple varieties, but at Thanksgiving we have our orchards press Golden Russets by themselves to make what many people consider the champagne of apple ciders.

If cider is bought fresh from a reputable supplier, it will keep in the icebox for a week to 10 days before it gets fizzy and starts to turn. It freezes well and will keep for a year; just be sure to allow space at the top of the jug to let it expand.

Where would Thanksgiving be without *cranberries?* Of course, the Indians were eating them and using them for medicines for centuries before the Pilgrims came, harvesting them as we still do from the sandy bogs along the New England coast and in northern Wisconsin in late fall. Be sure they're shiny, dark red, and not at all mushy—a perfect cranberry will bounce off the kitchen floor. Cranberries freeze well, but afterward they can be used only for cooking, not for stringing on the Christmas tree.

Fresh *kumquats* hide their tart pulp inside a sweet skin, and eaten whole, the taste is exhilarating, rather like a combination of an orange and a tangerine. They are traditionally cooked with duck, but they also add zest to pork, goose, and game birds and go well in fruit salads and sweet desserts.

Pears (see chart on page 242) ripen from the inside out, so they will almost always be fairly hard when you buy them. They're actually better if they're picked before they're ripe because they become grainy when they ripen on the tree. Keep them at room temperature until their stem ends have softened and their fragrance has developed. Pears make a rich cider, too—we sell a lot of it.

Persimmons, in season from October through Christmas, are rich in protein and vitamin A. Their silken flesh can be unbelievably sour if eaten too soon but is honey-sweet when ripe. Persimmons ripen easily at room temperature; the magnificent red-gold color won't change, but they will be soft to the touch, almost like jelly. They can then be cut in half like a melon and eaten with a spoon. The cultivated variety is the yellow-orange Japanese persimmon, or kaki, whose flavor is often compared to that of apricots, but there's also the tiny wild American persimmon: only about an inch in diameter, it is dull orange when ripe and has a gooey texture and a very rich, sweet flavor. It is wonderful in nut breads and puddings.

Pomegranates, which are actually a form of berry, come into the market in the early fall and reach their peak in November. They are handsome but forbidding on the outside; break them open to reveal ruby clusters of seeds encased in rich, juicy pulp. The white pith is bitter, but the seeds and pulp are good to eat or use as garnishes, or mash them in a sieve to extract their juice, which is the base for the liqueur grenadine. Don't spill the juice on anything important; it stains permanently.

The noble, ancient, apple-shaped *quince* has a small but dedicated following, particularly when it is made into jelly (the seeds are full of pectin). It cannot be eaten raw but can be transformed into excellent chutneys, tarts, and marmalades. Quinces yellow as they ripen, so choose the fruit showing the most vivid color.

Brussels sprouts, cabbage, and *cauliflower* are available in such abundance that you need never settle for any with outer leaves that are dry or brownish; cabbage and Brussels sprouts should be bright green and tightly wrapped, and cauliflower should be white, never rusty.

People who have never seen Brussels sprouts in the wild are startled when we sell these miniature cabbages still on the stalk. They protrude sideways from a heavy stem, looking like an ornate Gothic finial, and can be snipped off as needed. Brussels sprouts can often be harvested right through November; you can see them poking up through the snow in winter vegetable gardens. We cook them in a large quantity of boiling water until they're just tender, but they're wonderful steamed, too. Many people cut a cross in the stem end to help them cook evenly, although we're not convinced it makes much difference. The usual mistake is to cook them to mush; if they're still a little crunchy, they're terrific. Since Brussels sprouts grow above ground they'll be fairly clean when you get them home, but float them in cold water in case there are insects sheltering under the tight leaves.

Celeriac, the root of a cousin of conventional celery and the ugly duckling of the vegetable section, comes into its own in Céleri Rémoulade, cut into julienne strips and served raw in a mustard mayonnaise. It is also excellent baked, boiled, puréed, or diced and sautéed in butter. The lumps make it wasteful to peel, so choose the smoothest ones available.

"It was very exciting to roam the . . . boundless chestnut woods of Lincoln with a bag on my shoulder," Thoreau wrote. "I laid up half a bushel for winter." No more; *chestnuts* are trouble-free crops in Europe and Asia Minor, but the richer and sweeter American chestnuts were all but eliminated by the chestnut blight of the early 1900s. Most of the chestnuts in our markets now come from Italy, where there are at least three hundred known varieties and they have been a staple food for centuries; they are even milled into bread flour.

All imported chestnuts have been steamed or boiled before shipping, but they must be reheated to loosen their shells. Make an X in the outer shell, or cut a circle around the crown to keep the nuts from bursting, then roast for 10 minutes in a medium oven or cook for 10 to 20 minutes in boiling water, and both the inner and outer shells should peel right off. Lift them out of the water one at a time so the others will stay warm; if you let them cool off, the skins will be just as stubborn as they were before.

Leeks are easier to digest than the rest of their onion cousins and have been a European staple for hundreds of years, but they have only recently become readily available in this country. They are still expensive, but as they become more popular and more widely cultivated that situation is changing. If you buy them with their tops still on and a bit of earth still clinging to them, they will probably be fresher than if they are neatly trimmed in a package.

Because earth is mounded up around them as they grow to keep them white and tender, leeks are inevitably gritty, so they should be thoroughly washed. Cut the tops off carefully, keeping as much of the white and yellowish parts as possible, and save the tenderest of the green leaves to use in stock. Cut the roots off, halve the leeks lengthwise, and fan the leaves under running water. If you want to cook them whole, make a cut all the way down one side almost to the base and fan the leaves from there, then cook with the cut side down. Don't buy them if they are enormous; the centers will be woody, and they may well be from last year's crop. They are best braised by themselves, but they're also great in soups, stews, tarts, and entrées.

One of the particular pleasures of fall is the mossy forest smell of a basket of freshly gathered *mushrooms* (see chart on page 233). We have become so dependent on a reliable supply of conventional white cultivated mushrooms that it is hard to imagine cooking without them, but "wild" mushrooms of several varieties (chanterelles, cepes, shiitake, oyster mushrooms, golden oak, and enoki, for example) are now being cultivated, too, bringing a new world of richness into the market with them and making the old standby seem a bit bland in comparison. The exotic mushrooms are expensive, but remember that there are a lot of mushrooms in a pound, and most of them have such distinctive flavors that a little goes a long way.

All fresh mushrooms should be used as soon as possible after purchasing. They will keep for 6 or 7 days in the icebox if they're in a paper or cloth bag (plastic bags accumulate moisture, and the mushrooms will deteriorate rapidly). They should never be peeled, just brushed off; if you must rinse them under the tap, do so very briefly.

European pharmacies routinely put up charts showing poisonous mushrooms; we've seen them in Italy, Germany, Belgium, France, and Switzerland. It's a pity that we're a little more casual in this country, especially since recent interest in natural and exotic foods has renewed everyone's curiosity about what's out there in the woods. There are only about five lethal mushrooms in the United States, but there are plenty that can cause serious distress, and we have heard of a couple of very unpleasant incidents in the last year or so. Buy wild mushrooms only from a reputable dealer, and do not under any circumstances pick your own (except, of course, for young puffballs, which are superb sliced and sautéed in butter) without earnest and thorough study. Food gathering is fun, but poisonous mushrooms are no joke.

The two *potato* varieties most commonly asked for ("new" and "Idaho") aren't varieties at all; any freshly dug small potato is a "new" potato, and Idaho is a state—the potato grown there is Russet, and it flourishes in Maine, Nova Scotia, and the Pacific Northwest as well. Within the three categories of potatoes—high-, medium-, and low-starch—there are hundreds of varieties. Russet, or "Idaho," potatoes are the high-starch kind, whose low moisture content makes them fluffy when baked and ideal for french fries. Eastern Round Whites are an example of an all-purpose medium-starch potato, moister than Russets, that can be boiled, mashed, or fried and is often in demand for baking because less butter is needed to moisten it. Often called "new" potatoes, the small, smooth-skinned, red, low-starch Red Bliss are good boiled or in salads.

Potatoes can be stored for a few weeks at room temperature but will keep much longer in a cool, dark place; they will turn green if exposed to light, producing an alkaloid that is toxic if eaten in quantity. (The green part can be cut away, but the potato that remains will not be at its best.) Contrary to popular belief, potatoes are not fattening; the average potato contains only about 100 calories. Useless fatty calories are always added to it in the form of butter and sour cream, but the potato itself is nourishing and blameless.

Hard *winter squashes* (acorn, butternut, buttercup, Hubbard and the like), the great gift of the Indians, flourished on this continent long before the Pilgrims came. Plentiful and nourishing, they are almost as benevolent as the schmoo, which many of them resemble. They differ from their summer cousins in that their skins are always inedible, and they are harvested only when they are mature, after their skins have toughened. It takes cold autumn nights to develop their sugars and ripen them fully. All of them keep splendidly and are excellent baked or puréed or used in pies, breads, and soups. All the winter squashes are fine for cooking, but our favorite is buttercup, the homely one with the navel on the blossom end. Its golden flesh is of excellent, smooth quality and has a sweet, nutty flavor.

Unique among winter squashes, *spaghetti squash* must be boiled whole till it's tender, or cut in half and baked cut side down in ¼ inch of water. It is then split and seeded and the flesh combed out with a fork to produce long, crunchy strands that can be treated exactly like spaghetti and have very few calories; it's great stuff.

Watch it with *pumpkins*, by the way; the big ones grown for jack o'lanterns are tough and watery. They're not inedible, but they're not very good either. The smaller sugar pumpkins (they usually weigh less than 7 pounds) are grown for cooking, and they share all the virtues and versatility of the other winter squashes. To purée pumpkin for pies and breads, peel it and cut it in cubes, steam or simmer in water to cover till very tender, then drain it well and purée in a food processor or blender. Alternatively, bake large unpeeled pieces covered in the oven for 1½ hours at 375°F before scraping out the flesh and puréeing it.

There are two kinds of *sweet potatoes*: the one with the light skin and pale firm flesh that's in season in the fall, and the more common darker one with the soft orange-red flesh (referred to as a Louisiana yam) whose peak season is fall and winter but is available year-round. They're both considered "sweet" potatoes, although the white one is dry and mealy when cooked and sweet only when sugar is added; both are more nutritious than the other root vegetables, being up to 5 percent protein with substantial amounts of iron, calcium, and other minerals. The orange ones are hardy, but the whites bruise easily and should be handled with great care and eaten promptly. Both types should be kept in a cool, dark place and not refrigerated. Neither one is a real yam, although seventeenth-century slaves found the orange ones similar to the true yam of Africa (which doesn't hold a candle to a sweet potato and rarely reaches markets in this country) and named them accordingly.

There are still places where *wild rice* is harvested grain by grain from the marshes around the Great Lakes by Chippewa and Ojibway Indians in canoes, but most of it is grown commercially in rice paddies and harvested by machine. Not rice, actually, but the grain of a unique American grass, wild rice is richer in protein; it is the classic accompaniment to all kinds of game.

There are two traditional methods of cooking wild rice. The first method is to clean it by rinsing steadily in cold water, then simmering it partially covered with a little salt in lots of boiling water; as soon as the rice is puffy and the kernels are all opened, it is drained and then steamed to warm before serving. Proponents of the second method (this, we are told, is what the Indians do) insist that wild rice should never be boiled; the washed rice is covered with boiling water and allowed to stand till cool; any excess water is poured off and the process repeated three times more before the rice is drained and tossed with butter.

MUSHROOMS

COMMON NAME	SCIENTIFIC NAME	ORIGIN	PEAK SEASON	DESCRIPTION	BEST USES
CULTIVATED Common, White, Button, Field	Agaricus bisporus	Widely cultivated domestically.	Year-round	These common button mushrooms are familiar to us all. Usually snow white, sometimes fawny, with a tightly closed cap and fairly short stem. Usually 1 to 2½ inches in diameter. Mild flavor.	Soups, gravies, sauces, raw in salads, marinated, all-purpose.
ENOKI Enokidake, Enok, Velvet Stem, Snow Puff, Winter Mushroom	Flammulina velutipes	Grows wild in Japan and North America. Also cultivated in Japan and California.	Year-round	Tiny, delicate, snow white to beige, caps are about ¼ inch in diameter, with long, slender edible stems 3 to 4 inches long. Very mild flavor and crisp texture.	Stir-fry, tempura, raw in salads and sandwiches.
OYSTER Oyster Cap, Pleurottes, Chilblain	Pleurotus ostreatus	Cultivated domestically in Pennsylvania and on the West Coast, mostly on logs of poplar.	Year-round	Soft fawn to milky blue gray, cap nearly flat, roughly resembling an oyster shell or fan, generally 2 to 4 inches in diameter. Firm texture.	With roast pork, sausages, venison, and smoked meats.
SHITAKE Chinese Mushroom, Golden Oak (larger sizes)	Lentinus edodes	Grows wild and is cultivated in Japan; also in Oregon, northern California, and the northeast U.S. coast.	Year-round	Small to large caps, usually 2 to 4 inches in diameter. Mostly rusty brown with lighter patches and fissures. Stems are sometimes tough and fibrous. Meaty, beefy, earthy flavor.	Soups, sauces, gravies, stews, casseroles, sautéed, broiled, grilled.

MUSHROOMS (continued)

COMMON NAME	SCIENTIFIC NAME	ORIGIN	PEAK SEASON	DESCRIPTION	BEST USES
CAESAR's MUSHROOM	*Amanita caesarea*	Dry upland oak and pine forests of Europe, collected exclusively wild.	July–October	Considered by some to be second only to truffles in flavor and just as rare. Cap is warm sulfurous yellow-orange, stem somewhat more pale and partially covered with a light membrane.	Marinated raw, stuffed and sautéed in olive oil and butter.
CEPES King Boletus, Steinpilz, Porcini	*Boletus edulis*	Collected wild in coniferous and deciduous woods, e.g., chestnut-oak, beech in Europe and Pacific Northwest.	June–October	Generally quite large (3 to 10 inches) with a reddish-brown cap and white to creamy brown stalk, thickening at the base.	Good for prolonged cooking, e.g., stews, potatoes, risotto, sautéed with garlic and parsley, with prosciutto.
CHANTERELLES (large size), Girolles (smaller size), Pfifferling, Little Cockerel	*Chantharellus*	Collected from the wild throughout North America and Europe.	June–February	Deep golden orange, trumpet shaped, small to quite large (1 to 4 inches), deep gills with waxy margin, quite fragrant, reminiscent to many of apricots. Taste is mild to spicy-peppery.	Poultry, fish, veal. Cook slowly over low heat.
TRUFFLE, BLACK Black Périgord, Spoleto Truffle, Norcia Truffle, Truffe de Périgord	*Tuber melanosporum*	Collected from the wild in France, Italy, and other parts of Europe between 44' and 46' N. latitude. Grows underground, often in association with oaks.	Late autumn	Usually an inch or two in diameter, about the size of new potatoes, dark brown-black, slight "brainy" surface, lumpy, irregular shape, but easily recognizable. Often canned or dried.	Sautéed in dry white wine, pâté de foie gras, eggs, aspic, tartufi alla nurcina. Best cooked.

MUSHROOMS (continued)

COMMON NAME	SCIENTIFIC NAME	ORIGIN	PEAK SEASON	DESCRIPTION	BEST USES
TRUFFLE, WHITE Italian Truffle, Alba Truffle, Magnati Truffle	*Tuber magnatum*	Collected wild exclusively in Italy, in Piedmont and Emilia.	Late autumn	Generally similar to the Black Truffle, but putty colored and usually considered superior. Penetrating, unique, slightly garlic fragrance.	Very good raw, sliced thin for risotto, pasta, meats, eggs, cheese fondue, truffles parmesan.

(These mushrooms are found only in the spring.)

COMMON NAME	SCIENTIFIC NAME	ORIGIN	PEAK SEASON	DESCRIPTION	BEST USES
EARLY MOREL Wrinkled, Thimble Cap	*Verpa bohemica*	Light, sandy soils, along river valleys, Pacific Northwest.	Early spring, usually March	Very similar to Morel, but available 1 month earlier. First-time consumers should exercise moderation because some individuals are sensitive to this mushroom.	Eggs, omelets, soufflés, quiche, also gravies. Cook over low heat for only a few minutes.
MOREL Yellow Morel, Black Morel	*Morchella esculenta, Morchella elata*	Collected exclusively from the wild in Oregon, Washington, Wisconsin, and Michigan.	Spring, usually April–June	Spongy corklike caps, very short, hollow stem, earthy perfume and flavor, light brown to golden to dark cocoa brown. 2 inches wide x 2½–3½ inches long.	Eggs, cream sauces, Madeira sauces, in gravies and with beef.

NUTS

NAME	PEAK SEASON	PREPARATION AND HANDLING	BEST USED FOR
ALMONDS	June–October	Most almonds have a hard, brittle shell which is easy to crack open.	Cookies, cakes, tortes; slivered with green vegetables and savory dishes, poultry and pork.
BRAZIL NUTS	November–June	Brazils are among the most difficult to crack; their shells are tough and resilient. Use a good nutcracker.	Eating raw out of hand.
CASHEWS	All year	Cashews are always sold shelled; the shells contain an extremely irritating oil, and they must be shelled with great care.	Southern Indian cooking, hors d'oeuvres with cocktails, snacks, nut butters.
CHESTNUTS	September–November	For roasting, make a cut in the outer shell to keep nuts from bursting; they can be peeled after about 10 minutes in a medium oven or 15 to 20 minutes in simmering water.	Roasting, poultry stuffings, desserts.
HAZELNUTS	August	Easily opened with a nutcracker. The skins may be separated from the meat by blanching.	Poultry stuffing, cakes and tortes, soufflés, cookies, candy.
MACADAMIA NUTS	All year	Unshelled macadamia nuts are almost impossible to crack; they are almost always sold in jars.	Nut butters, cocktail and dessert snacks, candy, jams, soups.

NUTS (continued)

NAME	PEAK SEASON	PREPARATION AND HANDLING	BEST USED FOR
PEANUTS	August–November	Peanuts are actually not nuts but legumes, growing in pods beneath the soil. They shell easily.	Peanut butter, oil, candy, cocktail snacks, Oriental cooking.
PECANS	September–October	Easily opened with a nutcracker, they have a thin shell.	Pecan pie, cakes, candy.
PINE NUTS	Cones harvested November–March, dried till summer	Pine nuts have been removed from the cones and are ready to use.	Mediterranean cooking, especially Italian; pesto.
PISTACHIOS	June–October	The shells split when the nuts are cured and they are therefore easy to crack. Skins can be removed by blanching.	Stuffings, ice cream, pâtés; a rich complement to vintage port.
WALNUTS	September and October	Best opened along the seam with a good cracker. A nutpick may be handy. Skins may be removed by blanching.	Salads, candy, cakes, ice cream, oil.

Most commercial nuts are roasted in hydrogenated fats and are oversalted; nuts roasted at home are vastly preferable. Spread nuts on baking sheet, adding 2 to 3 tablespoons of vegetable or peanut oil for every pound of nuts. Toast slowly in preheated 300°F oven for 20 to 30 minutes or until golden brown. Brazil nuts need only 2 tablespoons of oil, and pine nuts need none at all. Nuts can also be browned in a skillet on top of the stove. Season after browning with coarse salt and cayenne pepper. Commercially packaged ground nuts lose flavor and aroma very quickly; they can easily be ground at home in a processor.

APPLES
(New England Apple-Growing Region)

APPLE	ORIGIN	HARVEST DATES	DESCRIPTION	BEST USES
RHODE ISLAND GREENING	Developed in Green's End, Rhode Island, by a tavern-keeper named Green.	September 1	A very hard, bright green apple. Briskly tart and flavorful. It has a fine-grained flesh and keeps well.	Great for all baking, especially pies, because apple slices will hold their shape. These are most often used cooked and sweetened because of their tartness.
MCINTOSH	First cultivated by John McIntosh, 1796, Ontario, Canada.	September 5	A New England tradition. Crisp, juicy, slightly tart, it is an aromatic apple. A bowl on the table will perfume a whole room.	Its sprightly flavor makes it a wonderful apple for applesauce and for most baking. It is perfect for eating and makes a very juicy pie.
SPARTAN	A cross between the McIntosh and Yellow Newtown in 1926.	September 5	A bright red apple, sweet-tart, crisp, and juicy. Limited availability in the Northeast. Good firm flesh.	Best for snacks, salads, and fruit cups.
CORTLAND	Result of scientific plant breeding between the McIntosh and Ben Davis, 1915.	September 15	Snow-white inside, skin is red with some green. It is very crisp and juicy, tart and flavorful. Flesh remains white and will not darken after slicing.	A perfect apple to eat raw, it is also suitable for pies and most baking. Gives off a lot of juice when cooked.
MACOUN	Developed by the New York State Experiment Station in 1923.	September 20	A crisp, hard apple, sprightly, aromatic, and tart-sweet. A deep almost purple color. Another old New England favorite.	It has a lively taste, perfect for snacks and salads. Makes delicious applesauce. Fine for cakes, breads, and pies.

APPLES (continued)

APPLE	ORIGIN	HARVEST DATES	DESCRIPTION	BEST USES
WEALTHY	Discovered by Peter Gideon in Excelsior, Minnesota, about 1860. Declining production and availability. Most are used commercially in processing.	September 25	Two-toned red and green, usually striped with red. Tart and spicy.	Good for applesauce and cooking but not suitable for whole baked apples.
WINESAP	Origin not recorded; believed to have been developed in New Jersey before 1800.	September 25	A deep, carmine red apple, very hard and crisp and fragrant.	A good apple for baking whole, its slices will remain firm in a pie. A good apple for cider because of its "winey" tart flavor. An excellent keeping apple.
STAYMAN	Originated as a seedling from the Winesap variety. Discovered in Kansas, 1866.	October 1	A bright red apple with purplish undertone, slightly russeted.	Good for puddings and cakes where a slightly less juicy but flavorful apple is required. Fine for applesauce and salads.
DELICIOUS-RED	Peru, Iowa, grown by Hiatt, 1872.	October 5	Dark red skin, striped or blushed with hard, juicy, sweet yellowish flesh.	Snacks and salads (used by Mr. Waldorf).
DELICIOUS-YELLOW	Mullins Farm, Clay County, Virginia, 1914.	October 5	A pale yellow-green to golden skin, sweet golden flesh.	Fine for all baking. Combine with more sour fruits (quince, rhubarb) for preserves.
JONATHAN	Jonathan was first grown in Woodstock, New York, 1800, from a seed of Esopus Spitzenburg.	October 5	Very rich-flavored, hard, slightly tart. A beautiful, bright red apple.	A good, all-purpose apple for snacks, salads, and all cooking. A poor keeper.

APPLES (continued)

APPLE	ORIGIN	HARVEST DATES	DESCRIPTION	BEST USES
EMPIRE	New York State Experiment Station, 1966. A cross between the McIntosh and Red Delicious.	October 10	A beautiful red apple, very hard, snappy, and flavorful. Has the aroma and taste of the Mac and the juice and beauty of the Red Delicious.	One of the best all-purpose apples. Perfect for snacks and salads and an excellent cooking apple.
BALDWIN	A chance seedling in 1740 on John Ball's farm in Wilmington, Massachusetts.	October 10	Once the most popular apple in the Northeast, now used mostly for commercial processing. Dull red or russeted.	Ideal for baking, sauce, and other cooking. A good cider apple. Keeps well.
NORTHERN SPY	Developed by Herman Chapin in 1800, from seeds from Salisbury, Connecticut.	October 10	Hard, moderately tart, crisp, juicy, with robust flavor. A red apple patched with green.	Highest in vitamin C of all apples, it is perfect for snacks and salads. Recommended for all cooking and baking. Keeps well.
YORK IMPERIAL	Discovered on Mr. Johnson's farm in the 1800's at York, Pennsylvania.	October 10	Creamy yellow flesh, very firm and hard, resists bruising. Has distinct lopsided appearance.	A good all-purpose apple. Great for apple rings, slices, sauce, pies, and eating. A very good keeping apple.
JONAGOLD	Raised at the New York State Experiment Station from Golden Delicious crossed with Jonathan. Introduced 1968.	October 10	A large bright yellow apple with a brilliant red flush. Hard, but fine-textured, flesh, sweet, juicy, flavorful.	A very fine apple that is excellent both for eating out of hand and culinary uses. Keeps very well.
SPIGOLD	Grown at the New York State Experiment Station from a Red Spy crossed with Golden Delicious.	October 10	Extra large with creamy white flesh that is crisp, juicy, and sweet but easily bruised.	Spigold combines the best features of both its parents and is the very best apple for pies and sauce.

APPLES (continued)

APPLE	ORIGIN	HARVEST DATES	DESCRIPTION	BEST USES
GRANNY SMITH	Believed to have originated from French Crab seeds discarded by Mrs. Thomas Smith, Ryde, Australia, around 1860.	October 15	Medium to large, bright green, sometimes with a pink blush, shiny and attractive. Flesh is greenish-white, juicy, tart, and very refreshing.	The perfect all-purpose apple, it requires a long season so is difficult to grow in New England. A welcome off-season import fresh from the Southern Hemisphere. Keeps well.
ROXBURY RUSSET	First noted in Roxbury, Massachusetts, 1649.	October 15	An old-fashioned all-purpose apple. Sweet-tart, distinctive flavor. Yellow, rough, brownish skin.	Ideal for baking, sauce, and other cooking. A good cider apple. Keeps very well.
ROME BEAUTY	First grown by Joel Gillett, Ohio, 1830.	October 20	Bright red, sometimes striped with light yellow-green. Very hard, mildly tart.	So firm—great for whole baked apples. Fair for other culinary uses, poor for eating. Keeps well.
GOLDEN RUSSET	One of the oldest varieties known, the Russet dates back to the Middle Ages.	October 20	Golden yellow with a brownish russet skin. Mildly tart with a very distinctive flavor and aroma.	An excellent all-purpose apple, important in cider making. A very good keeping apple.
MUTSU	The result of scientific plant breeding in Tokyo, Japan, in 1948. A cross between the Japanese Indo apple and the Golden Delicious.	October 20	A large golden yellow apple with sweet, yellow, juicy flesh.	A wonderful eating apple. Also good for all cooking, especially applesauce, cakes, and pies. A good keeping apple.
IDARED	Developed by Idaho Agricultural Experiment Station in 1935. A cross between the Wagener and Jonathan.	October 31	A very hard, sweet apple with a dark red skin. Flesh is white with traces of pink.	Especially good for whole baked apples, it will produce a rose-colored applesauce. Keeps well.

NOTE: Dates apply to the New England growing region. Generally, the later a variety is harvested the better its keeping qualities will be.

PEARS

VARIETY	SEASON	DESCRIPTION	COMMENTS	BEST USES
CLAPP'S FAVORITE	Early August–September	Medium to large with green to banana-yellow skin and typical bell shape. Similar to Bartlett but ripens earlier.	Has short storage life. They are disappearing from the commercial market. Still found in local orchards.	A good early pear for eating out of hand.
BARTLETT	August–December	Green to bright yellow skin, bell shape with prominent lenticels (freckles). Sweet, fine, juicy flesh with little granulations.	Ripe when color changes from green to full yellow.	Excellent for eating, cooking, and preserving.
RED BARTLETT	August–December	Identical to the yellow Bartlett in every way except color. This "sport" (as scientists call it) has bright red skin. Red sports of most of the other varieties listed are also being developed.	Very attractive fruit but some say not as flavorful as the regular Bartlett. Usually more expensive.	Excellent for eating and display.
APPLE PEAR	August–April	Looks like a large, russeted, yellow apple.	Has the firm, crisp texture of an apple with the sweet, buttery flavor of a pear.	Excellent for eating, salads, and fruit baskets.
DE VOE	October	Delicately slender with long, tapering neck. Large-size fruits, light yellow-green with slightly red blush at stem end.	A very good local pear. Not available in the commercial market because it is too delicate.	Very good eating out of hand.
SECKEL	October–December	A very small, roundish pear with thick, shiny olive-colored skin, blushed with red and bronze.	Both attractive and delicious. Makes a lovely garnish on serving platters.	Excellent eating and for cooking chutneys, preserves, and spiced conserves.

PEARS (continued)

VARIETY	SEASON	DESCRIPTION	COMMENTS	BEST USES
COMICE	October–March	One of the largest pears, bell-shaped, rotund. Green skin often rough and mottled, turning yellowish when ripe.	Very juicy, fine-textured, melting flesh with a nutty, buttery flavor. Very aromatic and sweet.	Considered the finest eating pear.
BOSC	October–June	Long, tapering neck. Skin starts green then turns yellow-brown. Eastern Bosc are completely russeted; fruit from the Northwest are lightly russeted.	Ivory flesh is nicely crisp and crunchy if slightly underripe and smooth when ripe.	An excellent eating pear and for all cooking.
ANJOU	October–June	Medium to large, plump, roundish grass green, sometimes with a rosy blush. Looks like a green Bartlett.	This pear is the favorite of supermarkets because it keeps well and does not bruise easily. It is uninteresting, however, and lacks flavor.	So-so for eating. Fair for cooking.
FORELLE	November–March	Small to medium-sized roundish fruit. Yellowish-green color with burgundy red blushy freckles or streaking. Smooth, white flesh.	A pretty pear for holiday fruit bowls. Best with other sweeter pears or fruit because it has a slightly astringent flavor.	Good in fruit salads or cooking.
PACKHAM TRIUMPH	March–July	A close relative to and looks exactly like our Bartlett. Imported during our spring and summer from the Southern Hemisphere—Chile, Australia, New Zealand, and South Africa, along with a Bosc variety.	A dependable fruit almost as good as the Bartlett and gives us a long pear season.	Very good eaten out of hand and for all cooking.

A ripening trick: Place in a brown paper bag at room temperature with a ripe apple. The apple provides extra ethylene to speed ripening.

Fall Menus

THERE'S a pause in October, and then the world slides pell-mell toward Thanksgiving and Christmas. Our fall menus offer feasts and smaller events to celebrate the turning season.

FIRST COLD NIGHT DINNER

It's cold tonight—there'll be frost on the grass in the morning. Here's an autumn dinner for the first night you're glad to be indoors. Pears make a nice combination of sweet and savory with the pork chops.

MUSHROOM-CLAM STEW   (*247*)

GINGERED PEAR GRILLED PORK CHOPS   (*279*)

CHEESE BAKED TOMATOES   (*281*)

CIDER APPLE PIE   (*299*)

THANKSGIVING FEAST

A change-of-pace Thanksgiving menu that is still traditional; our fore-bears found ducks as plentiful as turkeys. Pumpkin cheesecake is a spicy variation on an old theme.

SQUASH BISQUE *(250)*

ROAST DUCK WITH APPLES *(278)*

DUCHESSE SWEET POTATOES *(284)*

GLAZED CHESTNUTS *(287)*

BROCCOLI BRAISED IN WHITE WINE *(287)*

PUMPKIN PECAN PIE *(308)*

OR THANKSGIVING PUMPKIN CHEESECAKE *(309)*

HOLIDAY WEEKEND SUPPER

Thanksgiving is over, but the house is still full. Light the fire on Saturday night and serve a simple, elegant supper on a table by the hearth. Fresh cider is a natural for the children—or for everybody.

CROÛTE LANDAISE *(252)*

CALIFORNIA SALAD *(256)*

APPLE CIDER SORBET *(300)*

BUSY WEEKDAY DINNER

Days get dizzy, and work (and homework) seems endless, but don't cut corners—dinner is still important. None of this takes much time, and it will cheer everybody up a lot.

CHICKEN BREASTS PALACE *(276)*

SPAGHETTI SQUASH WITH LIME AND BASIL *(286)*

GREEN SALAD WITH GREEK DRESSING *(266)*

APPLE PANDOWDY *(296)*

QUICKIE

Anybody who expects to spend Saturday at Bloomingdale's would do well to prepare this meal in the morning and put it all together while the rice is cooking.

SHRIMP AND CRAB CREOLE *(273)*

STEAMED RICE *(20)*

APPLE OMELET *(297)*

FOOTBALL FARE FOR THE TUBE SET

In more households than anyone cares to admit everything is on hold during football season. But even diehards need nourishment, and this pasta is so pretty it may even seduce them from the tube to the table.

PASTA WITH LEEKS *(288)*

GREEN SALAD WITH ANCHOVY DRESSING *(265)*

PEAR BETTY *(301)*

ANNIVERSARY LUNCH

Here's a lovely light lunch to celebrate. What? Years at the job? Years in the neighborhood? Weeks since the hurricane? There's always something.

TOMATO SOUFFLÉ *(282)*

TARRAGON PEARS *(259)*

GRAPEFRUIT CUSTARD PIE *(306)*

RAINY WEATHER BRUNCH

Prescription for a gloomy Sunday: a bright, warm brunch, to be served with Bloody Marys.

APPLES STUFFED WITH HAM *(274)*

SPINACH AU GRATIN *(290)*

HAY DAY'S WHOLE MEAL BREAD *(314)*

FROZEN PUMPKIN MOUSSE *(309)*

Fall Recipes

MUSHROOM-CLAM STEW

This creamy variation on oyster stew gets a lot of character from the exotic mushrooms. Served with bread, salad, and a glass of white wine, it's a whole meal.

SERVES 4

2 tablespoons butter
2 tablespoons minced onion
2 tablespoons minced celery
1 clove garlic, minced
½ pound chanterelles, cepes, or morels, washed, dried, and cut up if very large
1 dozen fresh chowder clams, washed, drained, and chopped (reserve liquid)
¼ cup dry white wine
1 cup strained clam liquid
1¼ cups half and half

Salt and freshly ground black pepper to taste
1 tablespoon butter
Celery leaves for garnish

Melt the 2 tablespoons of butter in a heavy saucepan, add the onion and celery, and simmer 3 to 4 minutes until transparent. Add the garlic and the mushrooms. Sauté 4 or 5 minutes, shaking the pan from time to time. Add clams, wine, and clam juice. Simmer 3 minutes. Add half and half. Check seasonings and add salt and pepper to taste.

Heat for 4 or 5 minutes without boiling. Add 1 tablespoon of butter. Stir and serve very hot, garnished with celery leaves.

If large chowder clams are not available, use 18 cherrystone clams.

SOUPE AU PISTOU

This is a classic hearty French soup, redolent with garlic. The pistou is a French cousin of pesto, but without the pine nuts.

SERVES 8

1 pound dry white beans
¼ pound dry kidney beans
8 cups chicken broth (see page 8)
Salt and freshly ground black pepper to taste
¼ pound fresh green beans, cut in ½-inch pieces
3 large potatoes, diced
3 small zucchini, diced
2 carrots, sliced
3 large cloves garlic
⅓ cup fresh basil leaves
¼ cup grated Gruyère or Parmesan cheese
⅓ cup olive oil
2 ounces very thin dried spaghetti, broken into 1-inch lengths
Freshly grated Gruyère and Parmesan cheese

Soak dry beans overnight. Drain. Place beans in a heavy kettle. Add the broth, salt, pepper, and vegetables. Simmer gently for at least 1 hour, until the beans are very tender.

While the soup is cooking, drop garlic cloves, one at a time, into the bowl of a food processor. Add the basil and cheese. Add olive oil in a thin stream until mixture is thick and creamy.

Stir spaghetti into finished soup and simmer 10 minutes longer. Stir garlic and cheese paste into the soup and serve at once. Pass extra grated cheese and lots of crusty French bread.

CREAM OF WALNUT SOUP

Nuts can be much more widely used in cooking than many people realize. They add protein and rich flavor to soups and main dishes.

SERVES 4

1½ cups walnuts (broken pieces but not chopped)
3 cups well-seasoned chicken broth (see page 8)
2 cloves garlic
½ cup dry white wine
1 cup heavy cream
Salt and freshly ground black pepper to taste
3 scallions, well washed and the white parts finely sliced

Put walnuts and 2 cups broth into the bowl of a food processor. Process until smooth. Drop in garlic cloves with processor running and process until puréed. Strain into a saucepan, pressing to obtain as much liquid as possible. Discard the pulp.

Add wine and heat the soup to boiling. Simmer for 10 minutes. Add cream and season well with salt and pepper. Simmer for 20 minutes. Serve very hot, garnished with sliced scallions.

SQUASH BISQUE

Small and convenient acorn squash is good for this recipe; we
like its definite flavor.

SERVES 6

3 tablespoons butter
2 large onions, minced
2 carrots, minced
Salt and freshly ground black pepper to taste
2 medium potatoes, washed and cubed (but not peeled)
2 acorn squash, peeled, seeded, and cubed
4 cups well-seasoned chicken broth (see page 8)
1 cup heavy cream
Tabasco to taste
1 tablespoon butter

Melt the 3 tablespoons of butter in a heavy kettle. Add onions, carrots,
and salt and pepper. Cover and simmer gently for about 10 minutes. Add
potatoes, squash, and chicken broth and simmer for 30 minutes, or until vegetables are very tender.

Purée soup in a food processor, adding cream. Return to the kettle and
season with Tabasco. Heat thoroughly. Finish with 1 tablespoon of butter
beaten into the hot soup.

PORK AND APPLE TERRINE

Plan ahead for tailgate picnics. This is an easy pâté to make, and
if it is tightly covered, it will keep well for 2 or 3 days in the icebox.
Serve it with French bread, cornichons, and spicy mustard.

MAKES 1 TERRINE

*¾ pound lean pork (2 thick loin chops do well), coarsely chopped in the food
processor*
¼ pound bacon, finely diced

1 small tart apple, peeled, cored, and minced
1 small onion, finely minced
6 fresh sage leaves, chopped, or 1 teaspoon dried sage
1 teaspoon dried oregano
Salt and freshly ground black pepper to taste

Preheat the oven to 375°F.

Mix together pork, bacon, apple, onion, sage, and oregano. Season well with salt and pepper. Press into a 1-pound earthenware or china terrine. Cover and bake at 375°F for 2 hours. Remove from the oven and weight with a 2-pound can or a foil-covered brick until cool. Turn out just before serving.

Do not use a metal terrine.

APPLES AND CHEESE

This is an unusual way to start a company dinner. The leftover apple can be used for making applesauce or added to a fruit salad.

SERVES 6

3 large apples (Rome Beauty, Granny Smith, or McIntosh)
6 Crottins de Chavignol (goat cheese) or rounds cut from a log of Ste. Maure
  or similar cheese, lightly peeled if the crust is too hard
Whole fresh basil leaves
3 tablespoons extra-virgin olive oil
6 large lettuce leaves, washed and dried
Fresh roasted walnuts, for garnish

Preheat the oven to 350°F.

Wash the apples. Cut 2 rounds out of each apple, as if you were cutting toast rounds. Arrange them on a baking sheet. Top each one with a small cheese. Place 1 or 2 leaves of basil on each cheese and drizzle a little olive oil over each.

Bake at 350°F for 20 minutes. The cheese should be melted or very soft. Serve hot on a large lettuce leaf, topped with freshly roasted walnuts.

WALNUT SPREAD

Serve this spread on thin slices of pumpernickel raisin bread, or use it as a cocktail spread with crackers and fresh vegetables.

MAKES ABOUT 1 CUP

¼ pound (1 stick) butter, softened
½ cup blue cheese or Roquefort, softened
3 tablespoons Cognac, Armagnac, or bourbon
¼ cup finely chopped walnuts

Combine the butter, cheese, and brandy or bourbon in a food processor and process until smooth. Stir in walnuts. Allow to rest at least 2 hours, or, even better, overnight.

CROÛTE LANDAISE

Like foie gras and other marvels, Croûte Landaise comes from the rich Lande region of southern France. It makes a superb company lunch.

SERVES 6

6 thick slices of white bread, crusts removed and the centers
  slightly hollowed to create a shallow cup
4 tablespoons butter, melted
⅔ cup heavy cream

Salt and freshly ground black pepper
Pinch of nutmeg
1 tablespoon cornstarch, softened in
  1 tablespoon white port wine
½ pound fresh mushrooms, very thinly sliced, sautéed in
  2 tablespoons butter
1 tablespoon cornstarch blended with
  ¾ cup heavy cream
Salt and freshly ground black pepper to taste
1 egg yolk
½ cup bread crumbs
½ cup freshly grated Parmesan cheese
6 thick slices foie gras

Preheat the oven to 200°F.

Brush the bread cups well with melted butter. Place them on a cookie sheet and bake at 200°F until golden brown. Remove from the oven and set aside.

Heat the cream with salt, pepper, and nutmeg until bubbles form around the edges. Add 1 tablespoon cornstarch and port and simmer gently until thickened. Add mushrooms and keep warm. Blend the second tablespoon of cornstarch with the cream in a small saucepan and simmer gently until thickened. Season well with salt and pepper and beat in the egg yolk. Keep warm, but do not boil.

Combine bread crumbs and cheese.

Preheat the broiler.

Fill the bread cups with the mushroom mixture. Top each with a slice of foie gras. Spread 2 tablespoons of cream sauce over each cup and sprinkle generously with cheese and crumb mixture. Broil just until bubbly and golden brown. Serve very hot.

HAY DAY'S HARVEST SALAD

We sell a lot of this salad in the autumn; we designed it in colors that reminded us of fall, but it's good with any color of pasta. Don't make it if you can't get fresh dill; as far as we're concerned, the fresh and dried kinds are *never* interchangeable.

[253]

SERVES 6 TO 8

1½ cups Homemade Mayonnaise (see page 18)
¾ cup chicken broth, reduced to ¼ cup chicken broth (see page 8)
¼ cup chopped fresh dill
1 pound tomato pasta, cooked
3 stalks celery, sliced thickly
½ pint cherry tomatoes, cut in half
½ pound zucchini, cut in half, julienned
⅓ pound mushrooms, quartered
⅓ pound broccoli fleurettes, blanched in boiling water for 3 minutes
⅓ pound carrots, julienned, blanched in boiling water for 3 minutes
½ red pepper, cut in triangles
½ green pepper, cut in triangles
Salt to taste

Mix together mayonnaise, broth, and fresh dill. Toss dressing with remaining ingredients. Chill and serve.

GOAT CHEESE SALAD

Here is a California version of our Italian Caprese Salad (Mozzarella and Tomato Salad, p. 57).

SERVES 4

4 large tomatoes, cut into thick slices
*1 pound goat cheese from a large log such as Boucheron or Lezay, cut in
    ¼-inch slices*
¼ cup whole fresh basil leaves
4 tablespoons sun-dried tomatoes, cut into strips
1 teaspoon Dijon mustard
3 tablespoons oregano vinegar
Salt and freshly ground black pepper to taste
3 tablespoons olive oil
6 tablespoons safflower oil, or other very delicate salad oil

On a platter or large plate, overlap slices of tomato with rounds of goat cheese. Slip a fresh basil leaf between each slice. Scatter the dried tomato strips over the salad.

Beat together the mustard, vinegar, salt, pepper, and oils. Sprinkle the vinaigrette over the salad, let stand 15 minutes, and serve.

SAUCY MUSHROOM SALAD

Look for the whitest, plumpest mushrooms you can find, and just brush them off before slicing, so they'll stay light and crisp—they get awfully watery if they're washed. Serve this salad with cheddar cheese and thick slices of homemade bread for a good summer lunch.

SERVES 6

1 pound fresh mushrooms, cleaned but not washed, and sliced
2 tablespoons minced onion
1 clove garlic, minced
1 tomato, peeled, seeded, and finely chopped
1 large head leaf lettuce, washed, dried, and torn into serving pieces
½ cup olive oil
1 tablespoon walnut oil
¼ cup rice vinegar
Salt and freshly ground black pepper to taste
2 tablespoons chopped walnuts

Toss the mushrooms, onion, garlic, tomato, and lettuce in a serving bowl. Beat together olive oil, walnut oil, rice vinegar, salt, and pepper. Pour over salad and toss again.

Garnish with toasted walnuts.

SOUTHERN CUCUMBER SALAD

This light, tart salad is great with fried chicken or smothered pork chops. Serve in a glass relish dish.

SERVES 4

3 small cucumbers, peeled, cut in half, seeded, and thinly sliced
1 tablespoon salt
1 small onion, chopped finely
⅓ cup sugar
⅔ cup champagne vinegar or white wine vinegar
1 teaspoon finely chopped coriander
Freshly ground black pepper

Place cucumber slices in a deep bowl. Sprinkle with salt and toss well. Weight the cucumber slices with a plate and a weight. Allow to stand in the icebox for 1 hour. Drain thoroughly and dry with paper towels.

In a small bowl, mix onion and sugar with the vinegar until the sugar is completely dissolved. Add to cucumbers and sprinkle with coriander and pepper. Chill.

CALIFORNIA SALAD

Here is a version of the old-fashioned wilted salad. It bridges the seasons—combining the last bounty of the summer with the first of the fall—and the sweet bite of the oranges is a counterpoint for the bacon and lemon.

SERVES 4

2 large heads leaf lettuce, any combination
1 large orange, peeled and sectioned
Salt and freshly ground black pepper to taste
2 tablespoons sugar
3 tablespoons lemon juice
2 bunches scallions, thinly sliced
4 slices bacon, cut into ½-inch pieces

Tear lettuce into bite-sized pieces. Toss in a salad bowl and let stand at room temperature for 30 minutes. Toss with orange slices. Mix salt, pepper, sugar, and lemon juice with scallions. Toss with lettuce.

Cook bacon until crisp. Pour bacon and fat over salad. Toss lightly and serve at once.

APPLE AND POTATO SALAD

This crunchy autumn salad can be made ahead of time and kept in the icebox.

SERVES 8

2½ pounds red new potatoes, boiled and quartered
⅓ cup lemon juice
¼ cup olive oil
Salt to taste
1 teaspoon dried thyme leaves, or 1 tablespoon fresh thyme
½ cup Homemade Mayonnaise (see page 18)
⅓ cup plain yoghurt
1 large red apple (Rome Beauty, Empire, or similar variety), quartered, cored, and thinly sliced
2 ounces blue cheese, crumbled
Leaf lettuce
Fresh parsley for garnish

Toss the potatoes with lemon juice, oil, and salt to taste. Add thyme, toss again, and let stand for several hours, or overnight.

Just before serving, combine the mayonnaise and yoghurt, stirring until smooth. Spoon over the potatoes and toss. Add the apple slices and cheese and toss gently.

Serve in a lettuce-lined salad bowl, garnished with fresh parsley.

SPECIAL SALAD

Like many other cheeses, goat cheese is great in cooking. Here it is marinated and melted for a tangy complement to tomatoes. This recipe is really in two parts; the first must be finished at least 48 hours before the dish is to be served.

SERVES 4

2 Crottins de Chavignol (chèvre) cheese
½ cup fresh, well-flavored olive oil
1 clove garlic, minced
2 tablespoons each fresh basil, tarragon, and thyme leaves
2 large, very ripe tomatoes
3 tablespoons of the marinating oil
Leaf lettuce
Fresh basil
Fresh thyme
Freshly ground black pepper

Place cheeses in a small plastic, glass, or china container. Mix together with the olive oil, garlic, and herbs. Pour the oil mixture over the cheeses and allow to marinate at least 48 hours; several days to a week is preferable.

Drain cheeses, reserving the marinade. Cut them in half horizontally. Brush with the olive oil marinade. Arrange tomato slices in groups of three in an overlapping pattern on a lightly greased baking sheet. Top each trio of slices with half a cheese. Drizzle with a little more of the olive oil marinade. Broil for 3 to 4 minutes, or until the cheese begins to melt. Transfer the tomatoes and cheese to a bed of leaf lettuce. Serve at once, garnished with fresh herbs and freshly ground black pepper.

Use the remaining marinade for making a tasty vinaigrette salad dressing.

HAM AND PEAR SALAD

An unusual and delicious combination of salty ham and sweet pears.

SERVES 4

3 pears, peeled, cored, and sliced
Juice of 1 lemon
¼ pound salty baked ham, finely diced or ground
1 bunch scallions, the white parts very finely sliced
½ cup creamed cottage cheese
¼ cup sour cream
Salt and freshly ground black pepper to taste
1 head leaf lettuce, washed and dried
Fresh mint

Toss the pear slices in lemon juice. Mix ham and scallion slices with cottage cheese and sour cream. Season with salt and pepper. Pile the cheese mixture in the center of a lettuce-lined serving platter. Arrange pear slices around the cheese. Garnish with fresh mint.

TARRAGON PEARS

You don't usually think of putting tarragon with pears, but the combination works beautifully. Serve this salad with grilled cheese sandwiches for a super lunch.

SERVES 4

⅓ cup sour cream
1 tablespoon tarragon mustard
1 tablespoon tarragon vinegar
½ teaspoon fresh tarragon
Salt and freshly ground black pepper to taste
4 ripe but firm pears, peeled, cored, and thinly sliced
Leaf lettuce
¼ cup chopped pecans

Beat together sour cream and mustard. Beat in vinegar, fresh tarragon, salt, and pepper. Toss pear slices gently with dressing. Garnish a serving platter with lettuce leaves and mound the pear slices in the center. Top each serving with chopped pecans.

RICE SALAD WITH FENNEL

This salad would go easily to a tailgate picnic; it is an excellent accompaniment for cold poached fish or cold slices of roast beef or veal.

SERVES 6

2 cups cooked rice (see page 20)
2 bulbs fennel, peeled and sliced very thin
1 bunch scallions, the white part thinly sliced
1 tablespoon anisette
1 tablespoon Dijon mustard
⅔ cup Homemade Mayonnaise (see page 18)
Salt and freshly ground black pepper to taste
Tabasco to taste
3 hard-boiled eggs, quartered
¾ cup oil-cured black olives, pitted
2 tomatoes, quartered
Chopped parsley

Mix rice, fennel, and scallions in a large salad bowl. Beat anisette and mustard into the mayonnaise and add to salad. Toss well. Season to taste with salt and pepper. Add Tabasco if a sharper taste is desired. Refrigerate for several hours.

Garnish with eggs, olives, and tomato wedges and sprinkle with chopped parsley.

HAY DAY'S BROWN RICE SALAD À LA WALDORF

This was one of our first recipes, evolved because Alex wanted a fall salad for apple season; we added bright Red Delicious apples to our brown rice salad recipe, and we've been selling it ever since. Although we buy brown rice organically grown from Walnut Acres, it can be found in any supermarket; it takes longer to cook, but we like its flavor and firmer texture, which holds up well in salads. Don't overcook it.

SERVES 6

1 cup safflower oil
½ cup red wine vinegar
Salt and freshly ground black pepper to taste
1 cup cooked brown rice
2 tablespoons scallions, chopped
2 medium red-skinned apples, unpeeled, cut into ¼- to ½-inch dice
2 tablespoons parsley, chopped finely
3 stalks celery, diced
½ cup raisins
1 cup walnuts, coarsely chopped

Whisk oil, vinegar, salt, and pepper together and add to salad ingredients while rice is still warm. Marinate at least one hour before serving.

HAY DAY'S MARINATED BRUSSELS SPROUTS

This fall best-seller is incredibly easy to prepare. Herbes de Provence are marketed under that name by a number of companies; the mixture, which includes lavender and fennel, is more or less standard. Use red wine vinegar if sherry vinegar isn't available.

SERVES 4 TO 6

2 tablespoons sherry wine vinegar
1 teaspoon Dijon mustard
¼ teaspoon salt
½ teaspoon freshly ground black pepper
1 teaspoon herbes de Provence
2 tablespoons extra-virgin olive oil
¼ cup safflower oil

2 pints Brussels sprouts, trimmed, steamed but still crisp and green
2 plum tomatoes, seeded and cut into ½-inch pieces
⅓ cup chopped parsley

Blend vinegar, mustard, salt, pepper, and herbs in a bowl. Slowly whisk in oils. Mix with salad ingredients.

HAY DAY'S CARROT, CABBAGE, AND CELERY ROOT SALAD

You could call this Hay Day's version of coleslaw, but it's more glamorous than that. We love the color combination for fall or winter and the vinaigrette is not unlike our own honey vinaigrette that we sell in the store.

SERVES 8 TO 10

1 pound carrots, ends cut off and peeled
1 pound celery root, peeled (zucchini or jicama could be substituted)
½ head red cabbage
½ cup currants
3 tablespoons Dijon mustard

½ cup red wine vinegar
⅓ cup honey
1 teaspoon salt
2 cups safflower oil

Grate carrots and celery root with the smallest julienne blade of a food processor. Slice red cabbage with the finest slicing blade. Assemble carrots, celery root, cabbage, and currants in a bowl.

Blend mustard, vinegar, honey, and salt in a food processor. Gradually add oil. Pour over the salad ingredients and toss.

DILL SAUCE

This is a natural with cold poached fish, but it is also great with cold meats and pâtés.

MAKES ABOUT 1½ CUPS

1 cup Homemade Mayonnaise (see page 18)
1 tablespoon Dijon mustard
2 tablespoons dill or tarragon vinegar
Pinch of salt
¼ cup minced sweet pickles or cornichons
½ teaspoon Worcestershire sauce
Tabasco to taste
1 teaspoon chopped fresh parsley
3 tablespoons chopped fresh dill

Beat together all ingredients. Refrigerate, covered, for several hours.

CRANBERRY SAUCE

We are always amazed when people buy cranberry sauce in cans. Making it from fresh berries is almost effortless—and a lot tastier.

MAKES 3 CUPS

2 pounds cranberries, washed and picked over
¼ cup water
1½ cups sugar
½ cup white wine

Place cranberries in a heavy 2-quart saucepan. Add water, sugar, and wine. Simmer until the berries begin to pop. Reduce heat and simmer 5 minutes longer. Pour sauce into a bowl and chill until set.

CIDER APPLESAUCE

The fresh cider intensifies the flavor of the sauce and makes it a rich accompaniment for game or roast poultry, spareribs or roast pork.

MAKES ABOUT 3 CUPS

6 large cooking apples, peeled, cored, and cut into chunks
5 cups cider, reduced by boiling to 2½ cups
About 3 tablespoons sugar, to taste
2 tablespoons butter
1 teaspoon cinnamon

Add apples to reduced cider and gently simmer, covered, for about 45 minutes, stirring from time to time to keep from burning. Add sugar, butter, and cinnamon. Stir well and simmer for another minute or two. Mash with a fork or potato masher. This applesauce should be chunky. If there is too much liquid, simmer until thick, being careful not to let it burn.

SPICY PICKLED PEARS

This sweet and sour combination goes exceptionally well with a good, coarse country pâté.

4 pounds small, ripe Seckel pears (firm but not too hard)
1 tablespoon each whole allspice, cloves, and coriander seed
2 one-inch cinnamon sticks
2½ cups white wine vinegar
4 cups sugar

Wash the pears. Tie spices in cheesecloth. Bring the vinegar and sugar to a boil. Add the bag of spices. Add the whole pears and simmer very gently until tender.

Carefully lift out the pears with a slotted spoon and pack into hot sterilized jars. Remove spice bag and discard. Boil the vinegar for a few minutes to reduce it to a thick syrup. Pour over fruit and seal. Process jars in a boiling water bath for 15 minutes.

Crabapples can be prepared the same way, but cool the apples in the liquid overnight. Pack cold apples in hot jars and then boil the syrup until thick. Process the same way.

ANCHOVY SALAD DRESSING

Serve this dressing over a classic spinach, mushroom, and bacon salad, decorated with pieces of hard-cooked egg.

MAKES ABOUT ½ CUP

1 small can flat anchovy fillets, rinsed and drained
4 tablespoons olive oil
1 teaspoon sesame oil
2 tablespoons Dijon or Chinese mustard
2 tablespoons red wine vinegar
2 teaspoons capers

In a saucepan heat anchovies and oils over low heat for several minutes, stirring until anchovies dissolve. Turn off heat and beat in mustard, vinegar, and capers. Cool to room temperature.

GERMAN SALAD DRESSING

This is a good dressing for potato salad, mixed greens, or cold vegetables.

MAKES ABOUT ½ CUP

½ small onion, cut up
2 tablespoons parsley
2 tablespoons chives, chopped
2 tablespoons boiling water
2 tablespoons tarragon vinegar
1 tablespoon whole-grain mustard
Salt and freshly ground black pepper to taste
½ cup corn oil

Combine all ingredients, except oil, in a blender. Add the oil in a thin stream and blend just until smooth.

GREEK DRESSING

Serve this dressing with steamed vegetables that have been cooled to room temperature, or over small boiled new potatoes.

MAKES ABOUT ½ CUP

2 to 3 tablespoons lemon juice
2 tablespoons fresh thyme
1 tablespoon fresh dill
3 scallions, finely chopped
1 garlic clove, minced
½ cup extra-virgin olive oil
Salt and freshly ground black pepper to taste

Combine all ingredients in a blender. Blend for 10 seconds.

APPLE-TOMATO KETCHUP

The word can be kechup, catsup, or ketchup. Derived from the Malay *kechap*, it was originally a spiced fish sauce, but it has come to mean any of a number of condiments, many of them made with tomatoes. This is a great way to preserve the last of the summer crop.

MAKES ABOUT 6 PINTS

10 large apples, cored and chopped
10 large, ripe tomatoes, chopped
3 large onions, peeled and minced
¼ cup mustard seed
4 cups white vinegar
2 cups brown sugar
½ cup salt
½ red pepper, minced
1 cup raisins, plumped in rum and chopped
1 tablespoon turmeric
2 ounces fresh ginger, minced
1 tablespoon dry mustard

Boil apples, tomatoes, onions, mustard seed, and vinegar together until the fruit is very tender. Pour the mixture into a food processor, 2 cups at a time, and process until smooth. Add remaining ingredients to the purée. Simmer for 2 hours, stirring frequently. Do not boil.

Ladle into hot sterilized jars and seal immediately.

WILD RICE AND PECAN STUFFING FOR ROAST PHEASANT

Definitely a special event.

MAKES ENOUGH FOR 2 PHEASANTS

¼ pound (1 stick) butter
3 large yellow onions, chopped

> *1 cup chopped celery*
> *3 cloves garlic, finely minced*
> *¼ pound mushrooms, sliced*
> *¼ cup dry white wine*
> *3 cups cooked wild rice (see page 232)*
> *1 cup pecans, coarsely chopped*
> *¼ cup freshly chopped parsley*
> *2 tablespoons fresh sage*
> *2 tablespoons fresh thyme*

Melt the butter in a heavy skillet. Sauté onion, celery, and garlic until the vegetables are transparent. Add the mushrooms and wine. Add the wild rice, pecans, and herbs. Toss lightly. Cool completely and stuff the pheasants.

APPLE, ONION, AND CRANBERRY DRESSING

An unusual sweet and savory combination.

MAKES ENOUGH TO STUFF A 12- TO 15-POUND TURKEY

> *1 cup cranberries, boiled in ½ cup water until they begin to pop*
> *8 cups soft bread crumbs*
> *1½ sticks butter*
> *2 large yellow onions, chopped*
> *3 cloves garlic, minced (optional)*
> *½ cup chopped celery*
> *4 tart apples, cored and diced*
> *2 teaspoons salt*
> *1 tablespoon fresh sage, chopped*

Drain cranberries. Put cranberries and bread crumbs in a large bowl. Melt the butter in a heavy skillet. Sauté the onions, garlic, celery, and apples just until the vegetables are transparent, about 5 minutes.

Pour the vegetables into the cranberry and bread crumb mixture and toss with salt and sage.

SPAGHETTI WITH WALNUTS

This makes a very rich appetizer, so serve small portions.

SERVES 6

1 cup walnuts
5 garlic cloves, peeled
⅓ cup olive oil
1 pound fresh spaghetti (spinach pasta is exceptionally nice)
3 tablespoons chopped parsley
Pinch of nutmeg
4 tablespoons grated Parmesan cheese
Walnut halves for garnish
Freshly ground black pepper

Put walnuts in the bowl of a food processor. Process 20 seconds, until just well mixed. Turn on processor and drop in garlic cloves one at a time while the processor is running. Stop the processor as soon as the last garlic clove is added. Heat the oil in a large skillet. Add the walnut-garlic mixture and brown slightly.

Cook the spaghetti in boiling water for 2 minutes. Drain and turn into a serving dish. Stir the parsley into nut mixture. Turn hot nut mixture into pasta and toss well. Sprinkle with nutmeg and cheese. Sprinkle walnut halves over the top and serve very hot with freshly ground black pepper.

TORTELLI WITH PUMPKIN

Tortelli, like ravioli, are easy to form from sheets of fresh pasta. The flavor of whole wheat pasta goes well with pumpkin.

SERVES 6

3 pounds fresh sugar pumpkin, peeled and sliced
½ cup grated Parmesan cheese
Salt to taste
Nutmeg to taste

1 pound flat pasta sheets
¼ pound (1 stick) butter, melted
½ cup grated Parmesan cheese

Preheat the oven to 350°F.

Bake the pumpkin at 350°F until soft. Mash with ½ cup Parmesan cheese, salt, and nutmeg. Cut the pasta into rounds about 3 inches in diameter with a biscuit cutter. Put a tablespoon of the pumpkin mixture on each circle. Dampen the edges with water and fold the circles in half, like turnovers. Press the edges together well with the tines of a fork. Dry for several minutes on a rack, then cook in boiling water until just tender, about 3 minutes. Drain well.

Toss immediately with melted butter and Parmesan cheese, or toss with the Walnut Sauce in preceding recipe.

COUNTRY LASAGNE

A rustic version of classic lasagne, this is even better made ahead of time and reheated.

SERVES 6

2 tablespoons butter
1 small carrot, finely chopped

2 onions, thinly sliced
2 cloves garlic, minced
1 tablespoon chopped parsley
1 dried chili pepper, broken into pieces
1 pound lean pork shoulder, ground
¾ cup dry white wine
2 cups crushed tomatoes, or
*   6 large tomatoes, peeled, seeded, and finely chopped*
Salt and freshly ground black pepper to taste
½ pound hot pork sausage
1 pound fresh flat pasta sheets, cut into 2-inch strips
1 cup fresh ricotta cheese
4 tablespoons grated Parmesan cheese
6 ounces mozzarella cheese, grated

Melt butter and brown carrot, onions, garlic, and parsley. Add the chili pepper. Add the pork. Lower the heat and brown meat thoroughly. Add wine, boil until it evaporates, and then add tomatoes. Season with salt and pepper and simmer gently until pork is tender.

Preheat the oven to 350°F.

Twenty minutes before the pork is done (it should simmer a total of about 1 hour), add the sausage. Cook pasta, drain, and layer in a 2-quart baking dish with meat sauce, ricotta, and Parmesan, repeating the layers until the dish is full. Top with mozzarella and bake for 30 minutes at 350°F. Let stand 15 minutes before serving.

HAY DAY'S ROTOLLO WITH FRESH TOMATO BASIL SAUCE

Helen Brody developed this from an old recipe; our version has since been widely copied by local restaurants. It was originally intended as a hot entrée, but when people began asking for it in the summer we realized it can be served at room temperature as well. It requires sheets of fresh pasta, which can be bought almost anywhere. The recipe specifies rolling from the short side, like a jelly roll, but rolling lengthwise will produce smaller slices that are nice for appetizers.

SERVES 4 TO 6

1½ pounds fresh spinach, cooked and squeezed dry, chopped fine
1 pound ricotta cheese
½ cup freshly grated Parmesan cheese
½ teaspoon nutmeg
1 egg
½ teaspoon salt
½ teaspoon freshly ground black pepper
¼ teaspoon Tabasco
2 tablespoons melted butter
Egg wash (1 egg mixed with 2 teaspoons water)
1 sheet egg, tomato, or spinach pasta (11 x 18 inches)
⅓ pound prosciutto, sliced paper thin
2 quarts chicken broth (see page 8)
2 teaspoons extra-virgin olive oil
2 tablespoons freshly grated Parmesan cheese

Combine in a bowl the spinach, ricotta, Parmesan, nutmeg, egg, salt, pepper, Tabasco, and melted butter. Brush egg wash in a 1-inch rim around a sheet of pasta. Spread spinach-cheese mixture on pasta, leaving a 1-inch border. Place prosciutto over spinach-cheese mixture and fold edges over the mixture. Start rolling from short end, jelly roll fashion, keeping edges tucked in so filling doesn't leak out. Seal end with egg wash. Wrap in cheesecloth or cotton tea towel and tie ends very tightly.

Poach roll in simmering chicken stock for 15 to 20 minutes. Remove, drain, and cool for 3 hours or overnight in refrigerator. Remove towel, brush with olive oil, and sprinkle with Parmesan. Slice ¾ inch thick and serve warm or room temperature on Fresh Tomato Basil Sauce (see below).

FRESH TOMATO BASIL SAUCE

Plum tomatoes, the basis for this recipe, are the only kind that are available fresh virtually year-round. The sauce is great with fresh pasta. In a pinch, of course, you can use drained canned tomatoes.

MAKES APPROXIMATELY 3 CUPS

2 to 3 tablespoons olive oil
2 cloves garlic, peeled and crushed once with the side of chef's knife
2 pounds fresh plum tomatoes, stems cut out, coarsely chopped
¼ to ½ cup chopped fresh basil leaves

Heat olive oil in a heavy skillet. Add garlic cloves. Cook for about 3 minutes or until golden. Remove garlic and discard. Add tomatoes to oil and cook for 5 minutes. Add basil and cook 10 to 15 minutes more. Strain out the juice. Can be used warm or cold.

SHRIMP AND CRAB CREOLE

This variation on a Creole theme is great for special family dinners as well as for company. It should be good and spicy, so be generous with the Tabasco.

SERVES 4 TO 6

1 medium yellow onion, chopped
1 green pepper, diced
1 tablespoon butter
1 tablespoon flour
½ cup dry white wine
4 large tomatoes, peeled, seeded, and chopped
½ teaspoon thyme
1 teaspoon oregano
3 tablespoons fresh parsley
1 bunch scallions, sliced thin, including 1 inch of green
Salt and freshly ground black pepper
Tabasco
1 pound small shrimp, boiled 5 minutes with 2 tablespoons of
  crab boil spices, cooled and peeled
12 ounces lump crabmeat, well picked over

Sauté the chopped onion and green pepper in butter until transparent. Sprinkle with flour and stir for 3 minutes. Stir in white wine and cook for 5 minutes. Add chopped tomatoes, thyme, oregano, parsley, and scallions. Simmer gently 5 to 10 minutes.

Season with salt, pepper, and Tabasco to taste. Stir in shrimp and crabmeat and simmer until very hot. Do not overcook.

Serve with rice and extra Tabasco for those who like it hot.

APPLES STUFFED WITH HAM

Serve these apples with an omelet and a salad for lunch, or as an accompaniment for barbecued ribs.

SERVES 4

1 cup Virginia-style baked ham, diced or ground
2 tablespoons butter
¼ cup raisins
¼ cup chopped pecans
1 tablespoon rum
3 tablespoons brown sugar
4 large red apples, such as McIntosh or Empire, unpeeled and cored, leaving a
*   large center*
Cider vinegar

Preheat the oven to 350°F.

Mix together ham, butter, raisins, pecans, rum, and brown sugar. Fill the apple cavities with the stuffing. Place apples in a buttered baking dish and bake at 350°F for 45 minutes. While the apples are baking, brush them with vinegar from time to time.

STUFFED ONIONS

These stuffed onions are great on their own as a luncheon dish, or as a side dish with grilled or roasted meats.

FALL

8 large sweet onions (if Vidalia onions are available, use them)
2 slices white bread, crusts removed and broken up
½ cup hot milk
2 tablespoons butter
½ pound ground beef
⅓ cup ground cooked ham
2 whole eggs, beaten
1 tablespoon fresh basil, finely chopped
1 tablespoon fresh parsley, chopped
Salt to taste
Freshly ground black pepper to taste
¼ cup dry bread crumbs
¼ cup freshly grated Parmesan cheese
1 cup beef stock

Preheat the oven to 350°F.

Peel the onions. Place them in a large saucepan and add water to cover. Simmer, covered, for 10 minutes. Drain well.

Soak bread in hot milk. Heat 1 tablespoon butter in a small skillet and sauté the ground beef until browned. Remove from heat. Squeeze the bread dry and add to the beef. Add ham, eggs, herbs, salt, and pepper. Combine well. Scoop out the insides of the onions, leaving about a ¼-inch-thick shell. Chop onion pulp finely and combine with meat.

Stuff the onion shells and arrange them in a buttered baking dish. Sprinkle with bread crumbs and cheese and dot with the remaining 1 tablespoon butter. Pour stock around the onions and bake at 350°F for 30 minutes. Remove from the stock, drain, and serve very hot.

FRENCH CHICKEN SALAD

Serve this salad any time of the day or year—it is ridiculously simple and incredibly good.

SERVES 4

1 tablespoon wine vinegar
1 tablespoon Dijon mustard
Salt and freshly ground black pepper to taste
1 egg yolk
½ cup fine olive oil
2 cups cold roast chicken, cubed
1 large tart apple, cored and cubed but not peeled
3 heads Belgian endive, sliced
½ cup Gruyère cheese, diced
3 scallions, thinly sliced

Beat together vinegar, mustard, salt, and pepper. Beat in the egg yolk. Beat in the olive oil a little at a time, beating until the dressing is thick and creamy.

Toss remaining ingredients gently with the dressing. Let stand 15 minutes. Serve with buttered toast.

CHICKEN BREASTS PALACE

This recipe, or a variation of it, was served some years ago at the Palace Hotel in San Francisco. It is perfect for company, because most of it can be prepared ahead of time, and exceptional when accompanied by lightly steamed fresh spinach. Be sure to use a full-flavored salty ham—Virginia, Black Forest, or Parma—that will be an interesting contrast to the delicately flavored chicken.

SERVES 4

1 tablespoon butter
2 whole boneless chicken breasts, split in half

4 slices salty Virginia-style ham
1 cup heavy cream
⅓ cup sweet white wine (such as American Chablis)
1 tablespoon butter
1 tablespoon lemon juice
Salt and freshly ground black pepper to taste
12 whole mushroom caps
1 tablespoon butter
4 slices buttered toast, crusts removed

Melt 1 tablespoon butter in a heavy skillet. Sauté the chicken breasts until just cooked through, turning once. Just before the chicken is cooked, add the ham slices. Cook until heated through. Add cream and bring to a boil. Remove the chicken and ham and set aside. Reduce the cream by half and add wine. Reduce for 1 minute longer. Finish sauce with 1 tablespoon butter and 1 tablespoon lemon juice. Season with salt and pepper, tasting first. Keep hot. Sauté mushroom caps in a separate skillet in 1 tablespoon butter.

To serve, arrange toast slices on a serving plate. Top each with a slice of ham and then a chicken breast. Arrange mushroom caps on top of chicken and cover with sauce. Serve any remaining sauce in a separate dish.

RABBIT IN CIDER

Rabbit has been unjustly neglected in this country; its mild flavor takes readily to robust seasonings. Use good, fresh cider and cream for this version, which comes originally from Normandy.

SERVES 4

1 rabbit, cut up
½ cup flour
Salt and freshly ground black pepper
2 tablespoons butter
¼ pound thick-sliced bacon, diced
1 onion, sliced
¾ cup fresh cider
1 tablespoon fresh parsley, chopped
1 tablespoon fresh thyme, chopped

Salt and freshly ground black pepper
⅓ cup heavy cream

Toss rabbit pieces in flour seasoned with salt and pepper. Melt butter in a heavy skillet. Add bacon and onion and sauté until the onion is transparent. Remove bacon and onion with a slotted spoon and reserve. Brown rabbit in the same skillet, adding more fat if needed. Add cider and bring to a boil. Stir in herbs, salt, pepper, onion, and bacon.

Cover and simmer very gently for 1 hour. Remove rabbit pieces to a heated platter and keep warm. Stir cream into the pan juices and boil hard until the sauce is reduced by one-third. Check the seasoning and add salt and pepper to taste. Serve with fresh noodles and a hot spicy mustard.

ROAST DUCK WITH APPLES

This recipe is excellent with Long Island ducklings and even better with wild duck. Be sure the duck is washed well and dried before you start the recipe. If you use wild ducks, it is best to cook them covered for the first hour so that the steam can tenderize the meat. Uncover for the last 20 or 30 minutes, or until the ducks are well browned.

SERVES 6 TO 8

2 five-pound ducks
Salt and freshly ground black pepper
2 onions, peeled and quartered
4 stalks celery, cut up
½ cup chicken broth (see page 8)
6 apples, peeled, cored, and cut in half
¾ cup cider
¾ cup applejack or Calvados

Preheat the oven to 450°F.

Dust ducks inside and out with salt and pepper. In each cavity, place one onion, quartered, and two stalks of celery, cut up. If using tame duckling, prick ducks well with a sharp fork or knife. Place them side by side in a roasting pan. Pour chicken broth around ducklings. Roast at 450°F oven for 20 minutes. Reduce to 350°F and continue roasting for at least 1 hour and 30 minutes, until tender.

While ducklings are roasting, arrange apple halves in a well-buttered baking dish. Pour cider and ½ cup applejack or Calvados over them. Bake at 350°F for 20 minutes, or until tender but not mushy.

When ducklings are ready, cut them into quarters and discard vegetables. Arrange ducks skin up on a baking sheet and broil just until skin is crisp and crackling.

Skim the fat from the roasting dish. Place pan over burner and pour in ¼ cup applejack or Calvados. Deglaze pan, scraping up all browned bits from the bottom of the pan.

Serve duck quarters surrounded by apples and sauced with pan juices.

GINGERED PEAR GRILLED PORK CHOPS

Don't put the grill away just because summer's over. The flavor of charcoal is great in chilly weather.

SERVES 6

½ cup Pear Compote (see page 190)
2 tablespoons freshly grated ginger
½ cup apple cider
¼ cup applejack or Calvados
2 tablespoons lime juice
1 tablespoon teriyaki sauce
⅓ cup safflower oil

6 one-inch-thick center-cut loin pork chops
Salt and freshly ground black pepper

Blend together Pear Compote, ginger, cider, applejack or Calvados, lime juice, and teriyaki sauce. Slowly beat in the oil. Pour into a saucepan, bring to a boil, and simmer for 5 minutes.

Marinate the chops in the sauce in a glass dish for 1 hour at room temperature. Drain and dry the chops and season with salt and pepper. Grill or broil 5 minutes on a side. Continue to grill 15 minutes more on each side, brushing often with the marinade.

Serve with more Pear Compote.

VEAL KIDNEYS CHARVET

This treat for kidney lovers comes from Henri Charvet, a French chef of extraordinary talent and imagination.

SERVES 6

3 veal kidneys
5 tablespoons butter
Salt and freshly ground black pepper to taste
1 tablespoon Cognac or brandy
½ cup dried morels, soaked in warm wine to cover until plump, well drained
½ pound mushrooms, thinly sliced
2 large shallots, minced
2 cups heavy cream
1 tablespoon chopped parsley

Trim, or have the butcher trim, the kidneys, removing most of the fat. Cut the kidneys into ½-inch cubes. Melt 3 tablespoons butter in a sauté pan. Brown the kidneys. Add salt and pepper. Add Cognac, ignite, and remove the kidneys once the flames have burned out.

In the same skillet, add the remaining 2 tablespoons butter, morels, mushrooms, and shallots. Cook just until golden. Add cream and allow sauce to reduce until it is thick and creamy. Return kidneys to skillet, add chopped parsley, and heat thoroughly.

Serve with steamed rice.

CHEESE BAKED TOMATOES

Baked tomatoes go well with all sorts of meat dishes; try these with roast pork.

SERVES 4

4 large tomatoes
Salt and freshly ground black pepper to taste
¼ pound cheddar cheese, grated
2 egg yolks
⅓ cup heavy cream
Pinch of hot curry powder
Salt to taste
⅓ cup herbed dried bread crumbs
3 tablespoons butter

Preheat the oven to 350°F.

Cut tomatoes in half. Turn upside down and squeeze gently to remove some of the seeds and liquid. Place in a buttered baking dish, cut side up. Sprinkle with salt and pepper. Beat together cheese, egg yolks, cream, curry powder, and salt. Spoon about 2 tablespoons of this mixture onto each tomato half. Sprinkle herbed bread crumbs over tops and dot with butter.

Bake at 350°F for 20 minutes.

SAVORY STUFFED TOMATOES

It's great to cook outdoors on the last warm evenings as the days get shorter. These tomatoes are a wonderful side dish with grilled meats.

SERVES 4

4 large, firm tomatoes
4 tablespoons butter
1 medium yellow onion, chopped
¼ pound mushrooms, chopped

Salt and freshly ground black pepper to taste
1 tablespoon fresh marjoram, chopped (or ½ teaspoon dried)
2 cups fresh, soft bread crumbs
¼ cup grated cheddar cheese
½ cup heavy cream

Preheat the oven to 375°F.

Cut a slice off the stem end of each tomato. Scoop out the pulp and reserve. Melt the butter in a skillet. Sauté the onion until transparent. Add the mushrooms and sauté for 3 more minutes. Stir in the tomato pulp, salt, pepper, and marjoram. Simmer for 10 minutes. Stir in bread crumbs and stuff the mixture into the tomatoes. Sprinkle with cheese and arrange in a shallow buttered baking dish. Pour the cream around the tomatoes. Bake, uncovered, at 375°F for 30 minutes. Spoon the cream over hot tomatoes and serve.

TOMATO SOUFFLÉ

It sounds scary, but soufflés can be made ahead of time. Beat the egg whites till they're stiff, fold them into the cheese mixture, fill the soufflé dish, and cover it tightly with plastic wrap. It will be fine if set aside at room temperature for 30 minutes or an hour. Remember to preheat the oven before you put the soufflé in to bake.

SERVES 6

4 large tomatoes, peeled, seeded, and chopped
3 tablespoons olive oil
3 tablespoons finely minced onion
1 clove garlic, minced
Salt and freshly ground black pepper to taste
½ cup dry red wine
1 tablespoon butter
2 tablespoons butter
2 tablespoons flour
1 cup milk
5 eggs, separated, the whites beaten until stiff peaks form
¼ cup grated Parmesan cheese

Pinch of salt
Tabasco to taste
2 tablespoons grated Parmesan cheese

Preheat the oven to 425°F.

Drain tomatoes well. Heat the oil in a skillet and sauté the onion and garlic just until transparent. Add the tomatoes, salt, pepper, and wine and simmer for 15 minutes, or until nearly all the liquid has evaporated. Add 1 tablespoon butter and stir. Set aside and cool to room temperature.

Melt 2 tablespoons butter in a saucepan. Stir in flour and simmer 2 minutes. Stir in milk all at once and cook, stirring, until the mixture is thick and smooth. Remove the mixture from the heat and beat in the egg yolks one at a time. Stir in Parmesan cheese and season with pinch salt and Tabasco.

Butter a 1½-quart soufflé dish and sprinkle with 2 tablespoons Parmesan cheese. Stir tomato mixture into the cheese sauce. Carefully fold the beaten egg whites into tomato cream mixture and spoon into the prepared dish. Bake at 425°F for 30 minutes, or until soufflé is puffed and brown. Serve at once.

GINGERED SWEET POTATO PURÉE

Sweet potatoes are wonderful with fresh ginger; here they make a colorful purée that can be served in scooped-out orange shells or piped with a pastry bag onto serving plates. This recipe and the two that follow are Thanksgiving variations that will not stun the traditionalists.

SERVES 4

1 pound sweet potatoes, baked in the skins until very tender
4 tablespoons butter, softened
1 tablespoon freshly grated ginger
Salt and freshly ground black pepper to taste
About 2 to 3 tablespoons very heavy cream

Peel the sweet potatoes and drop into the bowl of a food processor. Add the butter and process 30 seconds. Add the ginger and process 10 seconds longer. Turn the purée into a saucepan and season with salt and pepper to taste.

Heat gently until potatoes are very dry but not burned, stirring from time to time. Stir in cream until the purée reaches desired consistency. Heat thoroughly and serve.

SWEET POTATOES AND APPLES

The combination of sweet potatoes with apples is a natural at Thanksgiving—the apples give a nice flavor and texture to a rich version of candied sweet potatoes.

SERVES 6

5 medium sweet potatoes, baked until very tender
¼ pound (1 stick) butter
⅓ cup granulated sugar
1 teaspoon cinnamon
3 large, sweet cooking apples, peeled, cored, and sliced into thin rings
½ cup light brown sugar
1 cup cider

Preheat the oven to 375°F.

Peel sweet potatoes and slice thickly. Generously butter a 1-quart oven-proof casserole. Mix together the sugar and cinnamon. Layer potato and apple slices, sprinkling each layer with both sugars and dotting with butter. Continue alternating layers, ending with a layer of apples. Dot with butter. Heat cider to boiling. Pour over apples and potatoes. Bake at 375°F for 40 to 45 minutes.

DUCHESSE SWEET POTATOES

Here puréed sweet potatoes are puffed with eggs, rum, and spices and piped as a rich, decorative border around the Thanksgiving turkey or a platter of sliced ham or grilled steak.

SERVES 6

4 large sweet potatoes, boiled in the skins
2 large egg yolks
3 tablespoons dark rum
1 teaspoon pumpkin pie spice (or ¼ teaspoon each
    cinnamon, nutmeg, mace, and allspice)
Salt and freshly ground black pepper to taste
4 tablespoons melted butter

Skin potatoes and purée in a food processor. Beat in egg yolks, one at a time. Beat in rum and seasonings.

Fit a pastry bag with a star tip. Fill the bag with the potato mixture. Pipe designs around the edge of the serving platter. Very carefully brush the surface of the potatoes with the melted butter and run the plate under the broiler for 2 minutes, just until the butter begins to brown. Serve immediately.

BAKED ACORN SQUASH

This old standby has always been a great way to persuade children to eat squash—it tastes almost as good as candy. Don't worry about the rum; it evaporates.

SERVES 4

2 whole acorn squash, washed and halved
4 teaspoons butter
4 teaspoons rum
4 tablespoons brown sugar
1 teaspoon freshly grated ginger
Salt and freshly ground black pepper to taste
½ cup water

Preheat the oven to 350°F.

Scoop out squash seeds and discard. Arrange squash halves, cut side up, in a baking pan. Fill each cavity with 1 teaspoon each of butter and rum, 1 tablespoon brown sugar, and ¼ teaspoon grated ginger. Season with salt and pepper. Pour ½ cup water around the squash in the bottom of the pan. Bake at 350°F for at least 1 to 1½ hours, or until the squash is tender.

SPAGHETTI SQUASH WITH LIME AND BASIL

A pesto variation made with lime is a tart counterpoint to the delicate flavor of the spaghetti squash.

SERVES 6

1 large spaghetti squash
2½ cups fresh basil leaves
1 cup Parmesan cheese
2 teaspoons sugar
1 large clove garlic, peeled
3 tablespoons fresh lime juice
½ cup olive oil
Freshly ground Parmesan cheese

Preheat oven to 350°F.

Rinse squash and pierce in several places with a fork. Place on a cookie sheet and bake at 350°F for about 1 hour, turning from time to time.

In the bowl of a food processor, combine basil, 1 cup of cheese, and sugar. Process until nearly smooth. Drop in the garlic clove while the processor is on. Add lime juice and then oil in a thin stream. Process until thick.

Split the cooked squash in half lengthwise. Pull out flesh with a fork and pile it in a serving bowl. Top with basil sauce and toss. Pass more cheese in a separate bowl.

BROCCOLI BRAISED IN WHITE WINE

Braising vegetables permeates them with the flavors of the liquid. This classic technique has been popular in Italy for generations.

SERVES 6

3 tablespoons olive oil
2 pounds broccoli, washed and trimmed, cut in fleurettes
1 clove garlic, minced
½ cup dry white wine
Salt and freshly ground black pepper to taste

Heat the oil in a wok or heavy skillet. Add broccoli and garlic. Sauté for 3 minutes, turning broccoli to coat with oil. Add wine and salt and pepper to taste. Cover, reduce to a simmer, and braise about 10 minutes. Remove cover and raise heat. Reduce liquid by half. Serve broccoli with sauce poured over it.

GLAZED CHESTNUTS

Glazed like turnips or potatoes, chestnuts are a traditional accompaniment for game or pork. For us they are a fall delicacy, but the irony is that they are a staple for the poor all over the world. Not only can they be boiled and eaten whole, or mashed, or puréed with sugar, or mixed with potatoes, they are also dried and milled into flour and then baked into bread.

SERVES 4

1 pound chestnuts, parboiled and peeled
1 cup well-seasoned beef stock
3 tablespoons butter
⅓ cup sugar
½ cup apple cider

Simmer the chestnuts in stock for 20 minutes, until tender. Remove the chestnuts from stock with a slotted spoon. Melt the butter and sugar in a small skillet. Add the cider and bring to a boil. Add chestnuts and continue to boil, shaking the pan often, until the liquid evaporates and the caramelized sauce coats the chestnuts. Serve immediately.

PASTA WITH LEEKS

For people who are just getting used to leeks, this is a fabulous—and very rich—introduction.

SERVES 4

4 tablespoons (½ stick) butter
5 large leeks, very well washed and the white part very thinly sliced
2 cloves garlic, minced
½ green pepper, thinly sliced
½ cup heavy cream
⅓ cup Feta cheese
Salt and freshly ground black pepper to taste
2 tablespoons chopped parsley
1 pound fresh pasta (linguine or fettucine)
Freshly grated Parmesan cheese

Melt the butter in a heavy skillet. Add leeks, garlic, and green pepper. Stir for 1 minute. Cover and simmer gently for 11 to 15 minutes, stirring frequently to prevent the vegetables from burning. Uncover and add cream and Feta cheese. Stir until the cheese is melted and vegetables are coated with sauce. Season to taste with salt and pepper. Stir in parsley.

Pour sauce over pasta cooked for 3 minutes in boiling salted water. Toss and serve very hot with freshly grated Parmesan cheese.

MUSHROOM BAKE

The Fontina melts well and has a delicate flavor that will not overwhelm the mushrooms.

SERVES 4

¼ pound (1 stick) butter
1½ pounds fresh mushrooms, thinly sliced
Salt and freshly ground black pepper
1 cup freshly grated Fontina cheese

Preheat the oven to 375°F.

Melt the butter in a heavy skillet and sauté the mushrooms until they are golden. Season with salt and pepper.

Arrange half of the mushrooms in the bottom of a small ovenproof casserole. Cover with half of the cheese. Add the remaining mushrooms and the rest of the cheese. Bake at 375°F for 15 minutes or until cheese is hot and bubbly.

STUFFED MUSHROOMS

Mushrooms are delicious served as a vegetable with fish or beef.

SERVES 6

20 medium mushrooms, cleaned and stemmed
¼ pound (1 stick) butter, softened
2 teaspoons each chopped parsley, chives, and shallots
¼ cup finely grated Gruyère cheese
Pinch of nutmeg

1 cup very heavy cream
Freshly chopped parsley, for garnish

Preheat the oven to 450°F.

Chop the mushroom stems finely. Mix with butter, herbs, cheese, and nutmeg. Fill mushroom caps with the cheese mixture and arrange side by side in a buttered baking dish. Pour heavy cream around mushrooms and bake at 450°F for 10 minutes.

Remove the mushrooms from the hot cream and keep warm. Pour the hot cream into a small saucepan. Reduce over high heat until only half the liquid remains. Spoon over the mushrooms and sprinkle with parsley. Serve very hot.

SPINACH AU GRATIN

We like to cook spinach with no additional liquid, so it keeps all its flavor and nutrients. We put it in a pot as soon as it is washed, cover, and let it wilt over low heat in whatever moisture remains on its leaves. This recipe is a slightly dressier variation on the same technique.

SERVES 4 TO 6

3 tablespoons butter or a mixture of butter and olive oil
2 pounds spinach, well washed, stemmed, and finely chopped
Salt and freshly ground black pepper to taste
1 clove garlic, minced (optional)
¼ cup dry bread crumbs

Preheat the oven to 375°F.

Butter a flat gratin dish with 1 tablespoon of the butter. Arrange spinach in the dish and season with salt and pepper. Sprinkle with garlic if desired. Spread bread crumbs over spinach and drizzle the remaining oil over it or, if using butter, dot the surface of the spinach with small bits.

Bake at 375°F for 20 to 25 minutes, until spinach is tender and crumbs are browned.

SPINACH ROLL

This crisp, spinach-filled pastry makes a terrific luncheon main dish, but it can be served as a vegetable at dinner, too.

SERVES 4

2 pounds fresh spinach, washed, stemmed, and steamed until tender
4 tablespoons butter
2 tablespoons finely chopped onion
1 cup fresh ricotta cheese
½ cup freshly grated Parmesan cheese
1 egg yolk
Salt and freshly ground black pepper to taste
½ package of filo leaves, thawed and unrolled, each leaf brushed with melted butter and stacked. Cover with a damp towel.
2 tablespoons melted butter

Preheat the oven to 375°F.
Drain the spinach, squeezing out most of the water. Chop.
Melt the butter in a skillet and sauté the onion until just transparent. Add the spinach. Sauté 2 minutes. Turn into a mixing bowl and beat in ricotta, Parmesan, and egg yolk. Season with salt and pepper to taste.
Lay the stack of filo leaves on a flat surface. Spread the spinach mixture over the surface. Roll the pastry into a tight cylinder. Slice in 1-inch slices. Arrange slices, cut side down, in a buttered baking dish. Drizzle melted butter over the surface.
Bake at 375°F for 45 minutes. Serve at once.
For cocktail appetizers, cut filo leaves in half, place 1 teaspoon filling on one corner, and fold like a flag. Bake on a greased baking sheet for 25 to 30 minutes.

FRIED SPINACH BALLS

These balls are excellent served as a vegetable, or make them a little smaller and offer them as a cocktail hors d'oeuvre.

SERVES 6

1½ pounds fresh spinach, washed, steamed, drained of all liquid, and chopped
2 tablespoons butter, melted
2 tablespoons minced onion
1 clove garlic, minced
4 tablespoons grated Gruyère cheese
Pinch of nutmeg
2 eggs
¼ cup water
1 cup fresh dry bread crumbs

Mix together the spinach, butter, onion, garlic, cheese, nutmeg, and 1 egg. Form mixture into 1-inch balls.

Beat the other egg with ¼ cup water until well mixed. Roll spinach balls in crumbs, then in egg, then in crumbs. Set aside to dry. Fry in deep fat until crumbs are golden. Drain and serve very hot.

APPLE CRÊPES

Caramelized apple slices wrapped in delicate crêpes and served with sour cream are irresistible; they make a lovely ending for a company dinner.

MAKES 12 7-INCH CRÊPES

2 eggs
1 cup milk
Pinch of salt
1 cup flour
4 tablespoons butter, melted
2 tablespoons butter
2 Golden Delicious apples, peeled, cored, and sliced thin
¼ cup brown sugar
¼ teaspoon cinnamon
2 tablespoons dark rum
Confectioners' sugar
Sour cream

Put eggs, milk, salt, and flour in a blender. Blend at high speed until smooth. While blending, add 1 tablespoon melted butter and blend well.

Heat a 6- to 7-inch crêpe pan until very hot. Add 1 tablespoon melted butter, turn to coat the pan, and pour excess back into the butter dish. Add 1 to 2 tablespoons batter. Turn the pan to coat evenly with batter and cook the crêpe until crisp and brown. Turn crêpe and cook 1 minute longer on the other side.

Stack crêpes on top of each other and repeat until all the batter is used up. Wrap in a towel to keep moist.

Heat 2 tablespoons butter in a shallow skillet. Add apples. Cook for 5 minutes. Toss together brown sugar and cinnamon and add to the apples. Cook gently until apples are soft and caramelized. Add rum and cook over high heat for 2 minutes.

For each serving, roll 1 tablespoon apple filling in each crêpe, making two crêpes per serving. Just before serving, sprinkle with confectioners' sugar. These are best if eaten very hot with a spoonful of sour cream.

APPLESAUCE

You can make applesauce with almost any apple, but we prefer McIntosh, Macoun, Stayman, and Wealthy. Idared will give it a delicate pink color.

SERVES 6

6 medium cooking apples (not Delicious) (see chart, page 238)
1 cup water or cider
½ cup sugar
½ teaspoon cinnamon
2 tablespoons butter

Peel, core, and cut up the apples. Place them in a saucepan with water or cider, sugar, and cinnamon. Boil gently, uncovered, until the apples are soft enough to mash, about 40 minutes. Stir with a fork to mash, leaving a few small lumps. Return to low heat. Stir in butter. Simmer until melted. Beat briefly. Serve hot, warm, or cool.

DUTCH APPLE PUDDING

Don't you remember certain dishes from childhood? This one has been a comfort as far back as we can remember.

SERVES 6

1 egg, well beaten
1 cup sugar
3 medium cooking apples, pared, cored, and diced
2 tablespoons flour
1 teaspoon baking powder
Pinch of salt
½ cup chopped pecans
Whipped cream

Preheat the oven to 350°F.
Butter a 9-inch pie pan.
Beat eggs and sugar together until light and frothy. Add apples, flour, baking powder, salt, and pecans. Spread in the pan and bake at 350°F until brown and crusty, about 25 minutes. Serve warm, but not hot, with whipped cream.

FLAN À LA NORMANDE

French children love to come home to this traditional confection after school.

SERVES 6

Pastry for 2 one-crust pies (see page 105)
2 tablespoons sugar
1 pound apples, peeled, cored, and very thinly sliced
4 tablespoons flour
½ cup sugar
3 eggs
2 egg yolks
2 cups milk
1 teaspoon pure vanilla extract

Preheat the oven to 375°F.

Roll out pastry and line 2 pie plates or tart molds. Make a fluted crust. Sprinkle sugar over the bottom of the pastry.

Arrange apple slices in a circular pattern in the bottoms of the pans. Mix flour and sugar. Beat the eggs and egg yolks together and then beat into the flour mixture. Beat in milk and vanilla extract.

Pour custard over the apples and bake at 375°F about 1 hour, or until the filling is set. Cool and cut in wedges to serve.

FLAMUSSE

This substantial pastry is a variation of an ancient Burgundian dish. Served with a big glass of milk, it is a good snack for a rainy fall afternoon.

SERVES 4 TO 6

3 tablespoons butter
4 apples, peeled, cored, and cut into thin rings
4 eggs
3 tablespoons dark brown sugar
1 tablespoon flour
1 teaspoon cinnamon
1 cup milk
3 tablespoons confectioners' sugar

Preheat the oven to 400°F.

Melt the butter in an ovenproof skillet. Brown the apple rings. Beat the eggs with sugar, flour, cinnamon, and milk. Pour batter over the apples. Cook 3 minutes on top of the stove, then place the skillet in a 400°F oven and bake about 15 minutes. Turn out onto a platter and dust heavily with confectioners' sugar. Serve very hot.

APPLE PANDOWDY

Haven't you always wanted to know what this was? It isn't easy—even the *Oxford English Dictionary* says "origin obscure." It's an old rustic American recipe for a one-crust apple pie; *American Heritage* suggests the dish was baked briefly and then "dowdied" by having the crust cut into the filling before the final baking, but that's the best we can do.

SERVES 6

4 large tart apples (such as Greenings), peeled, cored, and sliced
¼ cup sugar
1 teaspoon pumpkin pie spice
3 tablespoons dark rum
½ cup unsulfured molasses
1 cup flour
1 teaspoon baking powder
Pinch of salt
⅓ cup sugar
1 small egg, beaten
⅓ cup milk
6 tablespoons butter, melted

Preheat the oven to 350°F.

Butter an ovenproof baking dish. Toss apple slices with sugar and spices. Spread apple slices on the bottom of the dish. Mix the rum and molasses together. Pour over apple slices. Bake at 350°F for about 20 minutes.

Stir together flour, baking powder, salt, and sugar. In a separate bowl, beat together egg, milk, and melted butter. Stir into the flour mixture. Spoon the batter over apples and cut into the apples slightly. Do not stir batter into apples, simply make several cuts with a spoon to mix gently.

Bake at 350°F for 25 minutes. Serve hot, upside down, with the apples on top. Pass vanilla ice cream.

APPLE OMELET

This dessert omelet is less sweet than its ancestor, the old-fashioned jelly omelet; it is a nice way to end a light supper.

SERVES 4

4 tablespoons butter
2 apples, peeled, cored, and thinly sliced
1 teaspoon pumpkin pie spice
6 eggs, beaten
3 tablespoons heavy cream
Confectioners' sugar

Melt 3 tablespoons of the butter in a heavy saucepan. Add the apples and spice and cook over low heat until apples are soft, about 10 minutes. Cool. Beat together eggs and cream. Stir into the apples. Melt remaining tablespoon of butter in a large skillet. Pour in egg and apple mixture and cook over medium heat for 4 or 5 minutes. When the omelet is browned on the bottom, slide it onto a plate and invert it back into the skillet. Brown the second side. Serve at once, sprinkled with powdered sugar. Cut in wedges like a pie to serve.

DEEP DISH APPLE PIE WITH CHEESE CRUST

Apple pie is often served with a piece of cheddar cheese. For a savory twist, this recipe puts the cheese in the crust.

SERVES 8

2 cups flour
Pinch of salt
Pinch of cayenne pepper
¼ pound (1 stick) butter, chilled
¼ pound sharp cheddar cheese, grated
7 tablespoons ice water
1 cup sugar
4 large Granny Smith apples, peeled, cored, and sliced
1 teaspoon cinnamon
1 tablespoon flour
1 tablespoon lemon juice
2 tablespoons butter

Preheat the oven to 400°F.

Stir 2 cups flour, the salt, and the cayenne pepper together. Cut in the butter until the mixture resembles coarse meal. Stir in the cheddar cheese. Add the water gradually, pulling the mixture together with a fork, until a stiff dough is formed. Divide the dough into two pieces, one slightly larger than the other.

Roll out the larger round and line a deep dish pie plate.

Sprinkle ½ cup of the sugar over the bottom crust. Toss the apples with the remaining sugar, cinnamon, and 1 tablespoon of flour. Mound in the crust. Sprinkle with lemon juice and dot with butter. Roll out the remaining pastry and cover the pie. Cut slits to allow steam to escape.

Bake at 400°F for 10 minutes. Reduce heat to 300°F. Bake for 1 hour and 30 minutes. Serve hot.

CIDER APPLE PIE

The amazingly intense apple flavor in this old-fashioned American dessert comes from using fresh cider to rehydrate the dried apples. Dried apples make fabulous snacks, too; just peel and core them and cut in rings or slices, then spread them on a cookie sheet in a cool oven (180 to 200°F) until they are leathery.

SERVES 8

½ pound dried apples
3 cups fresh cider
½ cup sugar
1 teaspoon cinnamon
¼ teaspoon nutmeg
Pasty for a 2-crust pie (see page 105)
2 tablespoons butter
1 egg, beaten

Preheat the oven to 375°F.

Place apples and cider in a saucepan. Simmer gently until apples are tender and plump. Combine the sugar, cinnamon, and nutmeg, add to apples, and cook 10 minutes longer. The apples absorb most of the liquid.

Roll out half of the pastry and line a 9-inch pie plate. Pour in the apple filling. Dot the apple mixture with butter. Roll out the second half of the pastry and top the pie with a lattice crust. Glaze with beaten egg.

Bake at 375°F for 30 to 35 minutes, or until the filling is bubbling and the crust is browned. Serve warm with ice cream.

CANDY APPLE ICE CREAM

This tastes like old-fashioned taffy and brings back childhood memories.

MAKES 1 QUART

½ cup sugar
¼ cup dark brown sugar

Pinch of salt
1 tablespoon molasses
2 cups half and half
3 beaten eggs
1 cup heavy cream
1 cup finely chopped apples
½ teaspoon pure vanilla extract

In a saucepan combine sugars, salt, molasses, and half and half. Cook over low heat until the mixture is slightly reduced. Stir often. Beat about ¼ cup of the hot mixture into the eggs and then turn the eggs back into the hot mixture. Cook, stirring constantly, for about 1 minute. Cool. Stir in cream, apples, and vanilla.

Freeze in an ice cream freezer according to manufacturer's directions.

APPLE CIDER SORBET

Add a teaspoon of cinnamon to this cool, easy dessert for a spicier flavor.

MAKES ABOUT 1 ¼ QUARTS

6 cups fresh apple cider, simmered until reduced by half
2 teaspoons lemon juice
½ teaspoon ground cloves
¼ cup dark rum

Mix together cider, lemon juice, and cloves. Simmer over low heat until well mixed. Cool. Add rum. Freeze in an ice cream freezer according to manufacturer's directions. Let the sorbet rest in the freezer compartment for 1 hour before serving.

GRAPE SORBET

When this sorbet is made with wine grapes like Concord (or Cabernet Sauvignon, if they're available) the first taste is dark, rich, fragrant, and fabulous.

2 cups sugar
2 cups boiling water
2 cups grape juice (made by processing red or purple grapes in the blender or
  processor and then straining to obtain clear juice)
3 tablespoons lemon juice

In a heavy saucepan, dissolve sugar in water and bring to a boil. Simmer for 10 minutes and then cool. Add syrup to grape juice and then stir in lemon juice. Freeze in an ice cream freezer, following manufacturer's directions.

PEAR BETTY

Pears are easily substituted for apples in this adaptation of the classic Apple Brown Betty.

SERVES 6

½ cup sugar
1 teaspoon cinnamon
¼ teaspoon nutmeg
¼ teaspoon ginger
Juice of 1 lemon
6 large pears, halved and sliced lengthwise
3 tablespoons butter, melted
2 cups soft bread crumbs
Heavy cream, whipped (optional)

Preheat the oven to 350°F.

Stir together sugar and spices. Stir sugar and lemon juice into pear slices. Toss lightly. Pour melted butter into bread crumbs and stir with a fork. Place a layer of buttered crumbs in the bottom of a greased 2-quart baking dish. Spread with half the pears. Cover with more crumbs and the rest of the pears. Top with remaining crumbs.

Bake at 350°F for 25 minutes. Serve with whipped cream.

STUFFED PEARS

This recipe and the one that follows celebrate the natural affinity of pears and chocolate.

SERVES 4

2 cups water
1 tablespoon lemon juice
½ cup sugar
4 firm, ripe pears
¼ cup ground pecans
1 tablespoon sour cream
2 tablespoons brown sugar
½ teaspoon pure vanilla extract
1 tablespoon rum
1 cup heavy cream, whipped
1 cup Hot Chocolate Sauce (see below)

In a saucepan simmer water, lemon juice, and sugar for 10 minutes. Peel and core the pears from the bud end, leaving the stems intact. Gently drop pears into hot syrup and simmer until just tender. Cool fruit in syrup.

Mix together pecans, sour cream, brown sugar, vanilla, and rum. Stuff about 1 tablespoon of filling into each pear. Chill. To serve, spoon a little whipped cream into a serving dish. Arrange pears upright in the cream and spoon a little Hot Chocolate Sauce over them. Serve with remaining chocolate sauce on the side.

HOT CHOCOLATE SAUCE

MAKES ABOUT ⅔ CUP

2 ounces or 2 squares semisweet chocolate
¼ cup heavy cream
3 tablespoons sugar
3 tablespoons butter

Melt the chocolate in the cream in a saucepan over very low heat. Stir until smooth. Add the sugar and stir until the mixture begins to thicken. Remove the pan from the heat, and beat in the butter. Serve warm.

SAUTÉED PEARS IN CHOCOLATE SAUCE

This is a superb variation on Poires Belle Hélène, in which, instead of being poached, the pears are caramelized.

SERVES 4 TO 6

4 tablespoons butter
4 Bartlett pears, cut in quarters and cored
1 pint vanilla ice cream
1 cup Hot Chocolate Sauce (see page 302)
2 tablespoons chopped pecans

Melt butter in a heavy skillet. Sauté pears until they are tender and lightly browned. Arrange hot pears on a layer of vanilla ice cream in a serving bowl or individual dishes. Pour Hot Chocolate Sauce over the pears and serve at once topped with chopped pecans.

GRATINÉED PEARS

This goes very well with vanilla ice cream, but rum raisin ice cream is a natural, too. The liquid should evaporate as the pears cook, leaving them tender and crunchy.

SERVES 4

4 large firm, ripe pears, peeled, cored, and thinly sliced
½ cup sugar cookie crumbs
4 tablespoons brown sugar
2 tablespoons dark rum
4 tablespoons butter

Preheat the oven to 475°F.

Butter a shallow 1-quart baking dish. Toss pears with cookie crumbs and brown sugar. Arrange the pears in the prepared baking dish. Sprinkle the rum over all and dot with butter. Bake at 475°F for 30 minutes, or until hot and golden brown.

CRANBERRY PIE

Would it be too revolutionary to try cranberry pie for Thanksgiving this year?

SERVES 6 TO 8

1½ cups flour
½ teaspoon cinnamon
¼ teaspoon baking powder
Pinch of salt
¼ pound (1 stick) butter
⅓ cup sugar
1 egg yolk
¼ teaspoon pure vanilla extract
½ cup ground almonds
3 tablespoons dried bread crumbs
2 cups fresh cranberries, washed and picked over
½ cup Golden Syrup
1 tablespoon lemon juice
1 tablespoon butter

In a bowl, stir together flour, cinnamon, baking powder, and salt. In another bowl cream the butter with the sugar until light and fluffy. Beat in egg yolk and vanilla. Stir in the ground almonds and bread crumbs. Fold into the flour mixture and form a ball. Allow dough to rest in the refrigerator for several hours.

Press pastry into the bottom and sides of a 9-inch pie pan.

Preheat the oven to 400°F.

Mix cranberries, syrup, and lemon juice together well. Pour into pastry-lined pie pan. Dot with butter. Bake at 400°F for 30 minutes, or until pastry is well browned. If the crust begins to brown too rapidly, lay a piece of aluminum foil over the pie after ten minutes.

CRANBERRY-APPLE PIE

Tart cranberries simmered in cider counterpoint the sweet apples. This is another Thanksgiving natural.

SERVES 6 TO 8

2 cups fresh cranberries
¾ cup fresh apple cider
1 cup sugar
3 tablespoons cornstarch
½ teaspoon pumpkin pie spice
3 tablespoons dark rum
3 large apples (McIntosh, Empire, or similar variety), peeled, cored, and thinly sliced
Pastry for a 2-crust pie (see page 105)
1 tablespoon butter

Preheat the oven to 375°F.

In a saucepan combine cranberries and cider. Simmer and stir until cranberries begin to pop. Combine sugar, cornstarch, and pumpkin pie spice. Stir into hot cranberries and simmer until the mixture thickens, about 1 minute. Remove from heat. Cool slightly. Stir in rum and apple slices.

Roll out half of the pastry and line a 9-inch deep-dish pie pan. Pour in cranberry-apple mixture. Dot with butter. Roll out remaining pastry and make a lattice top crust for the pie. Bake at 375°F for 1 hour. Serve with whipped cream or Homemade Vanilla Ice Cream (see page 99).

PERSIMMON PIE

Don't try to eat a persimmon unless it's very, very soft to the touch—an unripe one can be agonizingly sour. The pulp should mash easily with a fork, like a ripe banana.

SERVES 6 TO 8

1½ cups pulp from very ripe persimmons
1 teaspoon freshly grated ginger
1 teaspoon lemon juice
Sugar to taste, about ½ cup
Pinch of salt
1½ cups heavy cream, whipped
1 prebaked Graham Cracker Crust, cooled (see below)

Beat together persimmon, ginger, lemon juice, sugar, and salt. Fold in whipped cream. Pile into cooled crust. Chill 30 minutes and serve.

GRAHAM CRACKER CRUST

The sweet crunch of this crust goes well with pies made with custards or cold fruit mousses.

MAKES 1 PIE SHELL

1½ cups graham cracker crumbs
½ teaspoon cinnamon
⅓ cup brown sugar
⅔ stick butter, softened

Combine crumbs, cinnamon, brown sugar, and butter. Press the mixture firmly on the bottom and sides of a 9-inch pie plate.
To bake ahead of time, bake at 375°F for about 10 minutes. Cool on a rack.

GRAPEFRUIT CUSTARD PIE

A surprising combination, this pie is great at the end of a special dinner.

SERVES 6 TO 8

1 cup sugar
2 tablespoons flour
1 tablespoon butter, softened
Pinch of salt
3 eggs, separated
Juice and pulp of 1 medium grapefruit
2 teaspoons grapefruit zest
1 cup half and half
1 9-inch unbaked Graham Cracker Crust (see page 306)

Preheat the oven to 350°F.

In a bowl, cream together sugar, flour, butter, and salt. Beat in egg yolks. Stir the grapefruit pulp and juice into the sugar mixture. Stir in zest and half and half.

Beat egg whites until they form soft peaks. Fold carefully into the grapefruit mixture and turn into the pie crust. Place the pie plate on a baking sheet and bake in a 350°F oven until the filling is set and lightly browned on top, 45 minutes or longer.

TEXAS PECAN PIE

There are as many variations of pecan pie as there are cooks. The cream in this one tempers the richness of the sugar.

SERVES 6 TO 8

1 cup dark brown sugar
½ cup light corn syrup
3 tablespoons dark rum
2 tablespoons flour
Salt
2 extra large (or 3 medium) eggs, well beaten
½ cup heavy cream
1½ cups pecan halves
½ teaspoon pure vanilla extract
1 unbaked pie shell (see page 105)

Preheat the oven to 400°F.

In a bowl combine brown sugar, corn syrup, rum, flour, and salt. Mix well. Add eggs and cream. Stir in pecans and vanilla. Pour into pie shell and bake at 400°F for 10 minutes. Reduce heat to 350°F and bake 35 to 40 minutes longer, until set. Cool before cutting.

PUMPKIN PECAN PIE

This pie creates the best of all worlds, with crunchy pecans giving a nice texture to the pumpkin custard.

SERVES 6 TO 8

3 eggs
¾ cup brown sugar
¼ cup light cane syrup
Pinch of salt
½ teaspoon nutmeg
½ teaspoon cinnamon
1 cup light cream
1½ cups puréed pumpkin (see below)
¼ cup chopped pecans
1 unbaked deep-dish pie shell (see page 105)
¼ cup pecan halves

Preheat the oven to 400°F.

Beat eggs, brown sugar, and cane syrup together with a whisk. Beat in salt, spices, cream, pumpkin, and chopped pecans. Pour filling into pie shell. Bake at 400°F for 40 minutes, or until the filling sets around the edges.

Remove pie from the oven and decorate with pecan halves. Cool thoroughly before serving.

To make pumpkin purée, simmer cubed, peeled, and seeded sugar pumpkin in water till tender, then drain well and purée in the food processor; or you can just seed the pumpkin, cut it in large pieces, and bake them with a little water for 1½ hours at 375°F, then scrape out the flesh and purée.

FROZEN PUMPKIN MOUSSE

Frozen desserts are a godsend for the make-ahead cook. This one is a nice way for the grownups to celebrate Halloween. Resist the temptation to use the big pumpkins that are sold for carving; sugar pumpkins are bred for cooking and have much more flavor.

SERVES 6

¾ cup water
¾ cup sugar
3 egg whites
Pinch of cream of tartar
1½ cups puréed pumpkin, well drained
1 teaspoon pumpkin pie spice
2 tablespoons rum
1 cup heavy cream, beaten until stiff peaks form

In a heavy saucepan, boil water and sugar until the syrup reaches the soft ball stage—238°F on a candy thermometer.

While the syrup is boiling, using an electric mixer, beat egg whites with a pinch of cream of tartar until stiff peaks form. With the mixer running, pour the hot sugar syrup into the egg whites in a steady, thin stream. Continue beating until the mixture is entirely cool—it may take more than 10 minutes. Fold in pumpkin and spice.

Beat the rum into whipped cream and fold into the pumpkin mixture. Pour into a soufflé dish that has been fitted with a paper collar and freeze at least 4 hours.

Remove the mousse from the freezer and place in the refrigerator about 30 minutes before serving. Spoon into dessert dishes and serve with ginger cookies.

THANKSGIVING PUMPKIN CHEESECAKE

Here's another variation for Thanksgiving that will please even the traditionalists.

SERVES 10

> 2 cups graham cracker crumbs, or ginger snap crumbs
> 3 tablespoons butter, melted
> 3 teaspoons sugar
> 5 eight-ounce packages of cream cheese, very soft
> 3 cups sugar
> 6 large eggs
> ¾ cup puréed sugar pumpkin (see note on page 308)
> 1 tablespoon lemon juice
> 2 teaspoons pumpkin pie spice
> ½ cup heavy cream

Preheat the oven to 450°F.

Toss together cracker crumbs, butter, and sugar. Press the mixture into the bottom of a 9-inch spring form pan. Beat the cream cheese with an electric mixer until very fluffy. Gradually beat in sugar. Beat in the eggs, one at a time, beating well after each addition. Beat in puréed pumpkin and lemon juice. Stir in the spice and cream. Turn into the spring form pan.

Bake at 450°F for 15 minutes. Turn the oven down to 325°F and continue to bake for 45 minutes. Turn off oven, but do not open oven door until cake is completely cooled. (This *should* prevent the top from cracking.) Chill. Serve with rum-flavored whipped cream, if desired.

Just before turning into the pan, stir ½ cup finely chopped pecans into the pumpkin mixture if desired.

CHESTNUT TART

This fall treat should appeal to lovers of pumpkin or sweet potato pie. Try it as an alternative at Thanksgiving or Christmas.

SERVES 8

> 1 pound chestnuts, roasted, shelled, and peeled
> ⅔ cup sugar
> ½ cup heavy cream
> ¼ cup rum

2 egg yolks
1 pie shell (see page 105), baked for 10 minutes
4 tablespoons butter, cut up
Heavy cream, whipped (optional)

Preheat the oven to 300°F.

Boil the chestnuts until tender, about 20 minutes. Drain and purée in a food processor until smooth. Mix the purée with ½ cup sugar, cream, rum, and egg yolks. Pour the filling into partially baked pie shell, dot with butter, and bake at 300°F for about 25 minutes.

Remove pie from the oven and sprinkle remaining sugar over hot filling. Cool to room temperature and serve with whipped cream on the side.

INDIAN PUDDING WITH APPLES

Early settlers enjoyed a cornmeal pudding like this, baked slowly in a Dutch oven or a brick oven as it cooled down after the bread had been removed. We like to lighten it a bit with fresh apples.

SERVES 8

5 tablespoons cornmeal
4 cups hot milk
2 tablespoons butter
⅔ cup unsulfured molasses
Salt
1 teaspoon cinnamon
2 eggs, well beaten
2 small apples, peeled, cored, and very thinly sliced

Preheat the oven to 300°F.

Stir cornmeal into hot milk. Cover and simmer for 15 minutes. Remove from heat. Stir in the butter, molasses, salt, cinnamon, and eggs. Stir in apple slices. Pour into a buttered 1-quart baking dish. Bake at 300°F for 1 hour and 15 minutes.

HAY DAY'S BOURBON PECAN CAKE

We sell hundreds of these at Christmas, generously laced with bourbon, wrapped in cheesecloth, then in plastic wrap, then in foil, and tied with ribbons.

MAKES 4 SMALL CAKES

½ pound (2 sticks) softened butter
2 cups sugar
6 eggs
2 cups flour
2 teaspoons baking powder
1 teaspoon salt
1 teaspoon cinnamon
½ teaspoon nutmeg
2 cups broken pecans or walnuts
2 cups currants
4 ounces bourbon
½ teaspoon grated lemon peel
3 tablespoons bourbon

Preheat the oven to 325°F.

Put the butter and sugar in a mixer and blend well. Add the eggs 1 at a time and mix until incorporated. Sift together the flour, baking powder, salt, and spices and add to the egg mixture. Add the pecans, currants, bourbon, and lemon peel and stir.

Pour the batter into 4 small loaf pans and bake for 1 hour at 325°F. Baste them with bourbon, wrap in cheesecloth, then in plastic wrap, then in foil, and tie with a ribbon.

RAISINÉ

This Burgundian recipe makes a fabulous pie filling and opens up new worlds as a substitute for jelly in a peanut butter sandwich.

MAKES ABOUT 2 CUPS

4 pounds ripe red grapes (Concord or Ribier), washed and stems removed
½ cup water
2 pounds Comice pears, peeled, cored, and thinly sliced
About 6 cups sugar

In a saucepan simmer the grapes with ½ cup water until they begin to pop. Press on the grapes from time to time. When all grapes are soft, strain through a sieve set over a bowl, pressing out all the juice. Reserve the juice. Poach the pear slices for about 4 minutes in boiling water just to cover. Drain. Measure grape juice and count 1 cup sugar to every cup of juice. Put the juice and sugar in a large kettle.

Bring the juice to a boil and simmer until reduced by about one-third. Add the drained pear slices and continue simmering, stirring until the pears break up and the mixture is thick. Stir thoroughly.

Pour into hot sterilized jars. Process in a boiling water bath for 10 minutes.

HAY DAY'S HONEY APPLE BRAN MUFFINS

Originally developed by the bakery in response to requests from customers, this is a real health food nut's muffin (it has no white flour, butter, or sugar) but is lighter than the granola version. It will take you through the day if it is served hot at breakfast with unsalted butter.

MAKES 16 MUFFINS

½ cup honey
½ cup safflower oil
1 teaspoon pure vanilla extract
2 eggs
1 cup bran
1½ cups whole wheat flour
2 teaspoons baking powder
1 teaspoon baking soda

½ teaspoon salt
1 cup buttermilk
1¾ cups finely chopped apple (Cortland or Northern Spy)
½ cup raisins
½ cup currants

Preheat the oven to 375°F.

In a bowl, beat honey and oil together. Add vanilla and eggs. Beat well. Put bran in a separate bowl. Sift flour, baking powder, baking soda, and salt into bowl with the bran. Add to the oil mixture in thirds with buttermilk. Do not overmix. Fold in apples, raisins, and currants. Fill muffin tins three-quarters full. Bake in 375°F oven for 20 to 25 minutes. Let cool in muffin tins for 10 minutes before removing. Serve warm with sweet unsalted butter.

HAY DAY'S WHOLE MEAL BREAD

Mimi Boyd developed this recipe years ago as a way of packing as much protein as possible into sandwiches for school and office lunches. Buy the blackstrap molasses (a rich source of iron) at a health food store, but don't be overzealous and substitute it completely for regular molasses—it will inhibit the action of the yeast. For even more richness, you can add 2 tablespoons of brewers' yeast, which also comes from the health food store; it won't change the character of the loaf, but it will add even more vitamin B.

MAKES 2 LOAVES

1 cup milk, scalded
1 cup cold water
¼ cup safflower oil or unsalted butter
¼ cup blackstrap molasses
¼ cup molasses (unsulfured)
1 tablespoon salt
1 tablespoon active dry yeast
¼ cup warm water
1 cup whole wheat flour

1 cup 12-grain flour (or whole wheat flour)
4 cups unbleached white flour (or more if needed)

Scald milk and pour it into a large bowl. Add water, oil, molasses, and salt. Stir to dissolve. Soften yeast in warm water. Add whole wheat flour and 12-grain flour to the liquids. Add yeast when proofed and mix well. Add enough unbleached white flour to make a stiff dough.

Turn the dough out on a floured surface and let rest for 5 minutes. Wash out mixing bowl and butter it generously. Knead dough for 12 to 15 minutes, adding more flour if necessary. The dough should feel smooth and elastic.

Put the dough in a buttered bowl, turning once to grease the surface. Cover with a clean dish towel and let rise in an oven that has been warmed for 3 minutes and turned off. When dough has doubled in volume, punch down and let rest a few minutes. Shape into 2 loaves and place in greased 9 x 5 x 3-inch pans. Let rise again in oven, covered with a towel, until doubled. When towel is rounded, take it off carefully. Turn oven to 350°F and bake bread for 45 minutes. The bread will continue to rise for the first 10 minutes of baking.

To test for doneness, tap bottom of loaf, and if the loaf sounds hollow, the bread is done. Remove from the pan and cool on a wire rack. This bread freezes very well.

WINTER

Up at 5:15 . . . the country seeming very beautiful and
cheerful after a light fall of snow. I am always humbled
by the infinite ingenuity of the Lord, who can make a
red barn cast a blue shadow.

E. B. WHITE, One Man's Meat

THIS is the skiers' season. They rejoice in it; everybody else battens
down. The wind howls outside, and indoors we bake bread and
make cassoulet and listen to the opera on Saturday afternoon, or page through
seed catalogs in the lengthening days and dream of Early Girl tomatoes, Sweet
Meat squash, and Cherry Belle radishes. We push along cross-country trails,
enjoying the clear air, the company of the winter birds, and the blue shadows
on the snow. Tea after that is a gift from heaven, and onion soup on Sunday
night or raclette cheese by a mountain fireside is celestial, too.

In the produce business, though, there's another side to winter—the intesti-
nal fortitude it takes to drive into the desolation of Hunts Point Market on a
bitter night in January. It's no picnic. There may be drearier landscapes than
the South Bronx, but they are hard to imagine. At midnight the lunar expanse of
gutted buildings between Edgewater Road and Bruckner Boulevard is pretty
close to the end of the world—and it's worse at dawn. But in the middle of all
that desolation is the New York City Terminal Market, Hunts Point, the
grimy three-hundred-acre hub of the produce business in the metropolitan
area.

It's a night world. Starting in the early evening, trucks unload produce
from all over the globe to be stacked and displayed at the commission houses.

Buyers come in around midnight to place orders or confirm those made earlier over the phone, and their trucks are loaded and gone by five or six in the morning. Work is over when the sun comes up.

Five nights a week, Hay Day sends two trucks and two buyers to the market. It's always crowded, and trucks maneuver all night among the docks, but on Sundays and Wednesdays (the major resupply nights) the tangle is unbelievable. If the trucks aren't parked at a loading dock by ten o'clock, we may end up cooling our heels for two hours waiting for a parking place, and that means losing the chance for the good stuff. A buyer has to be aggressive and be in a position to jump at opportunities, and you don't get anywhere when you're stuck out in the truck staring at the windshield wipers.

D'Arrigo. Armata. Square Produce Company. Finest Fruits. The displays stretch into infinity down the long docks, and some of them are fabulous. Apples and oranges, papaya and pineapples, eggplant and artichokes, are piled to the roof in boxes showing them off like jewels on plush. In the dreary setting, even onions are beautiful. Former rarities like arugula, radicchio, mâche, and haricots verts (the tiniest green beans) are plentiful. There are Daikon, Japanese eggplant, cardoons, tomatoes, and yellow and purple peppers. There are asparagus from Mexico, melons from Spain, and raspberries from New Zealand. Here in the South Bronx it is hard to imagine warm sun anywhere, but it's almost as if the vegetables bring their own radiance into this night world and give off solar energy by themselves.

The Hay Day stores carry about 350 produce items, and perhaps half of them will be on the list each trip. Moving along the miles and miles between broker displays takes time, and buying is a gamble—if you order all your Ruby lettuce from one house, there's always the chance that you're missing out on a better deal somewhere else. But over the years you not only develop an eye for quality, you also develop relationships with particular vendors which make the job less chancy—and cut down the time you spend slogging up and down the docks with a hand truck or a pallet jack.

After the deals are made, we bring the trucks up through the tangle of other behemoths to each dock in turn to pick up our purchases. We are usually loaded and out by six, and we turn into the first stop in Greenwich to be unloaded by seven, just when Hay Day's customers are climbing out of bed.

In the beginning, Alex Van Rensselaer and his produce manager used to make the trip themselves. A new company has a hard time getting credit, so they had to carry cash—six or seven thousand dollars between them. Now Hay Day is a major buyer and credit is arranged serenely over the phone, but some of the adventure has gone out of it—like scrabbling in the snow along the shoulder of Bruckner Boulevard trying to retrieve the hundred dollar bills that the wind had whipped through the gearshift hole in the floor of the first dilapidated truck.

Isn't there some other way to do it? Well, yes—there are plenty of distributors who will, in effect, go to market for us, and we do order from them from time to time. But by buying at Hunts Point you not only know that you'll get a fair market price—you find out what's really going on out there. People who love the produce business get a kick out of fabulous merchandise—nobody likes bruised fruit and droopy lettuce—and even if it is three o'clock in the morning you look forward to bringing back something terrific.

And so you line up with the trucks and join the brotherhood of the night people and go to market. But the good part is in the morning, when they're taking everything off the truck and somebody picks up a bunch of museum-quality radishes and says admiringly, "Hey, look at that!" It has its moments.

The Winter Market

THE arrival of the *citrus fruits*—grapefruits, oranges, tangerines, and the rest—highlights the winter marketplace. They're listed in the chart on page 334, but it's worth pointing out a few of our favorites. *Tangelos* are grapefruits crossed with mandarin oranges, and *Minneola tangelos* are the supreme example; they are deep orange, virtually seedless, often knobbed at one end—and unbelievably juicy. *Orchid Island grapefruit* come from one particular island in Florida near Vero Beach where soil and weather conditions are ideal for citrus; they are thin-skinned, rich, and juicy. Children often like to blindfold themselves and see if they can tell the difference between the flavors of pink and white grapefruit, but within the same variety—pink and white Orchid Island, for example—there isn't any.

Other citrus worthy of mention are *clementines*, a sweet cross between a Mandarin and a Seville, tiny enough for Christmas stockings; seedless *Jaffas* from Israel; tart-sweet *blood oranges* from the Mediterranean; bitter *Sevilles*, hard to get and the best for marmalade; and sweet, homely *uglis*, a cross between a grapefruit and a variety of tangerine.

All citrus should be glossy and firm and feel heavy with juice. They are often waxed to help retain their moisture and treated with ethylene gas to enhance their color, but both processes are harmless.

Freshly squeezed *orange juice*, one of the luxuries of winter, is best bought from a reliable source that does not crush the oranges so hard that bitter-tasting oils from the skin and fiber end up in the juice; you can make more juice that way, but the quality suffers. It's best bought from a local supplier, too; it will not only be fresher, but it will be made from a higher quality of fruit. Orange juice squeezed in the state of Florida is made from lower-grade fruit that cannot otherwise be shipped out of the state.

One depressing thing we just learned is that only a quarter of the vitamin C in citrus is contained in the juice; the rest is in the peel. If you can figure out anything to do about that besides making marmalade, we hope you'll let us know.

Many *tropical fruits* are in season during the winter. Although their real peak is in the spring, *pineapples* are plentiful now. A ripe pineapple will be heavy, slightly golden colored, and gently fragrant; if it smells sweet and fresh, it is. Since they can ripen only on the plant, they must be shipped ripe (the best ones are shipped by jet from Hawaii), and they have only a few days' shelf life. Pineapple contains an enzyme that dissolves gelatine and curdles milk; it must be cooked (simmered for 10 minutes with a little water) if it is to be used in a mold with other fruits or in a recipe containing milk or cream.

There are other tropical fruits to help dispel the gloom of February—many of these former rarities are now cultivated in this country and readily available. *Cherimoya*, the white-fleshed "queen of the tropical fruits" is also known as sherbet or custard-fruit. It is luscious eaten raw with a spoon, scraping away the custardy inside from the fiber and shiny black seeds. Buy them ripe, when they are even softer than a ripe tomato.

People who bother about fashions in food have now abandoned the *kiwi* as noisily as they took it up in the first place, but anyone who hasn't yet experienced the gentle flavor of its citrusy green flesh has something to look forward to. Kiwi is delicious eaten plain; peeled and sliced crosswise, it is translucent and decorative. Low in calories and full of vitamin C, kiwi keeps beautifully. It is slightly soft when ripe.

Originally found only in the East Indies, *star fruit* (Carambola) is now grown in this country and the Caribbean; it tastes a little milder than a lemon and makes a fine complement to poached salmon. Cut it crosswise and the slices are little stars; it's a lovely garnish for a fruit salad, or for beverages, or anything you'd use a lemon in.

We like *plantains* and *red bananas*, too, at this season. Red bananas are lovely, smaller than ordinary yellow ones, with a similar flesh and taste. They turn darker and softer as they ripen. Plantains, the staple food of the tropics and first cousin to the banana, are nourishing, digestible, and versatile—"the relief of all poverty," according to an eighteenth-century missionary. They are never eaten raw, but cooked in an astonishing variety of ways; they can be hors d'oeuvres, vegetables, main course, or dessert. Green plantains are starchy, rather like a mealy potato; they're yellow when they're half ripe, brown when they're ripe, black when they're super-ripe, and each stage has its uses. Plantains bought green will turn yellow in a week and black in two; their skins are tough, so even if they look bruised they're fine inside.

Although *chilies* are available from California, Florida, and Mexico year-round, it seems appropriate to highlight them during the chill of winter. To begin with, there's no such thing as chili peppers; the word *chili* means hot pepper. There's a vast range of them, from the sweet *bell* and *Italian* to the fiery *jalapeños* (see chart on page 329) and the general rule is the bigger, the sweeter. The hottest is the tubular dark green *Serrano*: not more than 2 inches long, it must be treated with great respect. Almost as lethally hot is its slightly larger, top-shaped relative, the *jalapeño*. The milder *Anaheim*, or California pepper, is considerably larger, lighter green, and good for Chiles Rellenos (stuffed chilies); it must be peeled before using. The Anaheim can be mistaken for one of our favorites—the mild, sweet *Cubanelle*, or *Italian pepper*, which is good cut in strips and fried in olive oil with garlic and a little onion; it is also wonderful in stir-fries.

When working with very hot chilies, be sure that you wash your hands scrupulously. If you happened to rub your eyes without doing so, the irritation caused by the enzyme capsaicin could be agonizing. Immature chilies are yellow, white, or green; they turn orange or red as they mature. Although they should be plump and fresh-skinned when you buy them, they're just as effective if the skins have become a little wrinkly.

To peel all peppers, put them in a hot oven or over high heat until the skins bubble all over, then place them in a paper or plastic bag for 15 minutes. The skins will then be loose enough to rub off easily.

Fennel, a favorite in Europe for centuries, is getting easier to find in markets in the United States. It looks like a bulbous whitish celery, with bright green feathery leaves, and has a fairly strong anise (licorice) flavor. Fennel is eaten in its entirety—the bulb is a vegetable, the leaves are an herb, and the seeds are a spice. It can be eaten raw with a dip or with a vinaigrette, or sautéed and braised in wine or stock. It should be bought fresh and firm and used soon afterward; it won't keep more than a week in the refrigerator.

Some people think *horseradish* grows in a bottle in the icebox door, but these gangly plants with their rough-skinned roots are a traditional late fall crop in New England and are available in the wholesale market through the winter. Horseradish can be bought dried or bottled year-round, but it is far more pungent fresh out of the ground, peeled, and grated into mayonnaise or sour cream, or added to a sauce for beef or pork.

Jerusalem artichokes aren't artichokes, and they are grown right here in New England, where they have been a substantial fall and winter vegetable for centuries. Sometimes sold as "sunchokes" from California (they're tubers of a relative of the sunflower), they are nourishing, low in calories, and though they may never be a staple of everyday life (some people find them hard to digest), they add variety to winter menus. When raw they taste rather like water chestnuts, when cooked they become starchy. They can be steamed or boiled in their skins and eaten like new potatoes, or peeled and served with hollandaise and other sauces. Avoid overcooking them—they get mushy very quickly. If they're too gnarly to peel easily, put them in boiling water for 5 to 10 minutes to loosen the skins, then shorten the cooking time in the recipe.

Mâche is a cold-weather salad green planted for centuries in Europe at the end of the summer; its small, delicate leaves grow slowly through the cold season and are flown from France and Belgium to winter markets in this country.

Mesclun, another import, is a rarity, but if it's offered, buy it. In Europe, its appearance at the greengrocer's is the first sign that spring is on the way. It is the very first cutting of a number of different wild greens (usually escarole, chicory, mâche, and dandelion or arugula) that are used in salads or wilted with bacon and coddled egg.

Oriental vegetables used to be exotic, but not any more; former rarities like Chinese broccoli, Napa, and bok choi are grown in California and available virtually year-round. We like to think of them in the late winter, though, when light and crunchy stir-fried vegetables are the answer to cravings for something green. Not unlike a cucumber with a shiny, wrinkled skin and a refreshing taste, *bitter melon* can be stir-fried with meats and fish; it should be sliced, seeded, and parboiled for about 3 minutes to avoid bitterness. *Bok choi*, the sweet, tender, versatile vegetable with long white stalks and green leaves, can be used in soup or stir-fries and requires very little cooking. *Napa* (also called Chinese lettuce or Tientsin cabbage) is an elongated head with firm, vertical white stalks and pale, yellowish-white leaves. Its taste is between that of lettuce and cabbage; it can be eaten raw in salads but is delicious stir-fried with beef, chicken, pork, or other vegetables. *Daikon* looks like an overgrown white radish, and it is. Stir-fried, it adds a subtle flavor and crunch to beef, pork, fish, and shrimp. Not unlike a watermelon on the outside, with a translucent white interior, *winter melon* needs very little cooking; it can be stir-fried as a vegetable or used in soups, which are often served by the Chinese in the carved shell of the melon. *Broccoli*, of course, is a highlight of the summer market in the East, but the crop from California is magnificent all winter.

You don't hear many people raving about *parsnips*, but they are superb and usually available fresh locally well into the winter. They should be treated just like carrots; peel or scrape and eat them raw with a dip, or cut them up to be steamed, boiled, or thinly sliced and sautéed with butter. They are wonderful in stews. Do not buy parsnips that are soft or shriveled; remove the green tops (which can draw out moisture) and use as soon as possible. They keep well in a plastic bag in the icebox.

Red and white *radicchio*, or Verona chicory, is a welcome ornament to winter salads. A close cousin of Belgian endive, it is (like its relative) a second-year crop. Its leaves are small and green the first year; only the second crop produces the characteristic tight, deep red head. Radicchio is best eaten raw; it can be cooked like endive but turns a rather grim rust color. It should be fresh and crisp when you buy it and will keep for a few days in the icebox if it is wrapped tightly in plastic.

Perishable native *rutabagas* are available unwaxed in the summer, but it is hard to imagine anybody cooking them in hot weather; in the winter, when they are waxed to preserve moisture and lengthen their shelf life, they come into their own with the rest of the root vegetables. They keep well in the icebox, and should be treated like turnips—peeled and cut in cubes or ovals and steamed or boiled and served with butter, or incorporated in soups and stews, or julienned with a mixture of other vegetables.

Salsify (oyster plant) and *scorzonera* are not synonymous, but these two root vegetables have enough in common to be interchangeable in most recipes. Often mislabeled in produce markets, both are long and carrotlike; scorzonera is thin and very dark brown (almost black), and salsify looks like a darkish parsnip. The faint oyster flavor that gives salsify its nickname must have been more pronounced in the centuries when it was commonplace in Europe—today you may not be able to detect it. Choose the smoothest, finest roots; they will keep several days in a plastic bag in the icebox but will dehydrate rapidly at room temperature.

Both salsify and scorzonera can be served like carrots or parsnips. They are good steamed or blanched and served with butter and parsley with lemon or garlic, and they are excellent in soups or stews. Their flesh will darken with exposure to air, so put them in acidulated water after peeling.

PEPPERS

NAME	DESCRIPTION	FLAVOR (1 = mild, 10 = hot)	USED FOR
BELL PEPPERS	4 to 6 inches long, 3 to 5 inches round with prominent ribs. Can be green, yellow, red, or purple.	1	General cooking: salads, stuffing, frying, broiling, pizza.
CUBANELLE (Italian Frying Pepper)	Pale yellow-green, twisted and tapered, 4 to 6 inches long, 1½ to 2 inches diameter.	1	Frying in olive oil with garlic, some general cooking.
ANAHEIM, CHILE VERDE	5 to 8 inches long, 1½ to 2 inches diameter. Bright green, tapered.	3–5	Charred and peeled, then stuffed or diced for Carne con Chile Verde.
When Dried CHILE DE LA TIERRA CHILE COLORADO CHILES PASADOS	Tough, dark, red-brown, 5 inches long, 1 inch wide.	3–5	Soaked and used as if fresh.
POBLANO	5 inches long, tapered, black-green and shiny; varies in appearance according to where grown.	3–6	Usually charred and peeled and used in Chiles Rellenos or Chiles con Quesa, or cut in strips.
When Dried ANCHO	Deep reddish-brown, wrinkled shiny skin.	3–6	Mostly soaked and ground for cooked sauces; sharp flavor. The most frequently used Mexican chili.
CHILACA	Blackish-green, 6 inches long, 1 inch wide.	Mild without seeds and veins, hot used whole.	Toasted and ground for table sauces, soaked and ground for cooked sauces.
When Dried PASILLA CHILE NEGRO	Long, slender, blackish, wrinkled.		
YELLOW CHILE	1½ to 2 inches long, ½ inch diameter, smooth, light yellow, tapered with pointed tip.	5	Ornamental, garnishes, table sauces.

PEPPERS (continued)

NAME	DESCRIPTION	FLAVOR (1=mild, 10=hot)	USED FOR
FRESNO	2 inches long, 1 inch diameter, red.	4–8	Hot sauces, salads, condiments and relishes.
HUNGARIAN WAX	4 to 5 inches long, 2 inches diameter, bright yellow.	7–8	Canning, pickling, relishes.
RED CHILE	1½ to 2 inches long, ¼ inch diameter, short, tapered, green, ripening to red.	7–8	Dried for seasoning.
HOT PORTUGAL	Scarlet, 5 to 7 inches long, 2 inches diameter, tapered.	8–9	Pickling.
CHILE CAYENNE	2 inches long, medium green, turning red, thin, pointed.	9 Seeds and veins very hot.	Not a Mexican chili; used fresh in Indian and Chinese recipes, but can be substituted for jalapeño and Serrano.
JALAPEÑO	Dark green, 2½ inches long, 1 inch diameter, straight, tapered, rounded tip.	8–9	Guacamole, salsa, nachos, garnishes; general Mexican cooking. Similar to serrano.
When Dried CHILE CHIPOTLE (Smoked)	Light brown and wrinkled, smells of smoke.	8–9	Albóndigas en Chipotle Quemado.
SERRANO	Small, green, smooth, longer and thinner than jalapeño, rounded, sometimes pointed.	9 Seeds and veins very hot.	Guacamole, all Mexican cooking. Should be smooth; they lose character when wrinkled.
CHILE DE ARBOL	1 inch long, 1 inch diameter, red, tapered, often sold on branches.	10	Table sauces, ornamental.
HABANERO	Lantern-shaped, 1 inch wide and 1 inch long, light green, ripens to orange.	10	Chopped raw in frijoles, used in many Jamaican and Haitian dishes.

Much of the information in this chart has been adapted from Diana Kennedy's superb *Mexican Regional Cooking* (Harper & Row).

POTATOES

NAME	TYPE	GROWN	PEAK SEASON	CHARACTERISTICS	USES
RUSSET	High starch	Idaho, Washington, Oregon, some from Wisconsin	Available year-round	Long, oval-shaped with russet brown rough skin. Flesh is dark, mealy, and fluffy.	The best baking of all. Also french fries and as a binder in soups when puréed.
EASTERN ROUND WHITES "All Purpose"	Medium starch	Maine, Long Island, Delaware, Canada	Fresh in fall, year-round from storage	Round with roughish light brown skin. Flesh is moist, keeps its shape.	"All purpose"—baking, mashed, fried, as chunks in soups; when baked, has moist flesh.
LONG WHITES	Low starch	California	Year-round	Long, oval-shaped like a Russet but with a smooth, pale yellow skin. Flesh is moist and will keep its shape.	Boiling, potato chips, home fries, potato salads.
RED BLISS	Low starch	Florida (spring), Minnesota, North Dakota (fall)	Spring and fall (fresh), from storage at other times	Small, round, smooth, very red skin. Flesh is wet, with waxy quality. Keeps its shape well.	Boiling, potato salads, sautés, au gratin, fried.
FINNISH POTATO	Low starch	Washington	Limited supplies October to February	Small, round potato with yellow, wet, waxy flesh. Lower in calories.	Boiling, potato salads, roasted.
FINGERLINGS	Low starch	Small East Coast farms	Limited availability October to November	Small, 1-inch diameter, fingerlike shape with yellow, waxy flesh.	Boil with jackets on; salads and roasts.

SWEET POTATOES

NAME	GROWN	PEAK SEASON	CHARACTERISTICS	BEST USES
WHITE SWEETS	Southeast	October–December	Pale yellow, dry flesh, less sweet	Baking
"YAMS" (Louisiana Yams)	Southeast	October–February (and year-round from storage)	Darker orange, moist flesh, sweeter	Baking

POTATO USE CHART

DISH	BEST POTATO TYPE
Baked	High starch
Boiled	Medium or low starch
Deep-fat fried	High starch
French fries	High starch
Home fries	Medium or low starch
Hashed brown	Medium or low starch
Mashed	High starch
Potato chips	Low starch
Potato pie	High starch
Roasted	Low starch
Sautéed	Medium or low starch
Soup, puréed	High starch
Soup, chunks	Medium or low starch
Salads	Low starch
Steamed	Medium or low starch
Straw mat	High starch

WINTER SQUASH

VARIETY	SIZE	DESCRIPTION	SEASON	BEST USES
ACORN	2 to 4 pounds	Oval with prominent ribs. Dark green to black skin, yellow, bright orange flesh.	Available all year but best September–December	Just right for two people, halved, baked, and stuffed with rice or meat.
BUTTERCUP	4 to 5 pounds	Round and stocky with a cap or button on the stem end. Dark green skin. Bright orange flesh.	September–November	Baked. Our favorite winter squash.
BUTTERNUT	2 to 6 pounds	Roughly bell- or pear-shaped. Pale yellow to creamy tan.	Available all year, but best September–December	Very good baked and mashed.
GOLDEN NUGGET	1 to 2 pounds	Like a small pumpkin, a little flat. Orange skin streaked with green; flesh is orange.	September–March	Another small squash excellent for baking and stuffing. Very sweet nutty flavor.
GREEN DELICIOUS	10 pounds	Round to heart-shaped. Dark green skin, orange flesh.	September–November	Best for freezing; use like Hubbard squash.
HUBBARD	12 to 15 pounds	Oval, heart-, or football-shaped. Blue, green, or orange skin, yellow-orange flesh.	September–March	Best for long storage; baked, boiled, purées, soups, pies.
RED DELICIOUS	10 pounds	More or less round, something like a pumpkin. Orange-red skin and flesh.	September–November	Baked, steamed, or mashed.
TURK'S TURBAN	3 to 4 pounds	Shaped like a turban; green to bright orange-red skin. Has orange-red flesh.	September–November	Ornamental. Can be stuffed with rice or meat and baked.

CITRUS

TYPE Variety Where Grown	PEAK SEASON	DESCRIPTION	COMMENTS
ORANGE Hamlin Florida	Mid-October, November, December	Medium size, round or slightly oval, dark yellow to orange color with a smooth rather thin peel.	Usually seedless. Produces a pulpy pale juice with a watery taste. Only fair in quality.
ORANGE Navel Florida	October, November, December, January	Large to very large, round to slightly oval, with deep yellow to shiny orange color.	Seedless. Pebbly, thick but easily peeled skin, sections well; we think the California navel is a better choice.
ORANGE Parson Brown Florida	November, December, January	Medium to large, perfectly round, light orange color. Skin is pebbly.	Has many seeds. Good flavor and fairly high juice content, but its seediness makes it unpopular.
ORANGE Navel California	November through June	Medium to very large, round, reliably bright orange with the characteristic navel at the blossom end. Skin is thick and pebbly.	Nearly seedless. One of the best eating oranges. Easy to peel and section. The only orange whose juice is undesirable because it turns bitter when exposed to air.
ORANGE Pineapple Florida	December, January, February, mid-March	Medium to large, oval or round with orange pebbly skin.	Has many seeds. A very sweet orange. Excellent juice content with good color and quality.
ORANGE Blood Spain	Late December, January, February	Small, orange to red-orange skin. Flesh may be red-orange, streaked, or a dramatic dark vermilion red.	Has seeds. Unusual blood-red color makes lovely salads. Flavor is a magnificent sweet-tart combination.
ORANGE Valencia Florida	March, April, May, June	Medium to large, oval shape; yellow to bright orange color sometimes streaked with green. Smooth, thin peel.	Usually seedless. Very high content of sweet, flavorful, and aromatic juice. We feel this is the very best juice orange available.

CITRUS (continued)

TYPE Variety Where Grown	PEAK SEASON	DESCRIPTION	COMMENTS
ORANGE Jaffa Israel	March, April, mid-May	Medium to large, oval shape, light orange color with a somewhat thick skin.	Only a few seeds. Peels well. A fine all-purpose orange with a flavor that's just a little less sweet than others.
ORANGE Pope Florida	May, June, and July	Medium-size fruit, yellow-orange in color with slightly paler interior flesh.	Has some seeds. In season with the Florida Valencia orange, which is the better choice.
ORANGE Valencia California	Early June through November	Medium to large bright orange-colored fruit with pebbly skin that is thicker than the Florida Valencia counterpart.	Has few or no seeds. An outstanding orange for eating or juicing during the summer and early fall.
BITTER ORANGE Seville Mediterranean	January, February, March	Variable size, yellow to bright orange, perhaps tinged with green and sometimes russeted. Tart but not bitter flavor.	Has many seeds. Known for the splendid marmalade it makes. Excellent for all culinary uses.
MANDARIN Robinson Tangerine Florida	October, November, December	Medium to large with the flat oval shape characteristic of all tangerines. Bright orange skin, smooth to slightly pebbly. A cross between the Clementine and the Orlando.	Has seeds. Very sweet and less acidic than other citrus fruit.
MANDARIN Sunburst Tangerine Florida	November–December	Large-size fruit, more round than most tangerines, with shiny, bright orange, smooth skin. A cross between the Robinson and Osceola.	Has seeds. The Sunburst ripens after the Robinson and before the Dancy and ships better than either.
MANDARIN Dancy Tangerine Florida	November, December, January	Small to medium, flat oval shape. Deep orange to almost red with a smooth, loose peel.	Has many seeds. Excellent sweet flavor, with a spicy fragrance. Very easy to peel.

CITRUS (continued)

TYPE Variety Where Grown	PEAK SEASON	DESCRIPTION	COMMENTS
MANDARIN Clementine Morocco and Spain	December, January	Small-size fruit with orange pebbly skin; knobby around the stem end. Not as flat as a tangerine.	Usually seedless. Small size and wonderful flavor make them a favorite for kids. Very easy to peel and section.
MANDARIN Mandarin California	December, January, February	Medium, round, orange to red-orange with fairly smooth and shiny skin. Thin, easily peeled skin.	Usually seedless. Sweet but sometimes lacks flavor. Usually sold with its leaves on.
MANDARIN Temple Florida	Mid-January, February, March	Medium to large oval with a lovely deep orange-red color and pebbly skin. Peels and sections easily. A cross between a tangerine and a sweet orange. Skin can be speckled or spotted with black.	Has lots of seeds. Very rich flavor and sprightly fragrance. Good for eating out of hand and makes a delicious bright-colored juice.
MANDARIN King Orange Florida	January, February, March	Large fruit, round but flattened at the ends. Skin is rough, very hard, orange to red-orange. Flesh is a dramatic deep orange color.	Has seeds. This orange has a hard, unattractive outside, but its flesh inside has superb texture and flavor. Excellent quality.
MANDARIN Murcott or Honey Tangerine Florida	January, February, March	A cross between a tangerine and a King orange, the fruit is small to medium, oval but with flat ends. Very thin, smooth, shiny, skin is orange-gold, sometimes with a little green or russeted with black spots. Peel comes off in little pieces.	Has many seeds. Flesh is deep red-orange, sweet, juicy, and aromatic. Excellent eating quality. The *only* variety of citrus for which a high skin color means superior quality.
TANGELO Early Kay Florida	October, November, December	Medium to large, round shape but flat at ends. Orange to deep orange. A tangerine-grapefruit hybrid.	Many seeds. Popular by virtue of its early season but of generally poor quality.

CITRUS (continued)

TYPE Variety Where Grown	PEAK SEASON	DESCRIPTION	COMMENTS
TANGELO Orlando Florida	November, December, January	Round to slightly flat and medium to large in size. Light to fairly deep orange and pebbly, moderately thick skin but peels easily and is very juicy.	Many seeds. This tangerine-grapefruit hybrid has fairly good quality but the later Minneola is the best buy.
TANGELO Nova Florida	December, January	Medium to large fruit. Tangerine-shaped with bright orange skin. Peels easily. A cross between the Clementine and the Orlando tangelo.	Many seeds. Better than the Early Kay and similar to the Orlando. Good but not equal to the Minneola.
TANGELO Minneola or Honeybell or Red Tangelo Florida	January	A cross between the Duncan grapefruit and the Dancy tangerine. Medium to very large fruit often with slight bulb at the stem end making them resemble a bell. Skin is a shiny deep orange to red-orange, somewhat pebbly. Very easy to peel and section.	A few seeds. We consider this the most outstanding of all citrus fruits. The Minneola's wonderful sweetness is balanced by a slight tartness and rich orange-tangerine flavor. Very short season.
TANGELO Minneola California	January, February, March	Small, very red-orange fruit with pronounced neck at the stem end. Thick skin is easy to peel.	Seedless. Flavor is an interesting tart-sweet combination. Good but no match for the Florida variety above.
GRAPEFRUIT Foster Florida	November–March	Pale yellow, medium size with a slight pink blush of color in the peel. Flesh color is dark pink.	Extreme seediness makes this fruit unpopular except that some are shipped early in the season.

CITRUS (continued)

TYPE Variety Where Grown	PEAK SEASON	DESCRIPTION	COMMENTS
GRAPEFRUIT Duncan Florida	November–May	Medium to large, smooth, pale yellow skin with pale yellow flesh. It is the oldest grapefruit variety still grown.	A very seedy fruit but has an excellent flavor and quality. Sections well. Is used extensively in Florida for juice.
GRAPEFRUIT Marsh Florida	November–May	Bright yellow, small to medium full, round fruit with pale yellow flesh. Skin can be thick. This is the most commonly grown grapefruit for the commercial mass market. Generally grown in the interior regions of Florida.	Considered seedless. Good quality during midharvest. Often has large open cavity in center of fruit. May acquire a bland flavor toward end of season.
GRAPEFRUIT Marsh Indian River region, Florida	December–May	Medium to extremely large, full, smooth peel, heavy fruit with very thin skins and large sections. Grown along the East Coast from Titusville to Fort Pierce, called the Indian River region. Heavy for their size and usually flattened at the ends. Both white and pink are available.	Considered seedless. This is our favorite grapefruit. The climate and growing conditions in the Indian River region produce the best eating Marsh variety grapefruit of all and the very best fruits of this region, in our opinion, come from a tiny area called Orchid Island near Vero Beach and are usually marked with stickers for identification.

CITRUS (continued)

TYPE Variety Where Grown	PEAK SEASON	DESCRIPTION	COMMENTS
GRAPEFRUIT Ruby or Redblush or Ruby Reds Florida and Texas	November–May	Small to medium fruits, round or slightly flattened at ends with a distinct pink blush and a light pebble in the peel. The flesh is crimson red but fades to pink late in the season. Usually has large open cavity in center of fruit.	Considered seedless. Excellent eating fruit with attractive red color. Particularly good when grown in the Indian River region. Usually identified with stickers.
GRAPEFRUIT Star Ruby Florida	December–May	Medium size with slightly flattened ends. Skin color is a deep yellow with a dark pink blush and a fine pebble.	Considered seedless. Another excellent fruit particularly at midseason from the Indian River region. Flesh is an intense deep red.
GRAPEFRUIT Thompson (pink Marsh) Florida	December–May .	Medium to large, smooth skin, round or slightly flattened at ends. Flesh is pale pink and fades as season progresses. Almost impossible to distinguish on the outside from the Marsh white variety.	Considered seedless. Another of our favorites when grown in the Indian River region or on Orchid Island. This is the pink version of the Marsh grapefruit.

NOTE: A few varieties of grapefruit from California come to market in July to September during the off-season in Florida but are usually poor eating, sour, and expensive.

MISCELLANEOUS CITRUS FRUITS

TYPE Variety Where Grown	PEAK SEASON	DESCRIPTION	COMMENTS
UGLI FRUIT Jamaica	October–February	Small to medium, flat at ends, knobby around the stem end, dark green turning yellow with knobby, lumpy, and ill-fitting skin. A cross between a tangerine and grapefruit.	Has seeds. Ugli is the word for this fruit, but the flavor is an interesting sweet-tart combination and delicious.
KUMQUAT Florida, California	October–January	Tiny 1 to 2 inch, egg-shaped, golden to bright orange fruit. Often sold with stems and leaves attached.	A few seed pods. Thick skin is sweet with a touch of bitterness and flesh is very sour. The combination is an extraordinary treat.
LEMON California	Almost year-round	Everyone knows what the common lemon looks like and all commercial varieties are almost identical. They should be bright yellow, shiny, smooth skinned, firm, and heavy.	All varieties have some seeds. The lemon season runs out just when the lime is at its peak so when one is expensive the other is usually a better value.
LIME Persian and Tahiti Florida, West Indies, Mexico	Almost year-round	Dark to light green, smooth, shiny, thin skin.	Considered seedless. This is the fruit that was carried on long sea voyages by British ships to prevent scurvy caused by lack of vitamin C, hence the term "limeys" for British sailors.
LIME Key Lime Florida Keys, Mexico	October–March	Small, spherical yellow fruit with some signs of light green. Skin is very thin, mottled, and dull.	Few seeds. More aromatic and tart than the Persian lime. Most Key Lime groves were destroyed in the 1929 hurricane and later by a serious fungus. Hard to find outside of southern Florida.

JUICE ORANGES HARVEST CHART

MONTH	OCT.	NOV.	DEC.	JAN.	FEB.	MAR.	APR.	MAY	JUN.	JUL.	AUG.	SEP.
QUALITY												
Fair		HAMLIN										
Better			PARSON BROWN									
Excellent				PINEAPPLE								
Excellent						FLORIDA VALENCIA						
Good									POPE SUMMER			
Excellent										CALIF. VALENCIA		
Excellent	C. VALENCIA											

NOTES: 1. As each new orange variety comes into the market, it is usually wise to wait several weeks into the season before switching to the next kind. The early fruit is always less sweet.

2. Skin color has nothing to do with ripeness and sweetness. Oranges showing green color can be just as ripe as those all orange in color.

3. Oranges with smooth thin skins have a higher juice content than those with thick coarse skins.

Winter Menus

FROM Christmas vacation well into March, we need nourishment for soul and body. Whether for a formal holiday dinner or a casual weekend brunch, we offer bright and substantial combinations for winter events at home or in the mountains.

HOLIDAY DINNER

This would make an elegant feast anytime during the holiday season, but we like to think of it with music and mumming on Twelfth Night, giving everybody something to look forward to when the tree is dismantled and the presents are history.

FOIE GRAS EN BRIOCHE *(349)*

SPICED ROAST VENISON *(371)*

BRAISED RED CABBAGE AND APPLES *(378)*

WINTER SQUASH SOUFFLÉ *(382)*

CRANBERRY SORBET *(400)*

CHRISTMAS DINNER

Here elements of the traditional menu come from all over the globe and remind us what a wonderful word *merry* is.

ANTIPASTO SALAD *(355)*

TINY TIM'S GOOSE STUFFED WITH SAGE AND ONION *(368)*

BAKED POTATO CAKE *(380)*

RUTABAGA AND GINGERED CARROT PURÉE *(378)*

HOT CABBAGE SALAD *(362)*

YULE CAKES À L'ORANGE *(397)*

BUSY NIGHT SUPPER

Some people are scornful about last-minute shopping, but what other kind is there? Assemble all this in the morning for an easy supper after it's over.

WINTER SALAD *(357)*

CHICKEN LIVERS VÉRONIQUE *(370)*

SOUFFLÉED BAKED POTATOES *(381)*

GRATINÉED ORANGES WITH COOKIES *(394)*

SUNDAY NIGHT SUPPER

If you were all alone up there doing your algebra, isn't this what you'd want to know was cooking in the kitchen? There's not much to clean up, either.

WINTER HOT POT *(370)*

RAINBOW SALAD *(361)*

GRAPEFRUIT SHORTCAKE *(395)*

SKI DINNER

The sun is out and it snowed last night, and the cook wants to spend the day on the mountain like everybody else. Make most of this meal ahead, let the Daube simmer all day, and go skiing; then put the pudding in the oven and pass the soup while the noodles are cooking.

BLACK BEAN SOUP *(346)*

DAUBE À L'ANCIENNE *(372)*

FRESH NOODLES

WILTED SPINACH SALAD *(361)*

APPLE BREAD PUDDING *(403)*

LUNCH FOR A SNOWY DAY

Schools are closed and nobody can get to the office; everybody's been up since dawn listening to the radio. Canadian Cheddar Soup is a rich, creamy restorative, with the tang of grapefruit for a nice contrast. Chestnut Flan is very light, almost a crème renversée flavored with puréed chestnuts.

CANADIAN CHEDDAR SOUP *(348)*

MOLDED GRAPEFRUIT SALAD *(357)*

CHESTNUT FLAN *(401)*

LUNCH FOR HOUSEGUESTS

You haven't seen each other since they moved, and there's a lot to catch up on. Here's what's for lunch.

LASAGNETTE VERDE WITH FONTINA *(364)*

JONATHAN'S GREEN SALAD *(360)*

ORANGE GRANITA *(400)*

CHRISTMAS HOLIDAY TEA

Late afternoon tea, one of Britain's major contributions to civilized life, is particularly welcome in the winter as the sun sets over the snow. We serve mulled cider and eggnog, too, and slide right on into cocktails.

TOASTED CHEDDAR SAVORIES *(356)*

CHRISTMAS CRANBERRY TARTS *(402)*

SOUTHERN FRUIT CAKE *(396)*

ALMOND CRESCENTS *(406)*

PEPPARKAKOR *(405)*

HOT MULLED CIDER *(393)*

EGGNOG *(393)*

BRUNCH FOR A BUNCH

Everybody thinks everybody else is away in February and huddles gloomily at home. Dig them out and serve a salad made with foie gras and pasta made with golden caviar, and send them home radiant.

SALADE FOLLE *(359)*

GOLDEN PASTA *(352)*

CHAMPAGNE SORBET *(399)*

Winter Recipes

BLACK BEAN SOUP

A great midwinter supper from as far south of the border as Argentina and Brazil, this soup gets much of its character from the chorizo, or spicy Spanish sausage.

SERVES 6 TO 8

1 pound dried black beans, soaked in water to cover overnight, drained
1 ham hock, or 3 smoked knuckles
2 quarts well-seasoned chicken broth (see page 8)
1 tablespoon dried oregano
Freshly ground black pepper to taste
1 bouquet garni made of bay leaf and parsley stems
2 tablespoons butter
2 cloves garlic, chopped
2 stalks celery, chopped

2 large carrots, chopped
2 large onions, chopped
1 pound hot chorizo sausage, cut up
⅓ cup dry sherry
Salt
Chopped parsley
2 limes, quartered (optional)

In a large kettle simmer the beans, ham hock, chicken broth, oregano, salt, pepper, and bouquet garni for 3 hours. Melt butter in a skillet. Sauté garlic, celery, carrots, and onions until transparent. Add the vegetables to soup and simmer for 1 hour longer. Purée half of the beans and vegetables in a food processor and return the purée to remaining soup in the kettle. Sauté the sausage and stir into the soup. Add sherry. Simmer 5 minutes, salt to taste, and serve in deep bowls. Top with chopped parsley and serve with lime juice, if desired.

PEANUT SOUP

The wondrous peanut, called a groundnut in Africa, is not only an important low-cholesterol source of protein for developing countries. Hulls from the nut have been used to make cloth and a number of other products. This recipe comes from the South, where the most succulent bacon and ham come from hogs fed on peanuts; it tastes like a rich bean soup, with roasted overtones. The peanut butter is easily dissolved into the chicken broth.

SERVES 6

¼ pound (1 stick) butter
1 small yellow onion, diced
2 stalks celery, diced
3 tablespoons flour
6 cups hot well-seasoned chicken broth (see page 8)
⅔ cup creamy peanut butter
Salt to taste
1 tablespoon lemon juice
½ cup fresh roasted peanuts, skins removed, ground in a food processor

Melt the butter in a heavy casserole. Add the onion and celery and sauté for 5 minutes or until transparent. Stir in flour and cook, stirring, until bubbly. Stir in chicken broth and simmer for 30 minutes. Remove from heat, strain, and discard vegetables. Add peanut butter, salt, and lemon juice. Stir well. Simmer about 10 minutes. Sprinkle each serving with ground peanuts.

CANADIAN CHEDDAR SOUP

Another hearty winter soup, this one is smoothed with melted cheddar. The sharper the cheddar you use, the tangier the finished product will be.

SERVES 6

1 large onion, minced
1 stalk celery, minced
2 tablespoons melted butter
1 tablespoon flour
1 teaspoon dry mustard
1 teaspoon paprika
3 cups chicken broth (homemade if possible) (see page 8)
2 cups half and half
2 cups grated cheddar cheese
Salt to taste
Minced dill to garnish

Sauté onion and celery gently in butter until transparent, about 8 minutes. Stir in flour and cook until mixture bubbles. Stir in mustard and paprika.

Slowly add broth, bring to a boil, and simmer for 10 minutes. Stir in half and half. Add the cheese a little at a time, stirring constantly until cheese is melted. DO NOT BOIL. Add salt to taste. Sprinkle each serving with chopped dill.

FOIE GRAS EN BRIOCHE

Fresh foie gras, which for us is perhaps the ultimate indulgence, is often available at Hay Day and other specialty food stores around Thanksgiving and Christmas. If it is not available fresh, use the best quality you can find in a can (the term in French is *en bloc*). Do not use mousse de foie gras because it melts when heated.

SERVES 8

½ *package dry yeast, or 1 cake fresh compressed yeast*
1 teaspoon sugar
2 tablespoons lukewarm water
¼ *pound (1 stick) butter, cut up*
2 cups flour
Pinch of salt
3 eggs, beaten to mix
11-ounce block of foie gras
1 egg yolk, beaten with a pinch of salt
Fresh parsley for garnish

Dissolve yeast with sugar in lukewarm water. In the bowl of a food processor, process butter, flour, and salt until the butter is cut into the flour. Add the yeast mixture and process until blended. Add the eggs and process just until dough forms a ball above the blade. Remove the dough from the processor and knead on a lightly floured board until smooth and elastic, about 5 minutes.

Let the brioche dough rise in a warm place until doubled. Punch down and knead the dough lightly. Butter a standard loaf pan. Roll the dough out onto a floured board to a 9 x 7-inch rectangle and set the foie gras lengthwise in the center. Roll the dough around it and pinch the edges to seal well. Turn the roll over so the seam is on the bottom and place in the buttered loaf pan. Cover with a damp cloth and let rise until the pan is almost full, 25 to 30 minutes.

Preheat the oven to 400°F.

Brush the brioche with the beaten egg glaze and bake until the dough is well browned and starts to pull away from the side of the pan, about 30 minutes. Remove brioche from the pan and cool on a rack. Serve at room temperature, or freeze.

To serve, cut loaf in ¾-inch slices with a serrated knife, cleaning the knife between each slice. Garnish with fresh parsley.

HAY DAY'S MOULES DIJON

This is one of the first and most successful appetizers we ever made; people buy it to serve for lunch, or as an hors d'oeuvre, or an appetizer. We almost always make it on weekends; we cook a couple of hundred pounds of mussels, and it takes two people hours to pick them out of the shells. You can use a dishtowel at home to strain the mussel juice, but we've had really good luck with a coffee filter.

SERVES 6 AS AN APPETIZER

1 cup dry white wine
10 black peppercorns
2 sprigs parsley
1 small onion, peeled and quartered
½ celery stalk, chopped (including leaves)
4 tablespoons butter
5 pounds mussels, washed and debearded
¼ cup mussel cooking liquid, if clean (or dry white wine)
1 cup Homemade Mayonnaise (see page 18)
⅓ cup Dijon mustard
1 cup celery, thinly sliced
⅓ cup scallions, cut in thin rings
3 hardboiled eggs, chopped
⅓ cup chopped parsley
2 tablespoons capers

Bring first six ingredients to a boil. Add mussels. Cover and cook until shells are fully open (about 8 to 10 minutes). Drain, straining and saving the juice, cool, shell, and refrigerate.

Mix remaining ingredients together and gently stir in the mussels. Serve on a bed of lettuce as an appetizer or hors d'oeuvre.

This appetizer improves if made a day ahead.

SALMON TARTARE

Serve this appetizer on lettuce leaves with buttered toast and lemon slices for a simple but elegant and very effective first course. It can also be packed in ramekins for a pot-luck supper. You could use lox, or Nova Scotia salmon, but Salmon Tartare is just like steak tartare—the higher the quality of the meat, the better it will taste.

SERVES 4

1 egg yolk
½ teaspoon tarragon mustard
1 teaspoon fresh dill, finely chopped
Juice of ½ lemon
2 tablespoons extra-virgin olive oil
2 shallots, very finely minced
½ pound finest quality smoked salmon, coarsely chopped with a knife
Salt and freshly ground black pepper
Tabasco to taste

Beat the egg yolk with mustard, dill, and lemon juice. Beat in olive oil, a little at a time. Beat in shallots. Stir in the chopped salmon. Season to taste with salt, pepper, and Tabasco. Stir gently. Serve mounded on a bed of lettuce, garnished with chopped parsley.

CITRUS CHICKEN SALAD

An excellent appetizer for a heavy winter dinner, this makes a nice way to use leftover roast or poached chicken.

SERVES 4

2 large grapefruit, peeled and sectioned
Leaf lettuce
¾ cup cooked chicken, minced
1 shallot, finely minced
1 teaspoon finely minced celery
4 tablespoons Homemade Mayonnaise (see page 18)
Tabasco to taste
Salt and freshly ground black pepper to taste
Freshly chopped parsley

Arrange grapefruit sections on four lettuce-lined serving plates. Combine chicken, shallot, celery, and mayonnaise. Season with Tabasco, salt, and pepper to taste. Pile chicken in the center of the grapefruit sections. Sprinkle with freshly chopped parsley.

GOLDEN PASTA

American golden caviar is attractive, readily available, and inexpensive enough to use in quantity; it can also withstand very gentle heating without bursting. This recipe is quick, dazzling, and delicious—a great first course for a celebration.

SERVES 4

1½ cups crème fraîche (see page 12)
4 tablespoons fresh dill, chopped
4 ounces American golden caviar
1 pound fresh angel hair pasta
Salt and freshly ground black pepper to taste

Bring the crème fraîche to a boil and add the chopped dill. Boil the cream until it begins to thicken. Meanwhile, bring the water to a boil for the pasta. When the cream has begun to thicken, remove from the heat and add caviar, reserving 2 teaspoons for garnish. Cover and keep warm. Cook the pasta in boiling salted water for 30 seconds. Drain well. Toss in a bowl with the caviar cream sauce and season with salt and pepper. Serve immediately, topping each serving with a spoonful of caviar.

RAVIOLI WITH RAISINS

This unusual sweet and savory combination has a North African ancestry.

SERVES 4

1 pound ricotta cheese, puréed in a food processor
2 tablespoons dry bread crumbs
1 teaspoon nutmeg
3 tablespoons parsley, chopped
2 eggs, beaten
⅓ cup raisins, plumped in white wine, drained, and chopped
Salt to taste
1 pound flat fresh pasta sheets
¼ pound (1 stick) butter
½ cup freshly grated Parmesan cheese

Beat together ricotta cheese, bread crumbs, nutmeg, parsley, eggs, raisins, and salt. Form the ravioli with the cheese and raisin mixture as filling. (See instructions for ravioli on page 67). Cook the filled pasta in boiling salted water for 3 minutes. Drain and toss with melted butter and grated Parmesan cheese. Garnish with more chopped parsley, if desired.

HAY DAY'S VEGETABLE LASAGNE

Children, grownups, vegetarians—everybody likes this; it was one of our first recipes, and we still don't get tired of it. Pasta in whole sheets can be bought to order at Hay Day or in any pasta store, but this recipe works with dried lasagna noodles, if that's all you can find. We generally leave the skins on when we cook eggplant. The sauce may seem thick, but that's on purpose; it is extra rich and helps keep the lasagne from becoming watery.

SERVES 8 TO 10

3¼ cups tomato paste
¼ cup brown sugar
1 tablespoon herbes de Provence
1 teaspoon oregano
2 teaspoons minced garlic
½ cup water
Salt and freshly ground black pepper to taste
1 medium eggplant, unpeeled and sliced in ¼-inch slices
½ cup olive oil
1 pound zucchini, sliced ¼ inch thick
½ pound mushrooms, thinly sliced
1 tablespoon herbes de Provence
2 sheets fresh egg pasta, cut to 9 x 11 inches
1 sheet fresh spinach pasta, cut to 9 x 11 inches
2 cups cottage cheese or ricotta
3 cups grated mozzarella cheese
2 cups grated Parmesan cheese
1 pound fresh plum tomatoes, sliced ¼ inch thick

Combine tomato paste, brown sugar, 1 tablespoon herbes de Provence, oregano, garlic, water, salt, and pepper in a saucepan and simmer over low flame for 20 to 25 minutes, stirring frequently to prevent scorching. The sauce will be thick.

Preheat oven to 325°F.

Grease a jelly roll pan with olive oil. Lay slices of eggplant in the pan, brush with ¼ cup of the olive oil, and bake for 15 to 20 minutes.

Heat the other ¼ cup olive oil in a sauté pan and sauté zucchini, mushrooms, and herbes de Provence until vegetables are tender.

To assemble the lasagne, spread ¾ cup of tomato sauce in a 9 x 11-inch lasagne pan. Place one sheet of egg pasta on top of the sauce and spread with another ¾ cup of the tomato sauce. Put eggplant slices on the sauce and on that put one-third each of the cottage cheese, the mozzarella cheese, the Parmesan cheese, and the sheet of spinach pasta. Repeating the layering, spread ¾ cup of tomato sauce on pasta, all the zucchini-mushroom mixture, then one-third each of cottage cheese, mozzarella, Parmesan cheese, and all the sliced tomatoes. Then add the final sheet of egg pasta, the remainder of the tomato sauce, mozzarella, and Parmesan cheese.

Lightly brush a sheet of foil with olive oil. Cover the pan loosely with foil, oil side down. Bake covered at 325°F for 1 hour and 15 minutes. Remove foil and increase heat to 400°F. Bake for 15 minutes.

ANTIPASTO SALAD

Antipasto Salad is a bright midwinter variation on Salade Niçoise.

SERVES 4 TO 6

3 medium new potatoes, boiled in the skins and cubed
1 small can water-packed tuna
½ pound small shrimp, cooked and cooled
⅓ cup oil-cured black olives
2 anchovy fillets, chopped
½ cup Homemade Mayonnaise (see page 18)
1 tablespoon Dijon mustard
1 tablespoon lemon juice
Salt and freshly ground black pepper to taste
1 tablespoon capers, rinsed and dried
2 to 3 tomatoes, quartered
4 hard-cooked eggs, quartered

Combine potatoes, tuna, shrimp, olives, and anchovies. Beat together mayonnaise, mustard, lemon juice, salt, pepper, and capers. Toss dressing with potato mixture.

Arrange salad on serving plates and surround with tomato and egg wedges.

SMOKED MOZZARELLA IN CARROZZA

With its delicate anchovy sauce, this is probably the ultimate grilled cheese sandwich.

SERVES 4 AS AN APPETIZER, 2 AS A LUNCHEON DISH

4 tablespoons butter
3 anchovy fillets, drained and chopped

2 tablespoons finely chopped parsley
1 teaspoon capers, chopped
1 teaspoon fresh lemon juice
8 slices homemade white bread, crusts removed
8 slices smoked mozzarella cheese
4 eggs
3 tablespoons milk
Salt and freshly ground black pepper to taste
Finely ground dry bread crumbs
Oil for frying: 3 tablespoons peanut oil with 1 tablespoon olive oil added for taste
Freshly chopped parsley

Melt the butter over low heat in a small saucepan. Stir in anchovies, parsley, capers, and lemon juice. Stir until the anchovies melt. Keep sauce warm.

Cut each slice of bread in half. Make sandwiches of the bread and cheese. Beat eggs, milk, salt, and pepper together. Spread bread crumbs on a large plate. Dip each sandwich in the egg mixture and then roll the edges in bread crumbs. (This keeps the cheese from leaking out.)

Heat oils in a heavy skillet. Fry sandwiches in oil until brown on both sides. Drain on paper towels and serve very hot, spooning anchovy sauce on top. Garnish with freshly chopped parsley.

TOASTED CHEDDAR SAVORIES

We serve these as hors d'oeuvres, but traditionally they would be the finale for an English menu; a "savory" was almost always served after the sweet.

SERVES 4 TO 6

⅔ cup shredded cheddar cheese
1 tablespoon grated onion
2 egg yolks
¼ cup dry bread crumbs

6 tablespoons softened butter
½ teaspoon dry mustard
1 teaspoon fresh tarragon, minced
Salt and freshly ground black pepper
4 slices bread, trimmed into triangles and toasted lightly on both sides

Combine the cheese, onion, egg yolks, bread crumbs, butter, and seasonings. Beat into a paste and spread over bread triangles. Broil until the cheese is melted.

WINTER SALAD

Offer this with hot muffins for an excellent company lunch.

SERVES 4

1 head leaf lettuce
2 medium grapefruit, peeled and sectioned
1 small onion, very thinly sliced
½ cucumber, washed and thinly sliced
1 sweet red pepper, seeded and thinly sliced
4 slices of smoked tongue
½ cup vinaigrette (see page 389), to which
   2 tablespoons Roquefort cheese have been added

Arrange washed lettuce in the bottom of a salad bowl. Alternate layers of grapefruit, onion, cucumber, and sweet pepper until all ingredients are used up. Roll up tongue slices and arrange on top. Serve vinaigrette separately.

MOLDED GRAPEFRUIT SALAD

Even people who regard molded salads with deep suspicion should try this one; served with curry mayonnaise, it is terrific with roast pork.

SERVES 6

2 envelopes of granulated gelatin
½ cup cold water
¾ cup boiling water
Pinch of salt
⅓ cup sugar
¼ cup lemon juice
Grapefruit juice
2 grapefruit, peeled, sectioned, and each section cut in 3 chunks, reserving juice
Leaf lettuce
1 grapefruit, peeled, sectioned, and tossed with 2 teaspoons sugar
Homemade Mayonnaise (see page 18) with curry

Soften gelatin in cold water. Add boiling water and stir until dissolved. Stir in the salt, sugar, and lemon juice. Add enough grapefruit juice to the juice reserved from sectioning the 2 grapefruit to make 1 cup. Add grapefruit juice to gelatin and chill until mixture becomes thick and syrupy.

Stir in grapefruit chunks. Pour into a mold and chill until set, at least 4 hours. Unmold onto a serving plate lined with leaf lettuce and garnish with remaining grapefruit sections.

Serve with Homemade Mayonnaise flavored with curry powder.

STUFFED GRAPEFRUIT

Serve these with hot bread and fruit-flavored butter.

SERVES 4

2 large grapefruit, halved and sectioned, reserving juice for another purpose
1 small green pepper, very thinly sliced
1 bunch scallions, very thinly sliced
1 tablespoon salad oil
¼ pound cheddar cheese, grated
1 tablespoon sugar

Toss grapefruit sections with the rest of the ingredients and fill hollowed grapefruit shells. Chill and serve.

SALADE FOLLE

According to the French title, which means "crazy salad," only a nut would put costly fresh foie gras in a salad. It may be crazy, but it's also fabulous.

SERVES 4

1 teaspoon Dijon mustard
1 tablespoon red wine vinegar
Salt and freshly ground black pepper to taste
⅓ cup very fine olive oil
1 pound very thin fresh green beans, tipped, steamed until crisply tender, and cooled to room temperature
Chopped parsley
4 ounces fresh foie gras, sliced

Whisk together mustard, vinegar, salt, pepper, and olive oil. About 30 minutes before serving, marinate the beans in the vinaigrette. Just before serving, drain off excess dressing.

Arrange the marinated beans on chilled serving plates, sprinkle with parsley, and top with foie gras slices. Serve with thick slices of hot, buttered toast.

Rounds of freshly steamed lobster tail can also be added.

ANJOU SALAD

White beans are popular in Anjou. This hearty salad is excellent with roast leg of lamb.

SERVES 6

3 cups cooked new potatoes, cubed and chilled
2 cups white beans, cooked until tender and chilled
2 cups green beans, steamed and cut into 1-inch lengths
1 bunch scallions, whites sliced into thin rounds
½ cup Vinaigrette de Dordogne (see page 391)
Freshly chopped chives

Toss together all ingredients except chives and marinate for at least 30 minutes. Serve topped with freshly chopped chives.

JONATHAN'S GREEN SALAD

This adaptation of a salad invented by Jonathan Waxman of JAMS restaurant in Manhattan is as popular made at home as the original is in the restaurant. The dressing is light and tangy—the mixture of nut oils with raspberry vinegar creates a perfect balance of tastes—and it goes beautifully with grilled steak or chops.

SERVES 4

2 tablespoons walnut oil
1 tablespoon sesame oil
¼ cup olive oil

3 tablespoons raspberry vinegar
1 teaspoon Dijon-style mustard
Salt and freshly ground black pepper to taste
4 teaspoons toasted walnuts, chopped
3 cups mixed leaf lettuce (such as curly endive, Boston, Romaine, Red-Tipped)

Put all ingredients except nuts and lettuce in a jar with a tightly fitting lid. Shake vigorously until thoroughly mixed. Pour dressing over greens and toss lightly. Top each serving with 1 teaspoon chopped walnuts.

WILTED SPINACH SALAD

The German and Eastern European custom of wilting greens like spinach and dandelions with a warm dressing may originally have been designed to tenderize tough leaves, but it works beautifully with young, fresh leaves, too.

SERVES 4

½ pound fresh spinach, washed, stemmed, and torn into bite-sized pieces
2 slices thick-sliced bacon, cut into ½-inch strips
2 tablespoons white wine vinegar
Salt and freshly ground black pepper

Arrange spinach in a serving bowl. Fry bacon until crisp. Remove bacon from the skillet with a slotted spoon and drain on paper towels. To the skillet add vinegar and salt and pepper to taste. Bring to a boil and pour over spinach. Add bacon strips and toss. Serve at once.

RAINBOW SALAD

Marinating the vegetables intensifies their flavor, contrasting with the delicate crispness of the spinach.

SERVES 6

1 pound zucchini, washed, trimmed, and thinly sliced
1 bunch scallions, washed and sliced
½ cup vinaigrette dressing (see page 389)
3 large sweet red peppers, washed, roasted, skins removed (see directions, page 57), and sliced into strips
1 pound spinach, well washed, stemmed, and torn into bite-sized pieces
Freshly ground black pepper

Marinate zucchini and scallions in vinaigrette for several hours before serving. Add pepper strips 1 hour before serving. Toss with spinach and pile in a salad bowl. Serve with freshly ground black pepper.

HOT CABBAGE SALAD

This is another variation on a German theme.

SERVES 4 TO 6

1 small head white cabbage, shredded
2 tablespoons olive oil
2 cloves garlic, minced
3 slices thick-sliced bacon, diced
2 tablespoons raisins
2 tablespoons wine vinegar
1 tablespoon dry mustard
Salt and freshly ground black pepper

Arrange shredded cabbage in a salad bowl. Heat olive oil in a skillet. Add garlic, bacon, and raisins. Cook until bacon begins to brown. Add vinegar and mustard. Remove from heat and beat with a whisk for 10 seconds, then pour the dressing over the cabbage. Season with salt and pepper, toss, and serve.

CAULIFLOWER SALAD

Try to buy cauliflower as white as possible. If it looks rusty, it isn't fresh.

SERVES 4

½ small, very white cauliflower, divided into fleurettes, and steamed until just tender
2 tablespoons wine vinegar
1 clove garlic, very finely minced
1 tablespoon chopped parsley
Salt and freshly ground black pepper to taste
⅓ cup fine olive oil
⅓ cup small oil-cured black olives
Freshly chopped parsley
Leaf lettuce

Chill cauliflower. Beat together vinegar, garlic, parsley, salt, and pepper. Beat in olive oil. Pour dressing over the cauliflower and toss gently. Toss with olives. Marinate 1 hour or more. Garnish with more chopped parsley. Serve on a bed of leaf lettuce.

HAY DAY'S ROQUEFORT CHICKEN SALAD

This is one of our favorites—we love Roquefort cheese. It looks pretty served on red cabbage leaves.

SERVES 6 TO 8

¼ cup fresh lemon juice
½ teaspoon medium curry powder
1 teaspoon grated onion
1 cup Homemade Mayonnaise (see page 18)
3 whole cooked boneless, skinless chicken breasts, cut in julienned strips
1 pound zucchini, cut in julienned strips
½ pound mushrooms, sliced thinly
3 stalks celery, sliced thinly
⅓ pound Roquefort cheese, crumbled

Blend lemon juice, curry powder, and grated onion into mayonnaise. Mix with chicken, zucchini, mushrooms, and celery. Gently fold in crumbled Roquefort cheese.

SPAGHETTI ALLA CARBONARA

Calvin Trillin wants to honor Columbus by making this the American national dish, to be served at Thanksgiving instead of turkey.

SERVES 4

5 ounces pancetta (Italian bacon), or good slab bacon
1 tablespoon extra-virgin olive oil
½ cup heavy cream
6 egg yolks, well beaten
¾ cup Parmesan or Gruyère cheese, freshly grated
1 pound fresh spaghetti
Freshly ground black pepper

Cut the bacon into thin strips and fry in the oil until nearly crisp. Remove the skillet from the heat and keep warm, leaving the bacon in the fat.

Beat the cream into the egg yolks and add two-thirds of the cheese. Cook the spaghetti for no more than 3 minutes in boiling salted water. Drain well and turn the spaghetti into a large mixing bowl. Pour off all but 2 tablespoons of fat. Toss spaghetti with hot bacon and fat. Pour the egg mixture over the hot pasta and toss quickly to mix. The heat from the pasta will cook the egg and melt the cheese. Serve on heated plates with freshly ground black pepper and remaining cheese on the side.

LASAGNETTE VERDE WITH FONTINA

Less filling than a traditional lasagne, this pasta and cheese pie is light enough to serve as a first course or as a main course for lunch with a tomato salad and fresh bread.

SERVES 6 TO 8

1 pound flat spinach pasta sheets, cut into 1½-inch strips
6 tablespoons butter
¾ pound Fontina cheese, sliced
Freshly grated Parmesan cheese

Preheat the oven to 450°F.
Cook the pasta, drain well, and toss with half the butter.
Butter a glass baking dish. Alternate layers of pasta and sliced Fontina, ending with pasta. Dot with butter. Sprinkle with 1 tablespoon Parmesan and bake at 450°F until Fontina melts and the top of the pie begins to brown. Serve with more Parmesan.

CARIBBEAN FISH SOUP

Travelers to Jamaica and the Bahamas will recognize this as a version of callaloo, a spicy fish or crab soup that is found in various incarnations all over the Caribbean. Spinach or swiss chard is often substituted for the original leafy, spinachlike vegetable that gave the soup its name.

SERVES 6

¼ pound bacon, cut into ½-inch slices and fried until crisp, reserve fat
1 pound fish fillets (flounder, haddock, bass, or the like), cut in 3-inch strips
Flour for dredging fish
1 pound fresh spinach, washed, stemmed, and chopped
4 cups well-seasoned chicken broth (see page 8)
1 clove garlic, finely chopped
½ pound tiny okra
2 tablespoons fresh thyme
Tabasco to taste
Salt

Dredge the fish in the flour, knocking off any excess. Fry until crisp in hot bacon fat. In a large stockpot place the spinach, chicken broth, and garlic.

Simmer until spinach is very tender. Add okra and fresh thyme and simmer 5 to 7 minutes longer. Stir in Tabasco and salt and add bacon and fried fish. Heat through and serve at once in soup bowls.

ROAST CHICKEN WITH 40 CLOVES OF GARLIC

Garlic roasted this way literally melts in your mouth. It doesn't linger on the breath, either, and is easily digestible. Have courage; cut off the ends of the roasted cloves and squeeze them onto a slice of toast—you will be rewarded. The lid of the casserole is sealed tightly to the pot with a paste of ½ cup flour and ½ cup water, so that no steam can escape.

SERVES 6

1 five-pound roasting chicken
1 bunch fresh thyme
1 tablespoon parsley
½ cup olive oil
40 cloves of garlic, unpeeled
Fresh rosemary, thyme, and parsley

Preheat the oven to 375°F.
Place thyme and parsley in the cavity and truss the chicken. Heat the olive oil in a heavy ovenproof casserole that has a tight-fitting lid. Roll the chicken in the hot oil. Surround with garlic and herbs. Cover and seal the

casserole with a paste of equal amounts of flour and water. Roast for 2 hours at 375°F.

Break the seal of the casserole with a sharp knife and arrange the chicken on a large serving platter surrounded by garlic.

BAEKENHOFE

This hearty Alsatian one-dish supper is great for after skiing. It can be assembled in the morning, then put in the oven at teatime to simmer during showers and cocktails. Bring it to the table piping hot in its own casserole.

SERVES 6 TO 8

1 pound boneless shoulder of lamb, cut in 1-inch cubes
1 pound boneless pork loin, cut in 1-inch cubes
1 pound beef chuck, cut in 1-inch cubes
4 onions, sliced
2 cloves garlic, peeled
1 bouquet garni (sprigs of parsley, thyme, celery leaves, and bay leaf tied together or tied in cheesecloth)
10 whole cloves
3 cups white wine (Riesling is traditional)
2 tablespoons lard or butter
4 large, all-purpose potatoes, peeled and thinly sliced
3 tablespoons flour
Salt and freshly ground black pepper to taste

Place meat cubes in a large glass or china bowl. Add 1 onion, the garlic, bouquet garni, and cloves. Pour the wine over all and marinate, covered, at least 12 hours. Turn the cubes occasionally.

Drain meat, reserving the marinade. Grease the bottom of an earthenware casserole with lard. Arrange half the potatoes in the casserole, top with half the meat and half the remaining onions. Repeat layering, ending with onions. Season with salt and pepper and pour in marinade.

Preheat the oven to 350°F.

Cover the casserole and seal the edges with a paste made of equal amounts of flour and water. Bake, without opening, for 4 hours. Serve very hot, directly from the dish, with large quantities of fresh, crusty bread.

TINY TIM'S GOOSE STUFFED WITH SAGE AND ONION

The fragrance of the sage in this classic stuffing is undoubtedly the reason the young Cratchits were in such a state; this is, truly, the great Christmas bird. Serve it with mashed potatoes—they are essential for the rich gravy.

SERVES 8

½ pound sausage meat
¼ cup minced shallots
2 medium onions, sliced
3 tablespoons fresh sage, chopped
4 tablespoons butter
10 slices dry homemade white bread, cubed
⅓ cup chopped parsley
Salt and freshly ground black pepper
1 apple, quartered (but not peeled) and cored
1 nine- to ten-pound goose
¾ cup white wine
¼ cup lemon juice
¼ cup red currant jelly
Salt
1 cup dry white wine
⅓ cup heavy cream

Preheat the oven to 375°F.

Brown sausage meat in a heavy skillet. Add shallots, onions, sage, and butter. Sauté until vegetables are transparent. Pour over bread cubes. Add parsley, salt, and pepper, and toss to mix thoroughly.

Stuff the goose. Place apple quarters over the stuffing, peel side up.

Simmer ¾ cup white wine, lemon juice, red currant jelly, and salt until jelly is melted and sauce is very hot. Roast goose at 375°F for 2 hours, basting every 15 minutes with wine mixture. Remove cooked goose and arrange on a heated serving platter.

Remove as much fat from the pan juices as possible. Deglaze the hot pan with 1 cup white wine, boiling until reduced by half. Add the cream and remaining basting liquid. Simmer until smooth. Serve separately in a sauce boat.

TURKEY EN DAUBE PROVENÇAL

A *daube* is usually made with beef and lots of dry red wine, but it's delicious with poultry, too, and for people who have never cooked a turkey other than roasted whole, it will be an awakening. Put it together early in the day, then bake it in the late afternoon and serve it with buttered noodles.

SERVES 8 TO 10

6 tablespoons lard, or butter, or a combination
1 eight-pound turkey (or large roasting chicken), cut into serving pieces
2 sprigs of fresh thyme
6 cloves garlic, crushed
½ pound salt pork, cubed and parboiled for 10 minutes to remove salt, drained, and dried
1 pound small white onions, blanched and peeled
3 leeks, the white part well washed and cut into 1-inch lengths
½ cup brandy
1½ cups dry white wine
1 cup well-seasoned chicken broth (see page 8)

Preheat the oven to 375°F.

Melt the fat in a heavy casserole. Brown the turkey pieces on all sides. Add thyme, garlic, salt pork, and vegetables. Pour in brandy, wine, and chicken broth. Cover and simmer 2 hours or more in a 375°F oven. The turkey should be very tender but not falling apart.

Remove turkey and vegetables and arrange them on a heated platter. Strain sauce and reduce the liquid to about 1½ cups. Spoon a little sauce over the turkey and serve the rest separately in a sauce boat.

CHICKEN LIVERS VÉRONIQUE

The word *Véronique* in a recipe generally means that it includes grapes.

SERVES 4

1½ pounds chicken livers, rinsed, dried, and trimmed
Salt and freshly ground black pepper to taste
4 tablespoons butter
½ cup dry white wine
1½ cups seedless green grapes
¼ cup heavy cream
4 slices buttered toast, crust removed and each slice halved

Season livers with salt and pepper. Melt butter and sauté the livers for 3 to 4 minutes, turning once. Remove livers to a heated dish and keep warm. Stir wine into the hot pan and boil until reduced by half. Add grapes and cream and heat through. Check seasoning. Return livers to sauce, toss gently, and spoon over buttered toast points.

WINTER HOT POT

Somewhere between a hearty soup and a stew, this is an adaptation of an old Pennsylvania Dutch one-dish dinner designed to be cooked slowly on the back of the wood stove all day long.

SERVES 8

4 tablespoons butter
4 pounds oxtail, cut into thick slices

1 pound lean fresh pork shoulder, cut in 2-inch cubes
1 cup white wine
8 cups beef stock
Salt to taste
1 green cabbage, washed and cut in wedges
1 pound carrots, washed, peeled, and cut in 1-inch chunks
½ pound small fresh turnips, peeled and quartered
3 whole onions, each stuck with 3 cloves
Salt and freshly ground black pepper

Melt butter in an ovenproof casserole. Brown meat a little at a time. Add white wine, then stock and salt. Simmer 1 hour. Add vegetables. Simmer 1½ hours. Season with salt and pepper.

Serve in bowls or soup plates—meat, vegetables, and broth at the same time.

Freshly grated horseradish in sour cream makes an excellent sauce for this dish.

SPICED ROAST VENISON

If you are lucky enough to know a hunter—or to be one—this spicy roast of venison is succulent and delicious. The dark, rich dish will have the texture of braised beef.

The dried berries of imported *genièvre*, or juniper, have a warm, pungent flavor and an aromatic scent, and they go well in sauces for game. (Dutch gin, of course, is flavored with varying amounts of juniper and derives its name from the corruption of the word.)

SERVES 8 TO 10

3 cups red wine
½ cup red wine vinegar
Freshly ground black pepper
½ teaspoon ground cloves
½ teaspoon ground cinnamon
1 tablespoon freshly grated ginger
3 tablespoons sugar

[371]

Fresh herbs (thyme, rosemary, sage, or a combination)
2 tablespoons juniper berries
4 pounds venison roast, from the shoulder or haunch
3 onions, peeled and sliced
¾ cup raisins, plumped in 1 cup of hot red wine
½ cup heavy cream

In a saucepan, bring to a boil the wine, vinegar, pepper, spices, sugar, fresh herbs, and juniper berries. Cool. Place venison in a glass or crockery bowl. Surround with sliced onions and pour marinade over all. Marinate overnight or longer, turning the meat two or three times.

Preheat the oven to 375°F.

Strain marinating liquid into a saucepan, reserving onions. Bring to a boil. Place venison in a covered casserole. Surround with sliced onions. Pour hot marinade over all. Add raisins and bake, covered, at 375°F for 2 hours, or more, until the venison is very tender.

Remove the roast from the pan and keep warm. Add cream to pan juices and reduce liquid until it begins to thicken. Slice roast and top with some of the sauce. Serve remaining sauce on the side.

DAUBE À L'ANCIENNE

This ancient dish is even better when made a day ahead and reheated. Use a very hearty red wine, like a Burgundy, Zinfandel, or Cahors.

SERVES 6 TO 8

3 pounds boneless stewing beef, chuck, or beef shank, or a combination of all
*   three, cut in 2-inch cubes*
4 medium onions, quartered
2 medium carrots, scraped and cut into thick slices
½ cup whole parsley
½ teaspoon thyme
1 bay leaf
1 bottle red wine (.75 liters)—the heartier, the better
¼ cup red wine vinegar

½ pound slab bacon, diced
3 cloves garlic, minced (or more, to taste)
Zest of 1 orange, cut into thin strips
10 whole peppercorns
Salt and freshly ground black pepper

Place the beef, onions, and carrots in a large bowl. Tie parsley, thyme, and bay leaf in a square of cheesecloth. Add to the bowl. Pour on the wine and vinegar. Cover and marinate in the refrigerator, turning occasionally, for at least 12 hours, better overnight.

Drain the beef, reserving the marinade and vegetables. Dry the meat with paper towels. Fry the bacon until crisp. Remove the bacon and set aside. Brown the meat in the hot bacon fat, a few cubes at a time. Set the meat aside and continue until all the meat has been browned. Pour off all but 3 tablespoons of the fat. Return the beef and bacon to the pot. Add garlic, orange zest, and peppercorns and pour in the marinade with the vegetables and bag of herbs. Add just enough water to cover the meat. Bring the liquid to a boil, reduce heat, and simmer, covered, until the meat is very tender, about 4 hours. Uncover and simmer 45 minutes to 1 hour longer until meat nearly falls apart. If sauce is thin, simmer uncovered for 15 minutes longer. Season to taste with salt and pepper.

Serve with fresh buttered noodles.

TOURNEDOS ROSSINI

Tournedos Rossini, the classic French preparation of slices of steak from the fillet with fresh foie gras, Madeira, and truffles, is rich, elegant, easy—and very expensive. Save it for a special occasion.

SERVES 8

1 small truffle, fresh if possible, canned if not
½ cup Madeira wine
½ pound (2 sticks) butter
8 small slices of homemade white bread, toasted lightly
8 tournedos, or thick slices of fillet of beef
Salt and freshly ground black pepper

½ cup well-flavored beef stock
1 eleven-ounce block of foie gras, cut into 8 slices
Watercress

Place the truffle in a small saucepan with the Madeira, cover, and simmer for 20 minutes. Cut the truffle into 8 slices and allow the slices to cool in the Madeira.

Melt 2 tablespoons of butter in a heavy skillet. Sauté the bread slices on both sides until browned. Keep warm. Season the tournedos with salt and pepper. Sauté in 3 tablespoons of butter until well browned outside and still quite rare inside. Remove from the pan and keep warm. Pour off all but 1 tablespoon fat.

Pour the stock into the sauté pan. Add the Madeira drained from the truffles and bring to a boil. Reduce by one-quarter. Whisk in remaining butter a little at a time.

Place toast slices on serving plates. Top each slice with a tournedo. On each tournedo, place a slice of foie gras and then a slice of truffle. Spoon the sauce around each. Serve at once, garnished with sprigs of watercress.

FRUITED PORK CHOP CASSEROLE

We cook with lemon all the time, so why not grapefruit? It is terrific with pork.

SERVES 6

1 tablespoon olive oil
2 tablespoons butter
1 yellow onion, thinly sliced
6 thick-cut loin pork chops
6 chorizo sausages
1 medium savoy cabbage, shredded
2 tart apples, peeled, cored, and diced
1 tablespoon brown sugar
Salt and freshly ground black pepper to taste
1 cup well-seasoned chicken broth (see page 8)
½ cup cider

½ cup dry white wine
2 grapefruit, peeled and sectioned

Preheat the oven to 350°F.

Heat oil and butter in a heavy skillet. Add onion and sauté until transparent. Add the chops and brown on both sides. Place browned chops and onions in an ovenproof casserole. Add the sausages to the skillet and sauté until just browned. Add to casserole. Pile savoy cabbage in the skillet and sauté just until wilted. Stir in diced apple. Cook 1 minute longer. Spread cabbage over chops. Sprinkle with brown sugar and salt and pepper. Pour the broth, cider, and wine over the cabbage. Cover the casserole and bake at 350°F for 1½ hours. Stir in grapefruit sections and simmer 15 minutes.

To serve, arrange cabbage on a platter and top with pork chops and sausages. Keep warm. Reduce the pan juices over high heat and pour over chops.

CHEESE FONDUE

There is a saying in Switzerland that fondue doesn't wait for people—the diners must wait for the fondue. Do not complete the fondue until everyone is seated. If it is not stirred and watched, it will burn or become a single great lump in the pot.

Traditionally made with a combination of Emmenthaler and Gruyère, fondue is best cooked in an earthenware dish called a *caquelon* that can withstand the heat of the stove and is glazed only on the inside. Some enthusiasts like freshly ground pepper added at the last minute; others like to dip the bread into a small glass of Kirsch before swirling it in the cheese mixture.

SERVES 4 TO 6 (CAN EASILY BE DOUBLED)

1 clove garlic
1½ tablespoons cornstarch
3 to 4 tablespoons Kirsch
2 cups dry white Riesling
1½ pounds cheese (ideally ¾ pound Swiss Emmenthaler and ¾ pounds Gruyère), shredded or cubed but not grated

Cut the garlic clove in half and rub the inside of the pot with the cut side. Dissolve the cornstarch in the Kirsch and set it aside. Pour the wine into the pot and set it over moderately low heat. Once it begins to simmer, add the cheese shavings by handfuls, stirring constantly. As each handful melts, add another, stirring all the time. The mixture will then form a large soft lump. Add the Kirsch and cornstarch mixture and continue to stir until the mixture is smooth and liquid.

Keep the mixture bubbling, set the fondue pot over a spirit burner, and serve immediately with chunks of crusty peasant or French bread.

For Fondue à la Tomate, follow the above recipe except add 3 cloves of garlic to the pot before pouring the wine. Add 1 cup plum tomatoes chopped well (or 1 cup canned crushed tomatoes) just before serving the fondue. Stir well to blend. Pour over boiled new potatoes.

FRIED PLANTAINS

Plantains, a starchy, less sweet cousin of a banana, are good served with meat dishes instead of rice or potatoes. Although unripe plantains have their uses, here they must be very ripe and almost black.

SERVES 4

3 tablespoons butter
2 large, very ripe plantains, peeled, halved lengthwise, and cut into 2-inch lengths
Salt and freshly ground black pepper

Melt butter in a heavy skillet. Sauté plantains in butter until tender and golden brown and crisp on the outside. Season generously with salt and pepper.

PASTA PANCAKES

This is a traditional Italian dish, but we suspect more distant Chinese origins that may go back to Marco Polo. Shrimp or crab-meat can easily be substituted for the lobster.

SERVES 6 AS A FIRST COURSE

1 pound fresh angel hair pasta
4 eggs, well beaten
½ pound cooked shelled lobster (or shrimp or crabmeat)
1 teaspoon grated onion
1 clove garlic, minced
Salt and freshly ground black pepper to taste
Olive oil

Cook pasta until al dente (1 minute or so), drain well, and turn into a large bowl. Add beaten eggs to pasta. Chop the lobster into small pieces and mix with pasta. Stir in grated onion, garlic, salt, and pepper.

Form pasta into small round pancakes and fry in hot oil. Drain well and serve very hot with a little Marinara Sauce (see page 186) on the side.

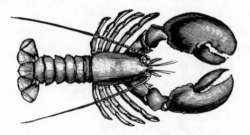

NUTTY CAULIFLOWER

Quick and easy, this is a great way to convince people who are not sure whether or not they like cauliflower.

SERVES 6

4 tablespoons butter
½ cup broken pecan pieces, chopped
1 large white cauliflower, broken into fleurettes and steamed until tender
Salt and freshly ground black pepper

Melt butter in a skillet and sauté pecan pieces until very crisp but not burned. Drain cauliflower and arrange in a serving dish. Pour nutted butter over it and toss gently. Add salt and pepper to taste. Serve very hot.

RUTABAGA AND GINGERED CARROT PURÉE

Called yellow turnip in some parts of the country, rutabagas are sweeter than white turnips and make a welcome addition to winter menus. Here they are served as a side dish like mashed potatoes or any other purée.

SERVES 6

1 pound rutabaga, peeled and cut into small chunks
4 carrots, peeled and cut in chunks
2 onions, coarsely chopped
1 tablespoon freshly grated ginger
Salt and freshly ground black pepper
4 tablespoons butter
About ⅓ cup heavy cream

Simmer rutabaga, carrots, and onion in boiling, salted water until tender, about 25 to 30 minutes. Drain and purée with the ginger in a food processor. Beat in salt, pepper, and butter.

Return purée to the saucepan and cook over very low heat until it is thick and very dry. Add cream until the purée is the desired consistency. Stir often to prevent the purée from sticking to the bottom of the pan.

BRAISED RED CABBAGE AND APPLES

Its sharp, slightly acidic taste makes this a nice accompaniment for duck, game, or roast pork.

4 slices bacon, cut in ½-inch pieces
2 tablespoons dark brown sugar
1 small yellow onion, chopped
1 very small head red cabbage, shredded
2 tart apples, cored and thinly sliced
2 tablespoons white wine vinegar
Salt and freshly ground black pepper
2 tablespoons fresh dill
Dry red wine

Preheat the oven to 350°F.

Fry the bacon until nearly crisp. Add the brown sugar and stir until it begins to brown. Add the onion and sauté until tender. Add remaining ingredients, using enough red wine to keep the cabbage from sticking to the bottom of the pan. Simmer 5 minutes. Spread the cabbage in a baking dish and bake at 350°F until very tender, about 40 minutes, stirring occasionally. Replenish the wine, a little at a time, to keep the cabbage from sticking.

Serve very hot.

STEAMED FENNEL

Fennel, with its delicate anise flavor, is a European winter staple. It goes well with fish, veal, or pork.

SERVES 4

2 bulbs fennel, trimmed, washed, peeled, and cut into small chunks
2 tablespoons butter
1 teaspoon sesame oil
1 tablespoon Dijon mustard
Salt and freshly ground black pepper

Steam the fennel over boiling salted water until crisply tender.

In a skillet or wok, heat the butter and oil until hot. Stir in mustard. Add fennel and toss well. Season with salt and pepper to taste and serve at once.

BAKED POTATO CAKE

A rich winter night accompaniment for roasts and chops, this can be assembled in advance and put in the oven while the roast is cooking. It goes well with grilled meat in the summer, too.

SERVES 6

6 tablespoons butter
2 pounds all-purpose potatoes, peeled and sliced very thin, soaked in cold water
  for 30 minutes
½ pound Gruyère cheese, sliced very thin
Salt and freshly ground black pepper to taste
1½ cups beef stock

Preheat the oven to 450°F.

Melt 3 tablespoons of the butter in the bottom of a shallow ovenproof dish. Layer the potatoes and cheese in the dish, starting and ending with potatoes. Season with salt and pepper. Pour the stock over the potatoes. Dot with the remaining butter. Cover with foil and bake at 450°F for 1 hour. Uncover and bake 20 minutes longer. Serve very hot, directly from the dish.

SOUTHERN FRIED APPLES

Try this dish with roast pork or roast duck on Saturday night, or with pancakes on Sunday morning.

SERVES 4

½ pound sliced bacon
3 large all-purpose apples, cored and sliced
⅓ cup sugar

Fry the bacon until crisp. Set aside and keep hot. Pour off all the rendered fat except 3 tablespoons. Using 1 tablespoon fat, brown half the apple slices. Remove from pan, add remaining fat and brown remaining slices. Return all slices to pan, sprinkle evenly with sugar, and cover. Cook over low heat until tender, remove, and turn up heat to evaporate juice, shaking the pan occasionally. Pour sauce over the apples.

Serve on a heated platter surrounded by bacon.

SOUFFLÉED BAKED POTATOES

These potatoes are terrific for brunch or lunch, or even as an accompaniment for grilled steak or roast beef. If you are serving them for brunch, try stirring several tablespoons of ground ham into the potato mixture.

SERVES 4

4 large baking potatoes, skins rubbed with oil and baked until tender
2 eggs, separated, the whites beaten until stiff peaks form
⅓ cup Gruyère cheese, grated
2 tablespoons butter
Salt and freshly ground black pepper to taste
Tabasco to taste
Freshly grated Parmesan cheese

Preheat the oven to 400°F.

Cut the tops off the potatoes. Scoop the insides of the potatoes into a large mixing bowl, leaving a shell about ¼ inch thick.

Mash potatoes well. Beat in the egg yolks, grated cheese, and butter. Season with salt, pepper, and Tabasco. Fold in beaten egg whites and mound the mixture in potato shells. Sprinkle with Parmesan cheese. Bake at 400°F for about 15 minutes, until the filling is puffed and golden. Serve immediately.

WINTER SQUASH SOUFFLÉ

Squash, the workhorse of winter menus, is transformed in this recipe into something elegant.

SERVES 4

2 pounds winter squash (any kind), peeled, seeded, and cut in cubes
Salt and freshly ground black pepper
¼ teaspoon dried thyme
2 tablespoons butter, melted
3 tablespoons heavy cream
¼ cup Gruyère cheese, grated (or more, to taste)
3 eggs, separated, the whites beaten until stiff peaks form

Preheat the oven to 350°F.

Boil the squash in salted water until tender, about 20 minutes. Drain well. Purée in the bowl of a food processor. Mix the squash with the pepper, thyme, butter, cream, and cheese. Beat in the egg yolks one at a time. Cool the mixture to room temperature. Fold egg whites into squash mixture. Turn mixture into a buttered 2-quart baking dish. Bake at 350°F for about 25 minutes. Serve at once.

WINTER

SQUASH WITH NUTS AND PRUNES

This dish is excellent with poultry and pork.

SERVES 6

2 pounds winter squash (any kind), peeled, seeded, boiled until tender, and then puréed
Salt to taste
2 tablespoons honey
Pinch of nutmeg
8 large seedless prunes, cut up
½ cup nuts (walnuts, pecans, hazelnuts, or almonds), finely chopped
2 tablespoons butter

Preheat the oven to 350°F.

Combine all the ingredients until well mixed. Butter a covered casserole. Turn the squash mixture into the casserole and bake, covered, at 350°F for about 30 minutes.

GIBLET GRAVY

Make this gravy any time you're having roast turkey. The stock can be made while the turkey is in the oven, then the gravy finished in the roasting pan while the bird is resting on its platter before being carved.

MAKES ABOUT 3 CUPS

1 turkey neck
1 turkey gizzard
1 turkey heart
1 turkey liver
2 cups water
1 cup white wine
Salt and freshly ground black pepper to taste
½ onion, cut up
2 tablespoons flour

Put all ingredients except the flour in a saucepan. Simmer for 2 hours, or until the meat is very tender and falling from the neck bone. Remove giblets from the liquid and shred the neck meat. Chop liver, heart, and gizzard. Strain the stock and set aside.

Pour off all but 2 tablespoons of the fat left in the roasting pan after the turkey has been removed. Set pan over medium heat. Pour in a mixture of 2 tablespoons flour beaten into ½ cup giblet stock. Stir into the roasting pan and scrape up all the dark bits on the bottom of the pan. When the mixture begins to thicken, stir in remaining stock. Simmer for 10 minutes. Season with salt and pepper. Stir in reserved meat and heat through. Serve at once.

CORN BREAD DRESSING

Some of us grew up in the South and remember chicken or turkey with this stuffing. The crunch of the corn bread is a nice counterpoint to the tenderness of the meat.

MAKES ENOUGH TO STUFF A 12- TO 15-POUND TURKEY

8 cups coarsely crumbled corn bread (see page 408)
½ pound bacon, cut into ½-inch pieces
3 large onions, chopped
1 pound hot sausage
2 tablespoons fresh thyme
2 tablespoons fresh sage, chopped
½ cup chopped parsley
Salt and freshly ground black pepper to taste
⅓ cup bourbon whiskey (optional)

Put the corn bread in a large bowl. Fry the bacon in a heavy skillet until almost crisp. Remove from the skillet with a slotted spoon and set aside. Sauté the onions and sausage meat in the bacon grease until lightly browned. Add herbs, salt and pepper, and bourbon, if using, and stir. Cook 1 minute. Pour the mixture over the corn bread crumbs. Sprinkle with the bacon and toss well to mix thoroughly. Stuff the turkey as usual.

HERBED BREAD CHESTNUT DRESSING

Aromatic and old-fashioned, this is a great stuffing for turkey and oven-roasted chickens, but it can also be covered and baked for an hour at 325°F, and served as a side dish.

MAKES ENOUGH TO STUFF A 12- TO 15-POUND TURKEY

½ pound thick-sliced bacon, cut into ½-inch strips
2 large onions, chopped
⅔ cup chopped celery
¼ pound (1 stick) unsalted butter
1 teaspoon dried sage
1 cup well-seasoned chicken broth (see page 8)
1 cup chestnuts, roasted, peeled, and chopped (see page 228)
6 cups two-day-old homemade white bread or herbed bread, torn into small pieces
Salt and freshly ground black pepper to taste

Fry bacon until crisp. Drain and set aside. Sauté onions and celery in butter until transparent. Add sage, chicken broth, and chestnuts. Simmer until chestnuts are tender. Pour over bread. Add salt and pepper to taste. Toss well. Loosely stuff both cavities of the turkey and truss the bird for roasting.

SAUSAGE AND CHESTNUT STUFFING

Try this rich dressing the next time you stuff a turkey.

MAKES ENOUGH FOR A 12- TO 15-POUND TURKEY

1 one-pound loaf of day-old bread
Salt and freshly ground black pepper
1 teaspoon each dried thyme and dried oregano
½ pound (2 sticks) butter
Turkey giblets, chopped
3 large onions, minced

1 pound country-style bulk sausage
⅓ cup parsley, minced
½ cup celery, minced
½ cup light cream
1½ pounds chestnuts, cooked, peeled, cooled, and chopped (see
  page 228)

Tear the bread into bite-sized pieces. Season with salt and pepper and herbs.

Melt the butter in a heavy skillet and sauté the giblets and onions until the onions are transparent. Add the sausage, parsley, and celery. Cook until the sausage is no longer pink. Pour the contents of the skillet over the bread and toss well. Add cream and chestnuts. Toss well and cool completely before stuffing loosely into both turkey cavities. Roast as usual.

CHESTNUT DRESSING FOR TURKEY

This elegant stuffing with a French accent is wonderful for wild goose or pheasant.

MAKES ENOUGH FOR A 12- TO 14-POUND TURKEY

¼ pound (1 stick) butter
2 red onions, peeled and diced
½ pound fresh mushrooms, sliced
Turkey giblets, raw, chopped
3 stalks celery, chopped
⅓ pound slab bacon, blanched and diced
1 one-pound loaf of day-old bread, torn into small pieces
2 tablespoons chopped parsley
Salt and freshly ground black pepper to taste
1 pound chestnuts, peeled, boiled until tender, and cut up (see page 228)
3 ounces foie gras, en bloc, cut in cubes (optional)

Melt butter in a heavy skillet and sauté onions, mushrooms, giblets, celery, and bacon until golden brown. Pour over bread, add parsley, salt, and pepper. Stir in chestnuts and foie gras, if using. Toss to mix completely.

Stuff both neck and body cavity with chestnut dressing, taking care not to pack too tightly. Truss bird and roast as usual.

OLD-FASHIONED BREAD STUFFING

A New England classic, updated with tarragon. What's the difference between stuffing and dressing? None, as far as we can tell.

MAKES ENOUGH TO STUFF A 12- TO 15-POUND TURKEY

½ pound (2 sticks) butter
¼ cup finely chopped shallots
1 bunch scallions, sliced
8 cups fresh bread cubes
2 tablespoons fresh tarragon
1 cup finely chopped parsley
Salt and freshly ground black pepper to taste
⅓ cup white wine

Melt butter in a heavy skillet. Sauté shallots and scallions in butter until transparent. Pour over bread. Add herbs, salt, and pepper. Toss well to mix. Add wine and toss well. Stuff the turkey as usual.

HAZELNUT HARD SAUCE

Hard sauce is traditionally served very cold with hot pie or plum pudding.

MAKES 1½ CUPS

1½ cups confectioners' sugar
1 teaspoon pure vanilla extract
6 ounces (1½ sticks) butter, softened and beaten until light and fluffy
⅓ cup brandy
⅓ cup finely chopped hazelnuts, pecans, or walnuts

Beat the sugar and vanilla into the butter until very smooth. Beat in the brandy, a little at a time, until all is absorbed. Stir in nuts and mound in a glass serving dish. Chill well. Serve with plum pudding or mincemeat pie.

CUMBERLAND SAUCE

A classic accompaniment for game, this also makes a superb sauce for turkey or ham. It's good for Christmas presents, too.

MAKES TWO ½-PINT JARS

2 large shallots, finely chopped
Zest and juice from 2 oranges and 1 lemon
1 cup red currant jelly
2 teaspoons Dijon mustard
⅔ cup Ruby port
2 teaspoons arrowroot
1 tablespoon water

In a small saucepan combine the shallots and zest. Cover with cold water, bring to a boil, and simmer for 5 minutes. Drain well and reserve juice. Melt jelly over hot water. Stir the citrus juices into the melted jelly. Stir in the mustard, blanched zest, shallots, and port. Simmer for 5 minutes.

Mix arrowroot to a paste with 1 tablespoon water. Stir into the jelly mixture. Simmer gently for 2 minutes. Pack in hot sterilized jars and seal.

CANDIED GRAPEFRUIT RIND

This is pretty when the grapefruit rind is as yellow as possible. Serve it with espresso, after dinner.

MAKES 1 ½ CUPS

Rind of 2 very yellow grapefruit
Water
Sugar

Peel the fruit and cut rind (with just a little of the white pith left on) into long, thin strips. Cover with cold water in a saucepan and bring slowly to a boil. Pour off water. Add fresh water and repeat boiling process two more times. Simmer the rind in the fourth water to cover until tender. Measure water and rind and add an equal volume of sugar. Simmer until the rind is clear and there is almost no more syrup. Drain the hot rind on absorbent paper and roll in granulated sugar. Spread on a baking rack and let dry. Pack in a tin lined with waxed paper.

GRAPEFRUIT MARMALADE

This is easy to make and an excellent Christmas present.

MAKES ABOUT 10 HALF-PINT JARS

4 large, thick-skinned grapefruit
4 large lemons, or limes
12 cups water
12 cups sugar

Scrub the fruit with soap, water, and a brush. Rinse it well and dry. Peel off rind, carefully leaving behind all the white pith. Cut the rind into very thin julienne and set aside.

Squeeze the juice of the grapefruit and lemons (or limes). Chop pith coarsely. Reserve seeds in a small cheesecloth bag. Add the juices, 12 cups water, bag of seeds and pith to a large kettle. Add julienned peel. Bring to a boil and simmer for about 2 hours. Remove the bag of seeds and pith from the kettle and add the sugar, stirring until it dissolves. Boil rapidly until 220°F on a candy thermometer, about 15 to 20 minutes. Do not allow to boil over.

Ladle the boiling marmalade into hot sterilized jars. Seal at once.

THICK VINAIGRETTE

This is especially good with vegetable salads, where the dressing should cling to the ingredients.

MAKES APPROXIMATELY I CUP

2 teaspoons balsamic vinegar
2 hard-cooked egg yolks, mashed
½ teaspoon dry mustard
Salt and freshly ground black pepper
2 teaspoons fresh chives, minced
2 teaspoons fresh chervil, minced
¾ cup extra-virgin olive oil

Whisk together all ingredients until smooth and creamy.

CARLY'S DRESSING

This slightly sweet dressing is perfect for a mixed salad of greens, tomatoes, cucumber, radishes, scallions, cheese, and boiled eggs. Add a little tuna, Feta cheese, and oil-cured olives for a Provençal-style salad.

MAKES I CUP

½ cup safflower oil
3 tablespoons lemon vinegar (or less, according to taste)
¼ teaspoon dry mustard
½ teaspoon curry powder
½ teaspoon sugar
Juice of ½ lemon
1 tablespoon freshly chopped tomato, peeled and seeded
1 clove garlic, crushed and minced
Salt
Dash of Worcestershire sauce
Tabasco to taste

Whisk together all ingredients, or shake vigorously in a jar, until thoroughly mixed.

VINAIGRETTE DE DORDOGNE

The Dordogne region in France is famous for walnuts, which really come into their own in a salad of mixed greenery.

MAKES APPROXIMATELY ½ CUP

1 teaspoon Champagne mustard
3 tablespoons red wine vinegar or
  2 teaspoons balsamic vinegar
Salt and freshly ground black pepper to taste
½ cup walnut oil or
  ¼ cup walnut oil mixed with ¼ cup safflower oil
2 tablespoons coarsely chopped walnuts

Whisk the mustard and vinegar with salt and pepper. Beat in oil. Stir in walnuts and chill for ½ hour. Whisk before using.

CUCUMBER DRESSING

Serve this creamy dressing with vegetable salads or cold poached fish.

MAKES APPROXIMATELY 2 CUPS

1 cup cucumbers, peeled, seeded, and minced
½ teaspoon salt
1 tablespoon Champagne vinegar (or other light wine vinegar)
1 tablespoon fresh chives, finely chopped
1 tablespoon fresh dill, minced
Freshly ground black pepper to taste
1 cup crème fraîche (see page 12)

Sprinkle minced cucumber with salt. Let it drain for ½ hour and then press out as much liquid as possible. Place cucumbers in a bowl. Add vinegar, chives, dill, and pepper. Stir in crème fraîche. Refrigerate 30 minutes or more.

CRÈME FRAÎCHE DRESSING

This dressing is delicious with endive, watercress, and mâche.

MAKES APPROXIMATELY ½ CUP

½ cup crème fraîche (see page 12)
1½ tablespoons raspberry vinegar
2 tablespoons chives, minced
Salt and freshly ground black pepper

Beat together all ingredients until smooth and well blended.

TARRAGON DRESSING

This has a very strong tarragon flavor, and should be used with substantial mixtures like salads made with fish or cold meats or potatoes.

MAKES APPROXIMATELY ½ CUP

1 tablespoon tarragon vinegar
⅓ cup olive oil
2 tablespoons heavy cream
¾ teaspoon sugar
1 teaspoon fresh tarragon, chopped
Salt and cayenne pepper to taste

Whisk all ingredients together until well mixed.

HOT MULLED CIDER

This is one of the things that makes winter worthwhile.

MAKES I QUART

1 quart cider
Juice of 1 lemon
Juice of ½ orange
⅛ teaspoon each of cinnamon, cloves, and nutmeg
⅓ cup raisins (optional)
¼ cup toasted slivered almonds (optional)
Rum (optional)

Simmer all the ingredients except rum together until steaming hot. Serve in mugs. Rum can be added just before serving.

EGGNOG

Once you've made eggnog yourself, you'll never buy it in a carton again. You will find this much lighter and less cloying than the supermarket version.

MAKES I QUART

4 tablespoons sugar
3 egg yolks, well beaten

3 egg whites, beaten until stiff peaks form
1 cup milk
1 cup half and half
3 ounces dark rum
1 cup brandy, or Scotch whisky, or bourbon
Nutmeg

Beat sugar and egg yolks until thick and lemon-colored. Fold whites and sugared yolks together. Gently stir in milk and half and half. Blend in rum and brandy. Chill until very cold. Pour into a large bowl and ladle into mugs. Serve topped with a dash of freshly ground nutmeg.

GRATINÉED ORANGES

A shirred egg dish is usually small (4 to 5 inches in diameter) and shallow, with two small extensions as handles, but any similar little heat-proof baking dish will do.

SERVES 4

4 large oranges, peeled and sectioned
4 egg yolks
⅓ cup sugar
⅓ cup heavy cream
Confectioners' sugar

Lightly butter 4 shirred egg or small gratin dishes. Arrange the orange sections in a pattern in the bottom of the dishes. Beat the egg yolks and sugar until thick and creamy. Beat in the cream. Pour a little of the mixture over the oranges. Broil for 2 minutes until puffy and golden. Sprinkle with powdered sugar and serve at once.

RED BANANAS FLAMBÉE

This is a variation on Bananas Foster, a New Orleans classic; using red bananas gives it a lot of character.

[394]

SERVES 4

4 tablespoons butter
½ cup brown sugar
4 red bananas, peeled and halved
¼ cup dark rum
2 tablespoons rum
Vanilla ice cream

Melt butter and sugar together. Simmer until thick and syrupy. Add bananas and ¼ cup dark rum. Simmer until tender, turning once. Heat the remaining rum, pour over bananas, and ignite. Serve bananas with vanilla ice cream. Spoon the sauce over all.

GRAPEFRUIT SHORTCAKE

Sometimes we get locked into grooves—we make strawberry shortcake in the spring and then forget about it. Why not make grapefruit shortcake in the winter?

SERVES 8

2 large pink Orchid grapefruit, peeled, sectioned, and drained well
⅓ cup sugar
2 cups flour
3 teaspoons double-acting baking powder
1 teaspoon salt
2 tablespoons sugar
4 tablespoons butter, cold
⅔ cup milk
1 cup heavy cream, whipped

Preheat the oven to 425°F.
Place the drained grapefruit sections in a bowl. Sprinkle with ⅓ cup sugar and allow to stand at room temperature for 1 hour.
Stir together flour, baking powder, salt, and 2 tablespoons sugar. Cut in butter until the mixture resembles coarse meal. Add milk gradually and stir

with a fork until it forms a soft dough. Roll or pat the dough out about ½ inch thick on a lightly floured board. Cut into rounds with a 3-inch cookie cutter and bake at 425°F for 15 minutes, or until golden brown.

While the cakes are still warm, split and fill with sweetened grapefruit. Top with whipped cream and more fruit. Serve at once.

This is also good made with tangerines or oranges. Use 6 to 8 smaller fruit.

SOUTHERN FRUIT CAKE

This old family recipe will please people who don't like lumps of preserved cherries and citron in their fruit cakes. The cakes can be soaked in bourbon and preserved for several weeks.

MAKES 2 CAKES

1 cup white sugar
1½ cups brown sugar
½ pound (2 sticks) butter
6 egg yolks, beaten
4 cups cake flour; reserve 1 cup for the fruit
4 teaspoons baking powder
½ teaspoon nutmeg
½ teaspoon cinnamon
½ teaspoon allspice
⅔ cup bourbon whiskey
½ cup molasses
1 pound seeded raisins (white, if you like)
1 cup dried figs, chopped
1 cup dates, chopped
½ cup currants
1 pound pecans
6 egg whites, stiffly beaten

Preheat the oven to 300°F.

Stir the sugars together until well mixed. Beat the butter until light and fluffy. Blend sugar and softened butter. Stir in the beaten egg yolks. Stir 3 cups flour with the baking powder and spices. Add flour mixture to the butter and sugar, alternating with the bourbon whiskey and molasses. Toss the fruit and nuts in the reserved cup of flour and stir them into the batter. (The flour will keep the nuts and fruit from sinking to the bottom of the cake during baking.) Carefully fold in egg whites and turn into 2 well-buttered tube pans (or 4 loaf pans).

Bake at 300°F for about 45 minutes and then increase to 350° for about 30 minutes, or until the cake is done. Allow to cool for 15 minutes in the pan, then turn out on a rack and cool thoroughly.

YULE CAKES À L'ORANGE

Serve these Scandinavian confections for breakfast on Christmas morning.

SERVES 6

2 cups very fine fresh bread crumbs
1 teaspoon pumpkin pie spice
⅓ cup sugar
1¼ cups heavy cream
4 eggs, well beaten
½ pound raisins, plumped in boiling water and then drained
2 tablespoons orange liqueur
6 tablespoons butter, melted
Confectioners' sugar
3 oranges, peeled and cut into segments

Beat the bread crumbs, spice, sugar, cream, and eggs together. Allow batter to stand for 15 minutes. Stir in the raisins and orange liqueur.

In a little melted butter, fry the batter into 3-inch pancakes, keeping them warm until all the batter is used. Arrange on serving plates. Sprinkle with powdered sugar and serve with fresh orange segments.

HAY DAY'S LEMON MOUSSE

This dessert has been incredibly popular. It's easy, with one caveat: when the recipe says "cool slowly to room temperature," don't hurry. If you put it in the icebox, the gelatin will start to harden and will make lumps when the whites and heavy cream are added. Just stir the lemon mixture for a little while with a whisk till it more or less reaches body heat, and you will have no trouble folding in the beaten egg whites and whipped cream.

You can make a gorgeous raspberry sauce by whirling a defrosted 10-ounce package of raspberries in a blender or processor with superfine sugar to taste and a tablespoon of Kirsch; it should be strained to remove the seeds.

SERVES 6

6 eggs, separated
1½ cups sugar
Juice and zest of 2 large lemons
1 package unflavored gelatin
¼ cup cold water
1 cup heavy cream, whipped until soft peaks form

[398]

Beat egg yolks and sugar until the mixture forms a ribbon when the whisk is lifted out of the bowl. The mixture should be fluffy and almost white. Add lemon juice and zest. Cook over simmering water in a double boiler until mixture coats a spoon. Stir constantly.

Dissolve gelatin in a measuring cup with ¼ cup cold water. Melt by putting the cup in a pot of simmering water. Beat the liquid gelatin into lemon mixture. Cool slowly to room temperature, stirring frequently. Beat the egg whites until soft peaks form. Whisk one-third of the egg whites into the cooled lemon mixture and then fold in the rest.

Fold one-third of the whipped cream into the lemon mixture. Then fold in the remaining two-thirds. Gently pour the mousse into a 1½-quart bowl and chill for 8 hours, or overnight.

Variation: This can be made into a cold soufflé by making a collar around a 1-quart dish. When mixture has become firm, remove collar. Decorate with whipped cream rosettes and serve.

CHAMPAGNE SORBET

Serve this between courses or for dessert; it is nice in tiny brandy glasses.

SERVES 6

½ bottle Champagne or other sparkling white wine
½ cup grapefruit juice
½ cup sugar
1 cup water

Mix wine and grapefruit juice. Boil sugar and water for 10 minutes until sugar is thoroughly dissolved and the mixture thickens a little. Cool thoroughly. Add syrup to the Champagne mixture just until it tastes sweet. Freeze as usual in an ice cream freezer.

Allow to stand in the freezer for 2 hours. Serve with more sparkling wine poured over each serving.

ORANGE GRANITA

Unlike a sorbet, which is smooth, a granita will have obvious ice crystals in it.

SERVES 4

1 cup sugar
2 cups water
1 cup fresh orange juice
3 tablespoons lemon juice
2 tablespoons orange liqueur

Stir sugar into the water in a small saucepan. Bring to a boil and simmer, stirring constantly, until all the sugar is dissolved. Cook for 5 minutes. Remove from heat and cool. Mix sugar syrup, orange juice, lemon juice, and orange liqueur together.

Freeze mixture in a 9-inch square pan until slushy. Every 30 minutes, turn slush into a cold bowl and break up the chunks with a fork. Repeat this process three times. Return the mixture to the pan and continue freezing.

If the granita becomes frozen solid, turn the mixture into the bowl of a food processor and process for 30 seconds with the steel blade.

CRANBERRY SORBET

A tart and colorful dessert any time cranberries are in season, or make it with the berries you stored in the freezer for a lovely warm-weather accompaniment for fruit salad.

SERVES 8

1 quart cranberries
2 cups water
1½ cups sugar
1 cup water
3 tablespoons vodka

Boil the cranberries in 2 cups water until soft. Drain. Purée mixture in a food processor and then strain to remove any seeds and skins. Add the sugar and remaining cup of water. Boil together for 5 minutes. Cool and chill. Stir in vodka and freeze in an ice cream freezer. Allow to rest in the freezer compartment of the refrigerator for at least 2 hours.

CHESTNUT FLAN

This is a lovely dessert. Imported chestnuts are cooked and ready to eat when you buy them; roasting adds flavor, of course, but like boiling, it is just a way of getting the shells off. Once they are peeled, the chestnuts should be puréed with the milk in a food processor.

SERVES 6

3 cups milk
2 inches of vanilla bean
4 egg yolks
4 eggs
½ cup brown sugar
25 cooked chestnuts, puréed with ⅓ cup milk
1 cup whipped cream
2 tablespoons brandy

Preheat the oven to 325°F.

Heat the milk to scalding with the vanilla bean. Beat egg yolks, eggs, and sugar until light. Stir in hot milk and simmer until mixture coats the back of a spoon. Remove from the heat and stir in chestnut purée. Pour the mixture into a well-buttered 2-quart baking dish and set dish in a pan of hot water. Bake at 325°F for 45 to 50 minutes, or until the center is set.

Allow the flan to cool completely. Chill and serve with whipped cream that has been flavored with brandy.

CHOCOLATE FONDUE

Cut up the prettiest fruits you can find in the market and dip them in chocolate to make this bright winter party dessert. This recipe can easily be doubled.

SERVES 4

8 ounces good-quality semisweet or bittersweet chocolate
½ cup heavy cream
3 tablespoons Kirsch or Grand Marnier

Melt chocolate with cream over medium heat until smooth. Stir in liqueur. Keep warm over a spirit burner.

Dip various fruits (bananas, pineapple, pears, apples, and strawberries, if available) and squares of day-old pound cake in the hot sauce, just as for a cheese fondue. Eat at once.

CHRISTMAS CRANBERRY TARTS

SERVES 6

1 cup Golden Syrup
2 tablespoons cornstarch
1 cup water
4 tablespoons grated orange rind
1 cup raisins, plumped in boiling water
5 cups fresh cranberries
1 cup coarsely chopped pecans
4 tablespoons butter
Pastry for 6 three-inch tart shells (one recipe for a 2-crust pie,
    see page 105)
1 cup heavy cream, whipped with 2 tablespoons brandy

Preheat the oven to 400°F.

Combine the syrup, cornstarch, water, and orange rind in a large saucepan. Mix well. Bring to a boil and stir in raisins and cranberries. Cover and reduce heat. Simmer until cranberry skins begin to pop, about 5 or 6 minutes. Stir in pecans and butter. Remove from the heat. Cool without stirring.

Roll out pastry and line tart pans. Spoon filling into shells. Bake at 400°F for about 20 minutes. Serve at room temperature topped with brandied whipped cream.

APPLE BREAD PUDDING

An unabashedly old-fashioned recipe, the kind of substantial dessert that kept the Stowes and the Alcotts going through long New England winters.

SERVES 6

8 slices of stale or toasted bread, cut into ½-inch cubes
½ cup raisins, plumped in rum and drained
4 Greening apples, peeled, seeded, and sliced thinly
3 cups scalded milk
⅓ cup dark brown sugar
2 teaspoons pumpkin pie spice
Pinch of salt
4 large eggs
Whipped cream

Preheat the oven to 375°F.

Butter an 8 x 12-inch baking dish (glass, preferably) and line it with the bread cubes. Sprinkle raisins over the bread and layer the apples over them. Combine the milk, brown sugar, spice, and salt. Beat the eggs together and beat into the milk mixture. Pour the mixture over bread and apples and let the pudding stand for 30 minutes. Most of the liquid will be soaked up by the bread. Bake at 375°F until the mixture is set, about 50 minutes.

Serve with sweetened whipped cream or vanilla ice cream.

TOURTEAU FROMAGE

The surface of this French cousin of cheesecake turns almost black when baked, but the interior is delicately sweet and makes a refreshing dessert. Serve it warm or cold, and lift off the blackened surface just before cutting. Fresh berries or other fruit and a little whipped cream can be served on the side.

MAKES 8 TO 10 SERVINGS

1 unbaked pie shell (see page 105)
½ pound fresh goat's cheese (Montrachet or similar cheese)
½ cup superfine granulated sugar
Pinch of salt
1 teaspoon pure vanilla extract
5 large eggs, separated, the whites beaten until stiff peaks form
⅓ cup flour
¼ cup cornstarch

Preheat the oven to 400°F.

Line the pie shell with waxed paper and fill with beans or rice. Bake at 400°F for 10 minutes. While the pie shell cooks, beat the cheese with the sugar, salt, and vanilla. If the cheese is a little dry, put all ingredients into the bowl of a food processor and pulse until smooth. Add egg yolks and then stir in flour and cornstarch.

Fold egg whites into cheese mixture. Empty pie shell of beans and waxed paper. Fill with cheese and egg mixture. Bake at 400°F for about 45 minutes, until the surface is black and nearly charred.

ZIMSTERNE

These cinnamon stars are traditional in Germany and Switzerland. Form a hole in one point before baking and thread ribbon through it afterward, so the cookies can be hung on the Christmas tree.

MAKES 5 DOZEN

2⅓ cups all-purpose flour
2½ teaspoons baking powder

1 teaspoon ground cinnamon
Pinch of salt
½ teaspoon nutmeg
3 tablespoons butter, softened
1½ cups confectioners' sugar
2 large eggs
1 large egg, separated, the white beaten just until frothy
1 teaspoon almond extract
1 cup very finely chopped almonds

Stir together the flour, baking powder, cinnamon, salt, and nutmeg. In another bowl, beat together butter, sugar, eggs, and egg yolk until light and fluffy. Beat in the almond extract. Stir in the flour mixture until well mixed. Stir in nuts. Chill until firm.

Preheat the oven to 375°F.

On a lightly floured board, roll out dough, one-third at a time, to ⅛-inch thickness. Cut with a 2-inch star cookie cutter.

In a small bowl, beat egg white with a fork until frothy. Brush a little egg white on each cookie. Bake 6 to 8 minutes until lightly browned. Remove from the oven and cool on wire racks.

PEPPARKAKOR

These traditional Christmas cookies are baked in enormous quantities in many Swedish kitchens.

MAKES ABOUT 8 TO 10 DOZEN COOKIES

1 cup sugar
½ pound (2 sticks) butter, softened
1 cup unsulfured molasses
1 teaspoon baking soda
1 teaspoon salt
1 tablespoon ground ginger
½ teaspoon freshly ground white or black pepper
3½ cups flour
Superfine granulated sugar

Preheat the oven to 350°F.

Cream sugar and butter until light and fluffy. Beat in the molasses. Stir together baking soda, salt, ginger, pepper, and flour, add to creamed mixture, and beat until well mixed. Chill the dough until easy to handle.

Shape dough into balls the size of large marbles. Roll in the sugar before placing on a lightly buttered baking sheet.

Bake at 350°F for 12 to 15 minutes, or until lightly browned. Cool on baking sheet for 1 minute and then transfer to a rack to cool completely. These keep for several weeks.

ALMOND CRESCENTS

These are one of our all-time favorite Christmas cookies.

MAKES ABOUT 4 DOZEN COOKIES

½ pound (2 sticks) butter, softened
⅓ cup sugar
⅔ cup ground almonds
Pinch of salt
1⅔ cups flour
½ cup confectioners' sugar

Preheat oven to 325°F.

Beat the butter with sugar until it is pale and fluffy. Stir in the almonds, salt, and flour. Wrap the dough in waxed paper and chill until firm.

Shape teaspoonfuls of the dough into crescents and place on an ungreased baking sheet. Bake 15 minutes until slightly firm to the touch. Do not allow them to color at all. Remove from the oven. Cool on a wire rack for a minute or two and then roll in confectioners' sugar, or shake gently in a bag full of confectioners' sugar. Cool completely.

PEANUT BUTTER CRISPS

These cookies are great for tea or after school, or serve them for dessert with fruit salad.

MAKES 3 TO 4 DOZEN COOKIES

¼ cup peanut butter
4 tablespoons butter, softened
½ cup granulated sugar
¼ cup dark brown sugar, firmly packed
1 egg, beaten
¾ cup flour
Pinch of salt
¼ teaspoon baking soda

Cream together peanut butter, butter, and sugars until light and fluffy. Add the beaten egg and mix well. Stir in flour, salt, and baking soda. Shape into a roll and wrap in waxed paper. Chill overnight.

Preheat the oven to 350°F.

Cut into ¼-inch slices, mark with a fork, and bake at 350°F for about 10 minutes.

QUICK CHRISTMAS BREAD

This quick bread—a cross between fruit cake and stollen—is a family tradition for us. We serve it with coffee or cocoa on Christmas morning.

MAKES 2 LOAVES

3 cups flour
1 cup sugar
Pinch of salt
3½ teaspoons baking powder
2 teaspoons ground cinnamon
2 eggs, beaten well
1½ cups milk
3 tablespoons melted butter
4 tablespoons dark rum
1½ cups broken pecans

1 cup white raisins, plumped in dark rum, drained, and dried
¾ cup chopped dates
¾ cup chopped dried figs
¼ cup currants
¼ cup flour

Preheat the oven to 350°F.

Stir 3 cups flour, sugar, salt, baking powder, and cinnamon together in a large bowl. Beat eggs and milk into the dry ingredients until well mixed. Beat in butter and rum.

Stir pecans, raisins, dates, and dried figs together. Toss with ¼ cup flour. Gently stir nuts and fruit into batter. Spoon into 2 loaf pans that have been lightly buttered and lined with waxed paper. Let the batter sit for 30 minutes. Bake at 350°F for at least 1 hour, or until a knife inserted in the middle comes out clean.

Cool bread on a rack.

SOUTHERN CORN BREAD

All corn breads are made with leavening, milk, and eggs, but unlike northern and western ones, southern corn breads have no sugar in them.

SERVES 8

1½ cups yellow cornmeal
¾ cup unbleached flour
¾ teaspoon salt
2 teaspoons baking powder
2 whole eggs, well beaten
½ cup buttermilk
1 cup milk
3 tablespoons butter, or lard, melted

Preheat the oven to 375°F.

Stir together cornmeal, flour, salt, and baking powder. In another bowl, beat eggs into the buttermilk. Stir in milk. Add egg mixture to the cornmeal mixture and stir with a fork until just moistened. Stir in melted butter or lard.

Heavily butter a 2-quart flat Pyrex dish. Pour in batter and bake at 375°F for about 25 minutes, or until golden brown on top. Cut in squares to serve.

HAY DAY'S OATMEAL BREAD

A good, hearty bread with a slight sweetness and a crunchy texture, this was originally developed by Mimi Boyd for her cooking class. Like any bread, it will keep for a day or two longer if raisins are added; they make this one into a stunner for cinnamon toast for tea.

MAKES 3 LOAVES

4 cups scalded milk
2 cups rolled oats
4 tablespoons unsalted butter
1 tablespoon active, dry yeast
¼ cup warm water
½ cup molasses
1½ tablespoons salt
5 cups whole wheat flour
4 to 5 cups unbleached white flour

Scald the milk, add it to the rolled oats and butter, and let stand for 30 minutes. Dissolve the yeast in warm water. Add the molasses, salt, and dissolved yeast to the milk mixture. Add enough of the flour to make a soft dough and knead it for 10 to 15 minutes. Put the dough into a well-greased bowl. Cover and let it rise until doubled in bulk. Turn it out onto a floured board and knead it until elastic, about 5 minutes. Divide the dough into 3 loaves and place in 3 buttered standard loaf pans and let rise again. Brush the tops with melted butter and bake in a 400°F oven for 45 minutes.

Add 1 cup raisins plus ½ cup sugar before adding the flour. Using the same dough, shape into rolls.

HAY DAY'S BROWN RICE BREAD

One of Mimi's favorites, this delicate bread with its unusual texture began as a solution for using up leftover rice. It's wonderful toasted—the rice stays whole and gives the bread a nice crunch.

YIELDS 2 LOAVES

½ cup milk, scalded
3 tablespoons unsalted butter, cut in pieces
3 tablespoons honey
2 teaspoons salt
3 cups cooked brown rice
1 heaping tablespoon active, dry yeast
¼ cup warm water
4 cups unbleached flour
1 egg white, beaten (for glaze)

In a large bowl, pour scalded milk over butter, honey, and salt. Add cooked rice. Dissolve yeast in warm water. When proofed, add to rice mixture. Add unbleached flour to make a stiff dough. Turn out onto a floured surface and knead until smooth and elastic, adding more flour if necessary.

Place dough in a buttered bowl, turning once to grease the top. Cover with a towel and let rise in a warm place until doubled. Punch down dough. Let rest 2 to 3 minutes. Then knead for a few minutes and shape into 2 small loaves.

Place in well-buttered loaf pans. Cover and let rise until doubled. Brush tops with an egg white glaze and slash with an X. Bake at 375°F for 40 to 45 minutes or until done. Cool on a wire rack.

INDEX

[411]

Index

Freelance writer MAGGIE STEARNS *lives in Fairfield, Connecticut, and spends part of the year at Opera Theatre of Saint Louis, St. Louis, Missouri, where she has been national press representative and program editor since 1979.*

A Smith College graduate, former English teacher, and magazine editor, she has been helping put together the monthly Hay Day Rural Times *since 1982. Her first and only professional experience in the kitchen came when she and her husband spent the first two years of their marriage managing two small country inns in Vermont.*

Apart from that, Ms. Stearns is by her own account an acceptable routine cook with occasional good days. Her husband is headmaster of Fairfield Country Day School; they have two daughters.

SALLIE Y. WILLIAMS, *born in Charlottesville, Virginia, is a graduate of Sweet Briar College, where she was elected to Phi Beta Kappa.*

The youngest child of a career naval officer, Ms. Williams has traveled extensively. She studied at Le Cordon Bleu in Paris and for two years was associate director of La Varenne cooking school, also in Paris.

Ms. Williams, who has served as consultant to the Hay Day Country Farm Markets for the past six years, is the author of The Art of Presenting Food, American Feasts, *and* Down Home Feasts, *among other books. She served as managing editor for* Forbes *magazine's* Restaurant Guide *and is a director of L'Academie du Vin in New York City.*

Ms. Williams lives with her husband and two sons in New York.

WESTPORT HAY DAY
1026 Post Road E.
Westport, CT 06880
Open Everyday – 8 to 7   Sunday 8 to 6
I 95, Exit 18 to the Post Rd.
Right ¼ mile on Right. Phone: 227-9008

GREENWICH HAY DAY
1050 E. Putnam Avenue
Riverside, CT 06878
Open Everyday – 8 to 7   Sunday 8 to 6
I 95, Exit 5, Left on US Rt. 1
¼ mile on Right. Phone: 637-7600

HAMDEN HAY DAY
2460 Dixwell Avenue
Hamden, CT 06514
Open Everyday – 8 to 7   Sunday 8 to 6
Wilbur Cross Exit 60, North on Rt. 10
(Dixwell Ave) 1 mile on Left. Phone: 288-3148

FAIRFIELD HAY DAY
1910 Black Rock Tnpk.
Fairfield, CT 06430
Open Everyday – 8 to 7   Sunday 8 to 6
From I 95, Exit 24, North on Rt. 58
1¼ miles on Right. Phone: 336-5865
From Merritt Pkwy., Exit 45, South on Rt. 58
2 miles on Left. Phone: 336-5865